Innovations in Landscape Architec

This inspiring and thought-provoking book explores how recent innovations in landscape architecture have uniquely positioned the practice to address complex issues and technologies that affect our built environment. The changing and expanding nature of 'landscape' makes it more important than ever for landscape architects to seek innovation as a critical component in the forward development of a contemporary profession that merges expansive ideas and technology applications.

The editors bring together leading contributors who are experts in new and pioneering approaches and technologies within the fields of academic and professional landscape architecture. The chapters explore digital technology, design processes, and theoretical queries that shape the contemporary practice of landscape architecture. Topics covered include:

- Digital design
- Fabrication and prototyping
- Emerging technology
- Visualization of data
- Systems theory.

Concluding the book are case studies looking at the work of two landscape architecture firms (PEG and MYKD) and two academic departments (Illinois Institute of Technology and the Rhode Island School of Design), which together show the novel and exciting directions that the landscape architecture curriculum is heading.

Jonathon R. Anderson is an Assistant Professor of Interior Design at Ryerson University in Toronto, Canada. He holds a Master of Fine Arts in Furniture Design from Savannah College of Art & Design, USA, and a Bachelor of Science in Architecture from Southern Illinois University, USA. Jonathon's work explores how industrial manufacturing and CNC technologies influence the design and making processes.

Daniel H. Ortega is an Associate Professor of Landscape Architecture at the University of Nevada, Las Vegas, USA. He holds a Bachelor of Landscape Architecture from the University of Nevada, Las Vegas, and a Master of Landscape Architecture from the Rhode Island School of Design, USA. His scholarly interests lie in the intersection between visual representation and the cultural factors that affect the crafting of our built environment.

INNOVATIONS IN LANDSCAPE ARCHITECTURE

Edited by
Jonathon R. Anderson and
Daniel H. Ortega

LONDON AND NEW YORK

First published 2016
by Routledge
2 Park Square, Milton Park, Abingdon, Oxon OX14 4RN

and by Routledge
711 Third Avenue, New York, NY 10017

Routledge is an imprint of the Taylor & Francis Group, an informa business

© 2016 Jonathon R. Anderson and Daniel H. Ortega

The right of Jonathon R. Anderson and Daniel H. Ortega to be identified as the authors of the editorial material, and of the authors for their individual chapters, has been asserted in accordance with sections 77 and 78 of the Copyright, Designs and Patents Act 1988.

All rights reserved. No part of this book may be reprinted or reproduced or utilised in any form or by any electronic, mechanical, or other means, now known or hereafter invented, including photocopying and recording, or in any information storage or retrieval system, without permission in writing from the publishers.

Trademark notice: Product or corporate names may be trademarks or registered trademarks, and are used only for identification and explanation without intent to infringe.

British Library Cataloguing-in-Publication Data
A catalogue record for this book is available from the British Library

Library of Congress Cataloging in Publication Data
Names: Anderson, Jonathon R., editor. | Ortega, Daniel H., editor.
Title: Innovations in landscape architecture / edited by Jonathon R. Anderson and Daniel H. Ortega.
Description: Abingdon, Oxon ; New York, NY : Routledge, 2016. | Includes bibliographical references and index.
Identifiers: LCCN 2015044177| ISBN 9781138860674 (hardback : alk. paper) | ISBN 9781138860681 (pbk. : alk. paper) | ISBN 9781315716336 (ebook)
Subjects: LCSH: Landscape architecture.
Classification: LCC SB472 .I56 2016 | DDC 712--dc23
LC record available at http://lccn.loc.gov/2015044177

ISBN: 978-1-138-86067-4 (hbk)
ISBN: 978-1-138-86068-1 (pbk)
ISBN: 978-1-315-71633-6 (ebk)

Typeset in News Gothic
by Saxon Graphics Ltd, Derby
Printed by Bell & Bain Ltd, Glasgow

CONTENTS

Notes on contributors   vii
Acknowledgments   xvii
Foreword   xix
BRAD CANTRELL
Introduction: the only thing we have to fear ...   1
DANIEL H. ORTEGA AND JONATHON R. ANDERSON

Part I
Innovative tools   7

1. L A N D script _ data S C A P E: 'digital' agency within manufactured territories   9
   JOSE ALFREDO RAMIREZ AND CLARA OLÓRIZ SANJUÁN
2. An interface for instrumental reconciliation   28
   ALEXANDER ROBINSON
3. Computational landscape architecture: procedural, tangible, and open landscapes   43
   BRENDAN HARMON, ANNA PETRASOVA, HELENA MITASOVA, AND VACLAV PETRAS
4. Get animated! Dynamic visualization and the site analysis process   60
   KEN MCCOWN AND PHIL ZAWARUS
5. The landscape as database   76
   CHRIS SPEED AND DUNCAN SHINGLETON
6. Discovering landform processes through creative 3D mapping and diagramming of form, pattern, and arrangement   90
   NADIA AMOROSO AND NADIA D'AGNONE
7. Data-driven landscape   102
   MING TANG

Contents

Part II
Innovative processes   123

8   Manufacturing resonance   125
     MICHAEL BEAMAN AND ZANETA HONG

9   Expanded 'thick description': the landscape architect as critical ethnographer   143
     ALISON B. HIRSCH

10   Urban morphology phenomena: post-industrial urban landscapes   164
     LAURA LOVELL-ANDERSON

11   Ecological urbanism: the synthesis of ethics, aesthetics, and cybernetics   171
     IMAN ANSARI

12   Engineering nature   189
     PATRICK FRANKE AND NICK CHRISTOPHER

13   Emergent convergent: technology and the informal urban communities initiative   205
     BEN SPENCER AND SUSAN BOLTON

14   Varying degrees of impermanence: art and landscapes as critical provocation   223
     ROBERTO ROVIRA

Part III
Innovative profiles   237

Interview I: Mikyoung Kim Design   239
     MIKYOUNG KIM

Interview II: PEG Office of Landscape + Architecture   246
     KAREN M'CLOSKEY AND KEITH VANDERSYS

Interview III: Illinois Institute of Technology (IIT)   254
     MARTIN FELSEN AND CONOR O'SHEA

Interview IV: Rhode Island School of Design (RISD)   263
     SUZANNE MATHEW

Index   271

CONTRIBUTORS

EDITORS

Jonathon R. Anderson is an Assistant Professor of Interior Design at Ryerson University in Toronto, Canada. Jonathon's research explores how industrial manufacturing and CNC technologies influence the design and making processes. His work is characterized by innovative and explorative methods that result in interconnected design, fine art, and technology solutions. From this non-traditional process emerges a provocative, complex design language that visually communicates at varied scales and emphasizes corporeal and phenomenological experiences. He holds a Master of Fine Arts in Furniture Design from Savannah College of Art & Design, USA, along with a Bachelor of Science in Architecture from Southern Illinois University, USA.

Daniel H. Ortega is an Associate Professor of Landscape Architecture at the University of Nevada, Las Vegas, USA. He holds a Bachelor of Landscape Architecture degree from the University of Nevada, Las Vegas, along with a Master of Landscape Architecture from the Rhode Island School of Design, USA. His scholarly interests lie in the intersection between visual representation and the cultural factors that affect the crafting of the built environment. As Principal Investigator at the Laboratory for Innovative Media Explorations (LIME), it is his ambition to engage students, academics, private, and public stakeholders in the use of digitally based technologies as platforms for making thoughtful decisions that affect the future development of the places where we live.

AUTHORS

Nadia Amoroso, PhD, ASLA, is an academic in landscape architecture and urban design. Her work focuses on visual representation, urban design, and creative mapping. She is an Adjunct Professor of Practice at the University of Guelph and the Director of Amoroso Studio in Toronto, specializing in landscape architectural representation, Geodesign, and creative mapping. She is the author/editor of a

Contributors

number of books including, *The Exposed City: Mapping the Urban Invisibles*; *Representing Landscapes: A Visual Collection of Landscape Architectural Drawings: Digital Landscape Architecture Now* and most recently *Representing Landscapes: Digital*.

Iman Ansari is an architect, urbanist, and a founding principal of AN.ONYMOUS. He is currently a faculty member at the University of Southern California's School of Architecture. Previously he has taught at the University of California, Los Angeles (UCLA) and the City College of New York. His work has been published widely and exhibited in international venues including the Museum of Modern Art (MoMA). Ansari holds degrees in Architecture and Philosophy from the City College of New York and in Architecture and Urban Design from Harvard University Graduate School of Design. He is pursuing a PhD in architecture at UCLA.

Michael Beaman is Co-Founder and Principal of Beta-field and GA Collaborative; Associate Editor for the *International Journal of Interior Architecture + Spatial Design* (*ii Journal*); Design & Technology Writer for *Architectural Record*; and Visiting Lecturer in Adaptive Reuse and Technology at the Rhode Island School of Design. His research, writing, and practice focuses on the relationships between adaptive environments and technologies in architecture and landscape, and its implications on design culture, sustainability, and socially conscious design practices. In 2012, the American Institute of Architects named Michael as an Emerging Practitioner; and in 2010, he was named the 2010–12 UVA Teaching Fellow in Architecture. Michael received a Bachelor in Architecture from North Carolina State University and a Master in Architecture from the Harvard Graduate School of Design.

Susan Bolton is a Professor in the School of Environmental and Forest Sciences, an Adjunct Professor in Civil and Environmental Engineering, and an Adjunct Professor in Global Health at the University of Washington. She has worked on innovative sustainable development infrastructure projects in Costa Rica, Bolivia, Peru, and Guatemala since 2000. She enjoys being a member of interdisciplinary, project-oriented teams and brings a rare combination of ecology, hydrology, engineering, and community development skills and experiences to her work.

Brad Cantrell is a landscape architect and scholar whose work focuses on the role of computation and media in environmental and ecological design. He received his BSLA from the University of Kentucky and his MLA from the Harvard Graduate

Contributors

School of Design. He has held academic appointments at the Harvard Graduate School of Design, the Rhode Island School of Design, and the Louisiana State University Robert Reich School of Landscape Architecture where he led the school as graduate coordinator and director. His work in Louisiana over the past decade points to a series of methodologies that develop modes of modeling, simulation, and embedded computation that express and engage the complexity of overlapping physical, cultural, and economic systems.

Nick Christopher is an architect and designer with Gould Evans. He has a passion for all aspects and scales of the built environment. Designing holistically, he considers the building to be just one opportunity to add value and places equal importance on the designed experience of the landscapes, interiors, furnishing, and construction systems. Nick has worked professionally in California, Illinois, and Missouri, and holds a Masters of Architecture from Clemson University. Believing that good design is a great investment he works to create environments that enhance the way we work and live.

Nadia D'Agnone is a landscape architectural designer and researcher. She was born in Toronto, Canada, and is now based in Venice, Italy, where she has recently completed her PhD research at the Università Iuav di Venezia. She has an Honours Bachelor of Arts from the University of Toronto in Fine Art Visual Studies and Architectural Studies and a Master of Landscape Architecture from the John H. Daniels Faculty of Architecture, Landscape, and Design, also at the University of Toronto. Her interests lie in exploring the interdisciplinary relationships between design, art, philosophy, and science through exploratory techniques in visual communication including creative mapping, modeling, and data visualization.

Martin Felsen is an Assistant Professor at Illinois Institute of Technology's College of Architecture where he teaches graduate studios with a focus on building technology and city design, urban infrastructures and social condensers, smart urban growth, and professional environmental responsibility. He is also Principle Architect of UrbanLab in Chicago, IL.

Patrick Franke is an architect with the design firm of Gould Evans in Kansas City, Missouri. He is a graduate of Tulane University, holding degrees in both Architecture and Urban Studies. A Kansas City native, Patrick's design agenda is strongly focused on community building and the potential for design to be impactful as a tool with which to bring people together.

Contributors

Brendan Harmon's research explores the role of creativity in traditional and digital design processes for landscape architects. With computer modeling and visualization we are better able to understand and represent landscape dynamics. However, interacting with computers can be unintuitive and can inhibit or transform creativity. Brendan is exploring whether advances in digital design, tangible user interfaces, and computer-aided manufacturing can enable a more intuitive design process that tightly couples creativity and rigorous analysis. Brendan has developed and teaches the graduate courses GIS for Designers and 3D Design.

Alison B. Hirsch, MLA, MS, PhD, is an Assistant Professor of Landscape Architecture at the University of Southern California and co-founder and partner of *foreground design agency,* a transdisciplinary practice working across the fields of landscape architecture, architecture, urbanism, and the visual arts. She is author of *City Choreographer: Lawrence Halprin in Urban Renewal America* (University of Minnesota Press, 2014) and co-editor of *The Landscape Imagination* (Princeton Architectural Press, 2014). Her research focuses on choreographic and participatory potentials of landscape architecture as emergent from the study of sociocultural processes and practices that activate the public realm.

Zaneta Hong is a Lecturer in Landscape Architecture at the Harvard Graduate School of Design; Editor of *Platform 8*; and Design Principal at Beta-field and GA Collaborative. In recent times, Zaneta was the 2013–14 recipient of the Daniel Urban Kiley Teaching Fellowship. Her research into landscape material systems, ecologies, and technologies has emerged in numerous publications including *Living Systems: Innovative Materials and Technologies for Landscape Architecture* and *Landscape Architecture Magazine*. Zaneta attended Cornell University before completing her Bachelor of Fine Arts in Industrial Design from the Rhode Island School of Design and a Master of Landscape Architecture from the Harvard Graduate School of Design.

For the last twenty years, **Mikyoung Kim** Design has crafted an exceptional body of work, spanning a wide range of landscape typologies in the United States, East Asia, and the Middle East. The firm has developed a reputation for culturally significant design work that serve as a powerful tool to heal and enliven the public realm. Their work addresses pressing environmental issues, while celebrating the beauty of our collective human experience through the use of contemporary materials and technologies. Today, Mikyoung Kim Design's work is defined by a

Contributors

seasoned understanding of material detailing and a whimsical celebration of the transformative and healing power of the natural world.

Laura Lovell-Anderson is a Doctoral Candidate in Design at North Carolina State University, researching urban deindustrialization phenomena and the emergence of landscapes of adaptation and residency. She holds Bachelor and Master degrees in Industrial and Sustainable Design from Savannah College of Art and Design, as well as a Master's degree in Law from Wake Forest University.

Helena Mitasova is a Professor in the Department of Marine, Earth and Atmospheric Sciences at North Carolina State University and a member of the Geospatial Science and Technology Faculty at the Center for Geospatial Analytics. Her research uses tangible geospatial modeling environments, dynamic simulations of landscape processes, and analysis of LiDAR time series data to investigate coastal evolution, soil erosion control, and sustainable land management. Helena has developed graduate courses based on Free and Open Source Geospatial software, including the Geospatial Modeling and Analysis course and an advanced special topics course on Multidimensional Geospatial Modeling.

Suzanne Mathew is an Assistant Professor of Landscape Architecture at the Rhode Island School of Design and a landscape designer with a background in both architecture and landscape architecture. Through her work in both teaching and professional practice, she has framed a series of research threads that mine the potential of multi-disciplinary practice. These research themes range from investigating models of hybridized and adaptive infrastructures as regenerative tools in declining cities to exploring new methods for visualizing dynamic phenomena that transgress the boundaries between architectural and landscape space. Mathew's work seeks to expand the cultural and architectural parameters for human environments and to create built environments that don't simply persist but respond to change with agility.

Ken McCown, ASLA, Associate AIA, Past-President, CELA, serves as the Chair of the Department of Landscape Architecture at Iowa State University where he is a Professor in the College of Design. His background includes an undergraduate degree in Landscape Architecture and a graduate degree in Architecture from the University of Illinois at Urbana-Champaign. These degrees provided a platform for integrative, interdisciplinary inquiry into the built environment through the

Contributors

integration of urban design, transition design/resilience and ergonomic/behaviour design in his collaborative works and teaching across disciplines.

Karen M'Closkey is an Associate Professor of Landscape Architecture and co-founder of PEG office of landscape + architecture, an award-winning design and research practice based in Philadelphia. PEG's work explores the potential for new media and fabrication technologies to produce novel relationships between organic and inorganic materials, often utilizing pattern as a means to heighten the perception of temporal and ephemeral phenomena.

Clara Olóriz Sanjuán is a PhD architect, tutor, and practicing architect. She developed her PhD on the relationship between architecture and technology, focusing on industrialized systems of production at the ETSAUN and at the AA. Currently, she teaches on the AALU Master's program as a design tutor and she works as a project leader in Groundlab. She has collaborated in several workshops and lectures worldwide in Mexico, Croatia, UK, Sweden, India, Switzerland, and Spain. She co-directs the AA Research Cluster 'Urban Prototypes' and the AA Bilbao Visiting School Program.

Conor O'Shea is a Visiting Assistant Professor at Illinois Institute of Technology's College of Architecture. Conor teaches studios and lecture courses in the Master of Landscape Architecture program where he uses landscape as a framework for rethinking emerging processes of urbanization. His current research situates logistical ecologies and logistical urbanization as territories for new landscape architectural strategies in North America. He is the Founder and Principle of Hinterlands Urbanism and Landscape in Chicago, IL.

Vaclav Petras's research includes landscape evolution analysis in coastal areas based on space-time cube concept, GIS-based environmental modeling of natural phenomena, web-based spatio-temporal visualizations for communicating research, and finally geospatial software quality assessment, which allows him and other scientists to test the proper functionality of various geospatial algorithms. Václav collaborates on free and open source software development, most notably development of GRASS GIS.

Anna Petrasova's research interests lie in interactive visualizations of multi-dimensional geospatial data using open source technologies. She also integrates dynamic geospatial modeling with tangible user interfaces. Anna is an active

Contributors

member of the international community of scientists developing open source GRASS GIS. Her peer-reviewed contributions, including tools for dynamic spatio-temporal data visualization, facilitate teaching and research throughout geospatial disciplines.

Jose Alfredo Ramirez is an architect, founder of Groundlab and director of the Landscape Urbanism (MArch/MSc) Graduate Program at the Architectural Association as well as the AA Mexico City Visiting School. He studied Architecture in Mexico City and Landscape Urbanism at the AA. Alfredo has worked and developed projects at the junction of architecture, landscape, and urbanism in a variety of contexts such as in China, Mexico, and Spain, among others. He concentrates mainly on large-scale developments like the Olympic Master Plan for London 2012 or the International Horticultural Exhibition in Xian, China 2011. Alfredo has lectured on the topic of Landscape Urbanism and the work of Groundlab worldwide.

Alexander Robinson is a landscape architect and an Assistant Professor at the University of Southern California in the Landscape Architecture program. He is the director of the Landscape Morphologies Lab and principal of the landscape design, research, and planning practice, Office of Outdoor Research based in Los Angeles. Robinson's research and practice is focused on the means necessary to advance the design and implementation of high performance landscapes and infrastructures. He is the co-author of *Living Systems: Innovative Materials and Technologies for Landscape Architecture* (Birkhauser, 2007), a treatise on landscape performance systems. The American Academy in Rome awarded him the Prince Charitable Trust Rome Prize in 2015.

Roberto Rovira is Principal of Studio Roberto Rovira, Associate Professor, and former chair of Landscape Architecture + Environmental and Urban Design at Florida International University. As a registered landscape architect with a design, engineering, and fine arts background, his teaching, research, and creative work explore the potential of landscape architecture in public space and the intersection of technology and living systems through projects like his Ecological Atlas. The Architectural League recognized him as one of eight 2015 Emerging Voices, one of the most coveted awards in North American architecture, which spotlights individuals and firms based in the US, Canada, and Mexico with distinct design voices and the potential to influence the disciplines of architecture, landscape architecture, and urbanism.

Contributors

Duncan Shingleton is a Research Associate and Digital Artist at the Centre for Design Informatics, where his research and practice negotiates theories relating to the attachment of data to objects, and the resulting role these objects might have in our networks. From apps to installations, his critical enquiry attempts to balance the seesaw that defines an object's relationship between its material and immaterial affordances. Working at the intersection of code and thing, Duncan explores how we might reexamine the Internet of Things as we begin to adopt an ablative approach to designing by data, with data, and from data.

Chris Speed is Chair of Design Informatics at the University of Edinburgh where his research focuses upon the Network Society, Digital Art, and Technology, and the Internet of Things. Chris has sustained a critical enquiry into how network technology can engage with the fields of art, design, and social experience through a variety of international digital art exhibitions, funded research projects, books, journals, and conferences. Chris is co-editor of the journal *Ubiquity* and co-directs the Design Informatics Research Centre that is home to a combination of researchers working across the fields of interaction design, temporal design, anthropology, software engineering, and digital architecture, as well as the PhD, MA/MFA, and MSc and Advanced MSc programs.

Ben Spencer is an Associate Professor in the University of Washington's Department of Landscape Architecture, an Adjunct Associate Professor in the University of Washington Department of Global Health, a director at Architects w/o Borders-Seattle, Architects Designers and Planners for Social Responsibility–USA and ARC-Peace International, and the co-founder of the Informal Urban Communities Initiative. Ben's work integrates research, practice, service, and teaching, explores the relationship between the built environment, ecology, and human well-being in developing urban communities and champions design as a vehicle for environmental regeneration and social justice.

Ming Tang, AIA, NACARD, LEED AP, is an Assistant Professor at the University of Cincinnati, a registered architect, and founding partner of TYA Design. He has won numerous design awards, including first place in d3 Natural System Competition, IAAC self-sufficient housing contest, and Chichen Itza lodge museum design competition. His research includes parametric design, digital fabrication, building information modeling, virtual reality, human–computer interaction (HCI), and performance-driven design. His book *Parametric Building Design with Autodesk Maya* was published by Routledge in 2014.

Contributors

Keith VanDerSys is a Senior Lecturer at PennDesign and co-founder of PEG office of landscape + architecture, an award-winning design and research practice based in Philadelphia. Through uses of new media and fabrication technologies, PEG's work explores methods of systemic patterning to expand landscape's expressive agency in the shaping of the public realm. He is co-author with Karen M'Closkey of the forthcoming book *Dynamic Patterns: Visualizing Landscapes in a Digital Age* (Routledge) which situates the emerging expressions of pattern in landscape architecture.

Phill Zawarus is a Visiting Professor of Landscape Architecture at the University of Nevada, Las Vegas, where he provides knowledge and expertise in the field of landscape architecture analysis, synthesis, and design through performative measurements and dynamic visualizations. Zawarus uses advanced computational methods for data collection and visualization for comprehensive communication of social and environmental assessments. His exploration of parametric modeling and interactive media provides opportunities in cohesive demonstrations of responsive design processes, with an emphasis on stormwater management and performative design.

ACKNOWLEDGMENTS

JONATHON R. ANDERSON

I would like to acknowledge my co-editor, Daniel Ortega, and all the contributors. This project would not have been possible without their dedication to landscape architecture and design. Thank you to the School of Architecture at UNLV and the School of Interior Design at Ryerson University for giving me the time to complete the project. Special thanks to Louise Fox and Sade Lee at Routledge for supporting the project and providing assistance. I am particularly indebted to my beautiful wife, Laura Lovell-Anderson, and my parents, Robert and Jessica, whose endless support and encouragement allows me to pursue my passions.

DANIEL H. ORTEGA

This project would not have been possible without the love, support, and patience of my family. A special thank you to my amazing wife Lisa Ortega for your love, strength, and encouragement throughout all of my endeavors. To my parents Henry and Alexandria Ortega, this is one more accomplishment made possible by your life-long encouragement to pursue my education and to work hard. I would also like to thank Dr. Jeffery Koep, former Dean of the UNLV College of Fine Arts for your commitment and support of this project. Additionally, I am extremely grateful to Louise Fox, and Sade Lee at Routledge Press for listening to our thoughts and ideas and guiding us through what may have otherwise been an extremely intimidating process. To every student and teacher that I have met on my journey, thank you! There are too many of you to name individually, but please know that you have each made valuable contributions to who I am as an educator and life-long learner. To all of the contributors who participated in this project, a grateful thank you for your time, expertise, and willingness to participate in this project. And last, but not least, to my co-editor, Mr. Jonathon Anderson, this book would not exist without the amazing effort and work ethic that you brought to the team, cheers!

FOREWORD

Brad Cantrell

In 1971, after seven months of spaceflight, NASA's *Mariner 9* spacecraft arrived in orbit around our neighbor, Mars. Over 11 months, *Mariner 9* recorded imagery of 70 percent of the planet, continuing the imaging of the Martian surface that was started by previous orbiters. These images provided the first tangible proof of water in the form of rivers, canyons, erosion, deposition, and ephemeral processes such as fog. During the last 40 years over ten missions have sent probes and rovers to Mars, building the case for a planet that is teeming with geological processes. Each successive mission has expanded humanity's knowledge of Mars and has guided the subsequent missions and explorations. Beyond the missions around and on Mars there are multitudes of experiments on Earth that are preparing humans for life on an alien world. This laser-sharp focus has produced a deep body of knowledge about our neighbor that is being queried to design and engineer the first human missions to the red planet. It is this form of extreme science, rigorous design, and cultural expansion that is pertinent to humanity finding a symbiotic future within the solar system in the next century.

How does landscape architecture stand side by side with the exploration of a distant neighboring planet? It is in spirit, the spirit that the discipline in which we practice has the capability and desire to shape the future. In the spirit of Frederick Law Olmsted's systemic strategies for Central Park and the Emerald Necklace, which pushed technological and theoretical innovation, and in the spirit which the discipline is redefining its contemporary role. As a profession, landscape architecture is enjoying greater relevance than any time in history and is attempting to address intractable problems around the globe. In this role, the profession is developing methods, techniques, and strategies that engage with the 21st-century environment. An environment that is technologically connected and ecologically precious. As with most disciplines, any new method, idea, or product has a direct correlation to the time in which it is situated. As landscape architects we are currently experiencing the collision of multiple paradigms that are shaping the envelope we operate within – increasing knowledge of climate change, maximization of current methods of extraction and energy production, and the expanding complexity of human settlement.

Foreword

It is important that as a profession we celebrate the edge of the discipline and then trace back from that edge to understand its connection with the core. The core of the profession is our evolved disciplinary knowledge, the foundation of the profession that finds its home in the LAAB, the first four semesters of professional education, and guides the operation of competent firms. The edge is where the profession is pushed as we expand our toolset and evolve our theoretical frameworks to take on problems that lack disciplinary definition. The contributions to this book explore the edge, and it is important that students, academics, and practitioners find ways to tie them back to the core. It is a necessary spirit we must maintain that forces us to consume the world that surrounds us and continue to explore how it pertains to our profession. It is an all-consuming task that requires a deep passion for the discipline and a high level of respect for the profession of landscape architecture.

The following chapters display the passion that exists in landscape architecture, not only in the formulation of beautifully designed and constructed physical landscapes but in the crafting of tools and theories that explore the unknown. On one hand, innovations come in the form of technological approaches, inventions of new technologies, or the repurposing and deployment of existing tools. Technological approaches are often seen as the heart of innovation, the production of new products or methods that leverage the bleeding edge. Today, this bleeding edge is increasingly digital and biological, and utilizes technologies that leverage computation and manipulate the living. The discipline is increasingly stitching these two realms, digital and biological, together as we discover the influences and potentials of connecting our methods of representation and construction. The profession is finding new and important ways to not only use the digital technologies that surround us but is also creating the tools necessary to push itself forward. This has been enabled by a greater facility in coding and new tools that tap into the visual heuristic of designers. Landscape architects are creating tools to perform new methods of analysis and form generation, and even more importantly, leading the conversation.

Beyond technological innovation, the profession has a renewed concern in the theoretical frameworks that help to shape disciplinary expertise. The influence of James Corner and Elizabeth Meyer (among many others) in the late 1990s has helped shape generations of landscape architects as they have been inspired by systemic approaches to territory and looked for new definitions of beauty. While much of the evolution over the past two decades has been centered on a form of ecological determinism, it is becoming increasingly clear that issues of culture and social justice must be addressed alongside design. The academy and practice are simultaneously embarking on these projects and looking for overlaps to inform one another. This form of innovation is a generational project, one where we evolve the profession to justify its importance to a more diverse group of clients and future practitioners, individuals with a broader range of experiences across the world and throughout the socioeconomic spectrum.

The project that confronts landscape architecture is about being more rigorous in our exploration of the edges. It is pertinent that we bring knowledge back to the core and evolve the profession to take on the issues that confront the world today. While this is a project I am fully embedded in, my work is a small step in a bright future. Similar to *Mariner 9*, we are formulating the knowledge that the next generation of practitioners will use. Innovation is not the small steps we all take, but is an aggregate that our students and employees will build upon. When *Mariner 9* sent back its 7000 images over the course of 11 months in 1971, it provided the evidence needed to discover fluid water from leachate patterns in high-resolution imagery in 2015. It is important that we all understand innovation through this lens as we build a body of knowledge to operate at the edge of the profession and bring that knowledge back to its evolving core.

Introduction

The only thing we have to fear …

Daniel H. Ortega and Jonathon R. Anderson

Our world now faces profound challenges, many brought on by innovation itself. Although optimism runs counter to the mood of the times, there are extraordinary new forces aligning around these great challenges, around the world. If you put together all that's going on at the edges of culture and technology, you get a wildly unexpected view of the future.

(Mau 2004, 15)

The subject of innovation and specific strategies used to promote innovation are widely disseminated in the business and technology driven sectors, yet, how we define and apply innovation within the context of landscape architecture is lacking critical examination. Perhaps that's because it is difficult to frame innovation within the discursive practice of the discipline. Suzanne Mathew, in her interview for this book, suggests that innovation in landscape architecture is a difficult topic to articulate because the discipline is not practiced within a fixed set of conditions. Maybe a critical examination of the innovation in landscape architecture is lacking because its practice deals with dynamic systems, shifting cultural conditions, and the need to respond to externalities that often prove difficult to predict, and, therefore, evade standardized methodologies for innovation. Or, possibly, it is because, by definition, innovation requires a dedicated effort to initiate new ideas or methods, and a profession-wide commitment to engendering change may encounter a bit of fear.

In his iconic 1933 presidential inaugural address, Franklin Delano Roosevelt delivered the powerful assertion that 'the only thing we have to fear is fear itself' (Roosevelt 1933). His sentiment was aimed at reassuring the American people that, as a collective group, we would indeed withstand the hardships imposed by the Great Depression. In many ways, we have recently sustained challenging economic, political, and cultural hardships borne of the most recent global economic collapse. While this book does not directly deal with the socio-economic impacts of our global economic condition, it does find itself in parallel with a portion of President Roosevelt's address that states,

Daniel H. Ortega and Jonathon R. Anderson

> *we now realize as we have never realized before our interdependence on each other; that we can not merely take but we must give as well; that if we are to go forward, we must move as a trained and loyal army ... because without such discipline no progress is made ...*
>
> (Roosevelt 1933)

It is that same commitment to the spirit of moving forward during a time that poses as many questions as it does answers, regarding the current condition of landscape architecture, which inspired us to pursue this project. In conceptualizing it, we felt that a gathering of varied intellectual ideas and approaches to practice was necessary to form a collective and interdependent voice that would articulate just how we can work together to progress the discipline of landscape architecture. This book presents a collection of essays that explore how recent innovations in landscape architecture have uniquely positioned the profession to address complex issues, ideas, and technologies that affect our built environment. Landscapes and landscape architecture extend beyond the ameliorative notion of the garden to include matters of: environmental sustainability, applied technologies, cultural processes, land use, infrastructure, and economic development. These issues have not replaced, but rather add to, the landscape architects' responsibility of applying material and conceptual processes; making it more important than ever for landscape architects to seek innovation as a critical component in the contemporary development of a forward-thinking approach to a discipline that merges expansive ideas with site-scaled applications.

ORGANIZATION OF THE BOOK

The chapters within are divided into three sections: innovative tools, innovative processes, and innovative profiles. We have arranged the book in a way that allows for a chronological reading from start to finish, or, individual chapters can be read to provoke thought and provide perspective on the profession's innovative progression. Our organizational strategy carefully reflects a cyclical methodology familiar to most designers, regardless of discipline, and explores digital technologies, design processes, and theoretical queries that shape the research and contemporary practice of landscape architecture. The chapters offer design actions that exemplify innovative agency as a means to expand the discourse of landscape architecture while serving as a catalyst for collaboration between landscape architects and allied design professionals; including architects, urban planners, landscape urbanists, critical theorists, entrepreneurs, and public artists.

INNOVATIVE TOOLS

This section of the book discusses the contemporary use of tools, such as software and fabrication technologies, through the lens of landscape architecture, and how innovative uses of these tools are emerging within the discipline. These chapters look to not only provide an overview of what is happening but also to provide a prospectus on how future evolutions of these tools directly impact their implied uses within the practice of landscape architecture. It should be noted that this book is not meant to be software or process specific; instead, it is intended to render perspectives that extend various technological conditions that are not bound by any single tool, yet how the tools act as vehicles to express innovative ideas and work.

Digital tools are evolving at a rapid pace, one that seems impossible to stay ahead of and fully comprehend how, and what, they offer to the profession. Regardless of the tool, data and information are always present. As evidenced in the chapter by Ming Tang, the speed at which data can be processed is allowing for complex performative datasets to act as input parameters in a scenario-based analysis system. He believes that a seamless and careful planning of rules, from both human and computer, is required for these systems to hold merit.

The exploration of highly innovative tools offers the opportunity to question both the parts and the whole of the systems that we design. Jose Alfredo Ramirez and Clara Olóriz Sanjuán reflect on the role of the designer in an increasingly digital age of scripting and processing of information while offering a perspective that is unique to the system that they have developed. Alexander Robinson explains how technology is used to develop interfaces that establish agency and celebrate society's connection to the tools that develop our landscapes.

Additionally, issues of representation and the use of visuals to express analytical information have always been a vital part of the landscape architect's responsibility. This begs the question as to how methods of representation will evolve as digital tools continue to push the limits of visualization, and gesture toward a new systemic, computational, parameter-based workflow. Nadia Amoroso and Nadia D'Agnone are searching for answers to this question and are looking to extract information from the landscape and make data that is not apparent to the untrained eye visible. Chris Speed and Duncan Shingleton believe that the extraction and visualization of both qualitative and quantitative information will broaden the capacity of the landscape architect.

Brendan Harmon, Anna Petrasova, Helena Mitasova, and Vaclav Petras's research on tangible landscapes looks to establish a closed loop system that integrates modeling, analysis, and simulation into one process. They argue that digital tools allow for real-time analytics and thus allow designers to make informed decisions through quicker ideation and rigorous testing. In a similar vein, Ken McCown and Phil Zawarus present ideas of how digital tools offer an unprecedented capacity to allow designers and landscape architects to challenge what is buildable and unbuildable. The collection of works focused on innovative tools provides insights into the technologies that transform the ways in which we process, make, and present the elements that combine to create landscape architecture.

INNOVATIVE PROCESSES

This section explores speculative and forward-thinking approaches to the design of our built environment. A recent surge of innovative processes has emerged and is providing an exciting interpretation of the discipline's future. The ideas and processes presented in this section vary in technique, scale, and form; yet, their connection to understanding the unknown helps to provide an interdependent perspective on where the profession of landscape architecture is heading. These newly charted boundaries are connecting complex issues while providing an innovative way of thinking and giving physicality to a nonlinear process.

Michael Beaman and Zaneta Hong's chapter examines the landscape as an open system that exchanges material information. This information, better defined as observational domain and operational domain, activates the material processes that define our landscapes. Alison B. Hirsch provides a strong theoretical framework and presents projects that recognize the cultural agency of landscape architecture. Her chapter builds on Clifford Geertz's definition of 'thick description' to include a broader context of political, economic, and social structures. Laura Lovell-Anderson presents a chapter that carefully examines a systematic approach to deindustrialization and urban morphology phenomena.

Iman Ansari investigates an interdisciplinary approach to ecological urbanism through the lens of cultural consciousness by focusing on ethics, aesthetics, and cybernetics. He argues that ecological urbanism is a promising approach to our complex global problems. Additionally, Patrick Franke and Nick Christopher provide a provocative chapter that looks at the relationship between architecture and landscapes in the 'over-engineered' form. They provide insight into the evolution of these ideas and encourage an ongoing debate between architecture and landscape architecture. Roberto Rovira's chapter offers a critical examination of how the temporal nature of both art and landscape offer powerful revelations in making as a way of understanding the processes that shape and create landscapes.

As academics, we understand and value how processing innovation extends into, and beyond, the classroom. Ben Spencer and Susan Bolt present the University of Washington, Department of Landscape Architecture's Informal Urban Communities Initiative (IUCI). Their chapter presents a pedagogy focused on emergent technologies, making, product landscapes, and the understanding of how these ideas deploy in urban slums. The projects and practices within this section propose new trajectories for landscape architecture by exploring and disseminating innovative processes as catalysts for constant change in landscape architecture as well as allied design disciplines.

INNOVATIVE PROFILES

The third section of the book is a collection of interviews that examine how professional practice and academic environments are challenging innovation. We traveled to these firms and universities to sit down and ask a series of questions that would provide insight into the innovative ideas that are being explored in both practice and academia. In the following chapters, you will find responses to the following questions:

1   How do you understand innovation?
2   How has innovation evolved your practice/program?
3   To what level does interdisciplinary define innovation?
4   How do you create a platform or infrastructure to facilitate innovation? Have you critically examined or assessed this?
5   What role does innovation play in our future practice/education?

As evidenced throughout the book, there is no defined path or prescription for innovation. Rather, we have offered critical revelations by dedicated people who, in many ways perform as an intellectual abstraction of FDR's 'trained and loyal army' (Roosevelt 1933), with the vision to advance the praxis of landscape architecture. The conversations are wide, but the value is clear. New boundaries of what landscape architecture is and can become are being defined daily, and without fear. As noted in the foreword, Brad Cantrell reminds us to celebrate and promote those working on the edge, as innovation is a key component to this rapidly changing profession. Commonalities are woven throughout the book, and a concentrated focus was made to locate ideas that re-conceptualize the field of landscape architecture not only as a technical pursuit but also as one that advances design and allied creative disciplines. Admittedly, this book offers only a small snapshot of innovative happenings within the discipline of landscape architecture, but we hope that the ideas presented here not only provoke thought but also provide insight into the profession's forward trajectory in a way that reminds us 'the only thing we have to fear, is fear itself' (Roosevelt 1933).

REFERENCES

Joint Congressional Committee on Inaugural Ceremonies. *Thirty-Second Presidential Inaugural Address by Franklin D. Roosevelt, March 4, 1933*. Accessed October 23, 2015, www.inaugural.senate.gov/swearing-in/address/address-by-franklin-d-roosevelt-1933.

Mau, Bruce. 2004. *Massive Change*. New York: Phaidon Press.

Part I

Innovative tools

LAND script _ data S C A P E

'Digital' agency within manufactured territories

*Jose Alfredo Ramirez and
Clara Olóriz Sanjuán*

Digital technologies influence the way we think, intervene and produce landscapes. Through the notions of landscript and datascape, this chapter reflects on the role of the designer and the new operative frameworks provided by simulation, geographic information and scripting software. It questions the reductive scientific approaches suggested by the objective and methodological procedures of digital technologies to then propose alternatives through two project theses developed at the AA Landscape Urbanism Programme which, through the meaning of *techne*, suggest a different form of agency and production to intervene within given landscapes and territories, acknowledging and stressing their manufactured and machinic nature.

Jose Alfredo Ramirez and Clara Olóriz Sanjuán

New technologies constantly change and re-shape the way we think, design, and produce our environments and territories. Our impulse to control the surroundings in which we are immersed and live has triggered many of the innovations in technologies and methods that are now widely available to designers today. The invention of geometry, for instance, was triggered by the necessity to provide certainty to the distribution, property, and taxation of productive land around the Nile that shifted with every annual flooding – a fact on which the fertility of the land and thus, their living also depended on (Gardner 2009). More recently, the development of contemporary cartography, concomitant of the emergence of innovative surveying tools, provides a reliable technical tool for states and governments to ensure the control and delimitation of land, resources, and management of territories within and beyond their frontiers.

Along these lines, digital cartographic tools provide precise and accurate readings of the world based on their capacity to seamlessly handle and assemble vast amounts of information from multiple fields in the generation of territorial datascapes. Methodologies based on these innovative tools imply abstract systems of organization that provide frameworks to develop and script concrete interventions and management schemes into given territories. However, the processing capabilities of digital technologies have stressed the accuracy and objectiveness of information. The apparent objectiveness, efficiency, and pragmatism of these methodological approaches have detached these technologies from their purpose (a tool to project the future rather than analyze the present) while the procedural rigor has accentuated the scientific claims of design in the validation of management decisions. On this basis, we argue that this operative framework blurs and questions the role of the designer, and its capacity to engage territories and the dynamics that shape them. In these conditions, digital tools can exacerbate the designer's detachment from contemporary conditions (as a mere observer) while diminishing its direct participation and implication from reality.

This chapter attempts to put forward alternative and novel ways to handle the potential of digital tools, both from the point of view of analysis and intervention, addressing the question of the designer's agency within the scope of what we define as landscape and territorial projects. In order to do that, it proposes the re-engagement of designers in the idea of land-script and data-scapes, as a way forward to acknowledge the power of digital tools in the hands of the creative and critical stance of the designer. Both land-script and data-scapes share common etymological roots with the landscape. From a broader understanding of the latter, as a social and cultural construct, we intend to re-articulate our relation to the former terms.

LAND script _ data SCAPE

LANDSCRIPT

Digital scripting in the last decades has opened up possibilities for designers to generate an array of infinite variations from one original set of instructions. To feed these instructions, contemporary data mining is used in the form of input parameters to generate multiple configurations, reducing considerably the time and effort to produce each of them. Through a set of instructions fed by the set of supplied measurements, the scripting produces iterations adaptable to every parametric variation.

In Carpo's view, these digital tools are rapidly outdating the procedures we have been conventionally using to design and produce architecture. The Albertian paradigm, as defined by Carpo, led architecture to pursue 'identicality' (Carpo 2011, 35–48) – between the set of instructions reflected in the architectural drawings and the constructed product – as the crucial feature that defined its practice in the last centuries. The architectural drawing, and associated conventions, is the tool whereby the architect can design and control architecture without being on the construction site – 'allographic practice.' This design process allows the designer to claim full authorship over the single end product: the building. However, digital tools are radically affecting this production mode: from a set of instructions they are capable of producing not only one single end product – object – but an indefinite number of similar variations, which are not identical copies – algorithm. There are a number of potential advantages in this paradigm shift such as the rise of non-standard production systems and the emergence of new material properties. However, Carpo warns us that 'for the same reasons the emerging non-standard environment is bound to be meaningless' (Carpo 2011, 106) as the decision making process is more frequently entrusted to the parameters of the algorithm and less to the critical discernment of the designer(s).

An interesting reference between the relationship of a technology, such as the script, and landscape can be found in David Leatherbarrow's proposition to use Landscript or Landgraph as a substitute for the word landscape. In his essay 'Levelling the land' (Letherbarrow 1999, 172–175) he refers to the Greek myth by Pherecides of Phyros whereby Zeus threw a matrimonial veil over the head of the goddess of the underworld on which he wove the lines and divisions of the earth, the ocean, and the houses of the ocean. Leatherbarrow describes this veil as a map or mat, an artifact constructed through artistic work. In this sense, landscript is understood as a veil, generated and mediated through the intention and agency of a designer – Zeus – that makes the previously 'uncharted and unnavigable' ground 'livable.' It represents a form of control over the Earth that makes it habitable. This understanding of a landscript as a set of instructions for a constructed artifice with embedded intention is highly relevant with regards to the advancement of new technologies and the fact that almost the entirety of Earth's surface has been modified, intervened, or manufactured by humans, as the current discussions to assign the term Anthropocene (Sample 2014) to our age suggests.[1]

These authors pose several questions related to the designer's agency.[2] On the one hand, the control of the Greek fabric makes us aware of the agency of digital tools in governing landscape and territory as well as the validation of decisions. On the other hand, the landscript embodies the idea of landscape as the modelling and control of given conditions and dynamics that in turn affect the way they are 'draped.' The third interrogation that is suggested in Carpo's paradigm shift is from the multiple variations offered by the script: What are the criteria for selection? Is it parametric efficiency or optimization? How do those variations acquire meaning?

DATASCAPES

Today's gathering and monitoring of data, such as market data mining and more specifically related to Geographic Information Systems (GIS), has radically transformed the digital capacity of producing knowledge about landscapes, cities, the environment and its inhabitants based on the ability to cross-relate multiple and complex sets of data. Picon states that the digital permeation in the landscape disciplines 'lies in the capacity to accumulate and intersect all kinds of data' making it 'more and more difficult to distinguish between landscape and *Datascape*' (Picon 2013, 126). Furthermore, the digital capacity to compute data enables a dynamic understanding of processes, their abstraction through time, and thus, the simulation or prediction of behavioural patterns in future scenarios.

The availability and accuracy of data enables the production of scientific readings that are based on objective facts, mathematically related through algorithms and formulas that unveil legible patterns and potential developments in the territory. Digital tools stress the need for accuracy and the translation of conditions into quantifiable factors, radically transforming our approaches towards map-making and landscape representation. GIS, according to Corner – as well as simulation software and scripting methods – are presented to us as 'devices of inventory, quantitative analysis and legitimization of future plans' (Corner 1999, 221). This status of digital mapping, or 'accelerated technological change' in J.B.

Harley's words strengthens 'its positivist assumptions' (quoted in Corner 1999, 221) which can be read as a continuation of a trend initiated in the reasoning behind scientific urban maps of the Enlightenment.

Dennis Cosgrove describes eighteenth-century graphic design as undecorated simplicity that 'articulates goals of cartographic accuracy and objectivity by erasing evidence of human intervention between survey instrument and printed image' (Cosgrove 2006, 154). These maps built the grounds for 'the emerging science of urban statistics, by which expanding state capitals, and new industrial cities were to be regulated' (Cosgrove 2006, 154).[3] Cosgrove's portrayal of the Enlightenment approach towards map-making and Corner's description of contemporary digital tools pose several questions for us in the fabrication of datascapes: they stress the claims for objectivity or 'the erasing of the human hand' but, at the same time, they warn us about the agency of mappings in managing cities (Picon 2013, 126) and the legitimization of plans. Thus, within the supposedly analytic and selective process of gathering and relating data for the uncovering of territorial patterns and fabrication of datascapes: what is our role as designers? Is it merely collection of facts or does it construct a synthetic and subjective image of a city or territory? Does it acquire a regulatory or enacting role that validates management decisions?

These two sets of questions related to *landscript* and *datascapes* are going to be addressed through two design theses from the Landscape Urbanism programme from the Architectural Association (AALU) where we put forward critical cartographies – using GIS and simulation software – to not only identify overarching questions and alternative readings of various sites across Europe, but also to construct an argument that outlines the designer's approach and understanding of these particular territories. Throughout the following two examples, we will outline AALU's principles as part of an approach towards the territory that understands digital technology as an operative framework that re-claims the notions of agency and specificity through the recovery of the notion of 'techne'. This notion is of special relevance for us to propose alternatives to the methodological and reductive understanding of digital tools and the critical questioning of their application in specific contexts. Thus, we propose a constant feedback process between strategies based on general principles and context-related decisions through its actualization or acquisition of meaning within specific territories in time.

Jose Alfredo Ramirez and Clara Olóriz Sanjuán

COASTAL FUTURES

To further explain one particular approach towards the role of the designer in the use of digital tools, we will use a project called *Coastal Futures* by Valeria Garcia and Yunya Tang. In their design thesis, Valeria and Yunya examine contemporary flooding scenarios and the possibility to use coastal erosion, caused by extreme storms and surge conditions, to develop tidal creeks. Flooding scenarios in turn will gradually build the tectonic grounds to propose alternative productive spatial territories from where land formations can be then re-articulated.

The proposal makes use of the so-called catastrophic events, such as costal dynamics, floods, and tidal forces, as the engines to suggest alternatives to the problem-solving construction of eventually obsolete defenses. These alternatives understand and embrace the cultural and social implications of infrastructural interventions in given territories. In doing so, they build the foundations for a gradual change in the socio-economic conditions of isolated coastal communities in the south of England, deeply affected by London's centralization; by promoting emergency not as a threat but as a potential to shape alternative futures.

The principle behind the project is the acceptance of coastal erosion and the imminent impact on the shape of coastal territories. It means not the building of barriers, but the retreat of land. This acknowledges the capacity of waterscapes to be the force behind the future of these coastal territories. The proposal is thought from the five-year government funding scheme to deal with coastal erosion. This budget initiates the infrastructure required to control the formation of creeks that will absorb and diffuse flooding events and it then uses tidal forces to continue the construction and extension of the channels and streams.

Within their project, Valeria and Yunya used Caesar, a two-dimensional flow and sediment transport model, to simulate the formation of tidal creeks (Figure 1.1) through the use of algorithms and cellular automata. However, these techniques and the Caesar software simulation tools cannot be taken in isolation, as form generation or as an end in themselves, neither are the conditions in which they are inserted taken as a blank canvas. On the contrary, they are informed by, actualized, and further specified in their negotiation with the existing territorial conditions (Figure 1.2). The principles of tidal formation are intersected with the existing social, political, and physical conditions of the site. Tidal creeks are designed as a constructing device with the capacity to articulate and orchestrate human and geomorphological interaction in the town of Sandwich. For example, the project simulates the tidal processes and how long it takes for a creek to

LAND script _ data SCAPE

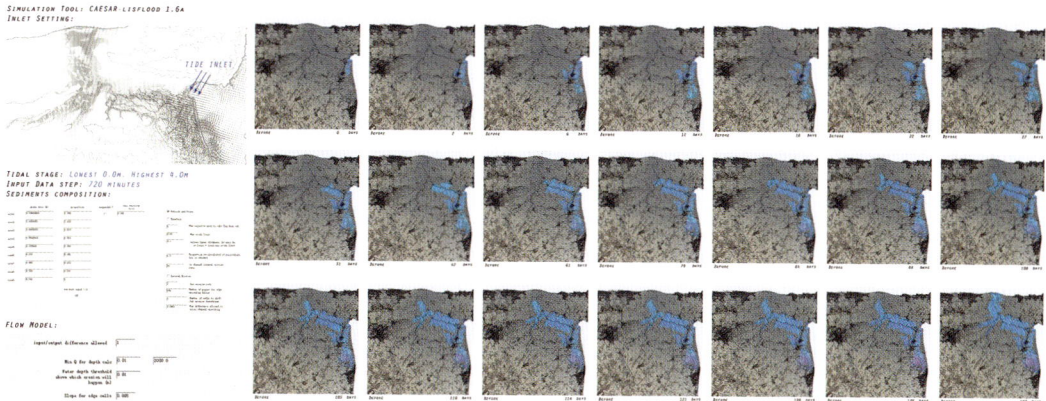

Figure 1.1   Tidal creek simulations performed via Caesar software.
Source: drawn by Valeria Garcia and Yunya Tang.

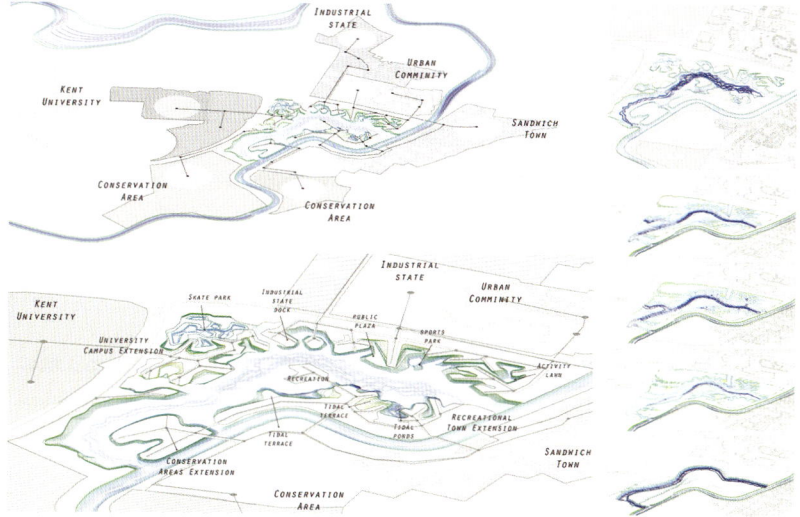

Figure 1.2   Actualization of tidal creek formations in accordance to specific social
dynamics in the area of Sandwich, southeast England.
Source: drawn by Valeria Garcia and Yunya Tang.

emerge within these particular sites. It then tests various landscape techniques – such as the construction of channels and dykes – to manipulate these formation processes so that they can accommodate a number of conditions required by the specific context. The areas taken over by the creek formation are gradually transformed into fish farms, hybrid agriculture, town services, and local infrastructures among others. The tidal creek simulations as a landscript become a generative tool that is appropriated and modulated in accordance with their physical requirements but also with the specific social purposes that condition their formation.

Valeria and Yunya wove social conditions, such as productive economies and administrative regulations in the area, existing government funding for coastal zones, and insurance policies, with the proposed tectonic grounds, proposing hybrid programs such as: agro/aqua culture scenarios or the possibility to integrate knowledge services, such as a university, within an expanded water infrastructure that serves as the spine for its future development. This approach is read through the multi-scalar intentions of the project, at a more strategic level and at a larger scale. The patterns of land ownership and resource exploitation are overlapped with the tidal dynamics to design a series of negotiated conditions in each particular area of the site, resulting in a manufactured territory that is gradually informed through specific goals (Figure 1.3). *Coastal Futures* represents an example of landscripted territories actualized through digital tools, in the form of algorithmic simulations of geomorphological processes and GIS data mining of existing patterns of land ownership and social formations, to subvert and re-invent existing productive dynamics within the new proposed tectonic grounds.

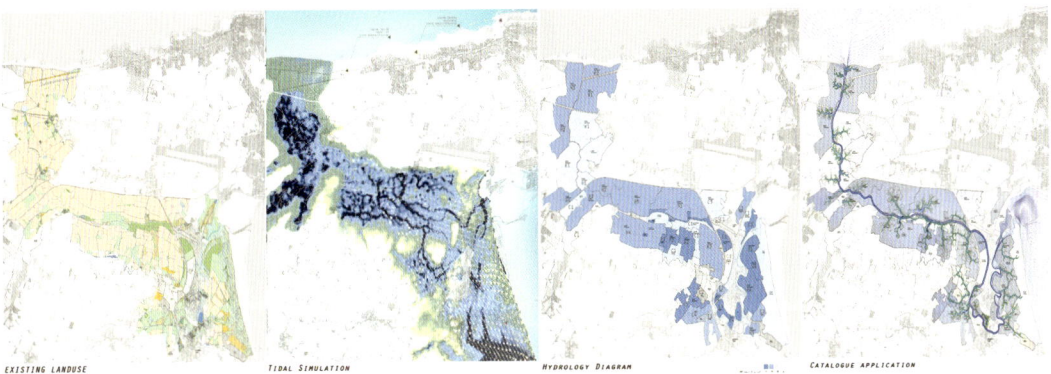

Figure 1.3 Overlapping of existing land uses (a) and tidal simulations (b) to produce a hydrology strategy (c) and actualize the catalogue of tidal creek typologies on site (d).

Source: drawn by Valeria Garcia and Yunya Tang.

L A N D script _ data S C A P E

SHIFTING SANDS

Digital technology understood as a method produces logic and static forms, regardless of their scripted potential geometrical variations. This idea is explored by this second example in which the re-activation of static and decaying dunes is made possible through their re-linkage and association to the existing territory, as a *landscript* or draped cloth. The establishment of negotiation regimes between sand dynamics and human activity patterns such as forestry, tourism, and existing villages is developed through the compromises and controlled interactions designed for the dune landscape inhabitation. It has been intrinsic to the historical nature of the Curonian Spit, a territory located in the boundary between Lithuania and a Russian exclave Kaliningrad, and now through UNESCO conservationist policies, both human activities and dune dynamics are constrained, or rather, sentenced to disappear. The way Niki Kakali and Anastasia Kotenko (2014) defined the argument for their project is as follows:

> *From a line on the plan, the political border between Lithuania and the Russian ex-clave becomes a territory of negotiations involving diverse interests in-between counteracting forces. Our proposal is to open active corridors for dunes, an inherent dynamic landscape trapped within fixed environments and UNESCO's conservation policies, which shift according to their time cycle and that of forest formations, thus negotiating between the cultural, social and economic land values in the Curonian territory.*

From their intentions behind the project, there are several aspects that can be extracted and can shed some light on the way we understand the agency of the designer within landscape digital tools and how that in turn can produce novel approaches to the way we understand landscape tectonics. Dune dynamics are researched through an abstraction of the principles of particle movement scripting. Gradually, several artificial obstacles are introduced into the research to unveil the potentials of the various forms of interaction in the construction of the landscape. In parallel to these studies, Niki and Anastasia investigated the site's existing economic activities and their cultural and social understanding of the dunescape that surrounds them.

This dual research uncovers two main drivers for the project. On the one hand, the odyssean mutual control and influences that both dynamics exert into each other: the way dunes constrain and prevent human forms of inhabitation and the various techniques used by humans to establish borders with the dunes. Understanding these conflicting interests in the territory through time reveals the potential of a cyclical articulation of territorial dynamics (Figure 1.4) in which sand paths are, for example, open through a 50-year-old forest according to wind directions and land ownership management patterns and closed through forest plantation cycles. This temporal reading of particular conflicting site conditions entails the challenging of conventional static conceptions of land ownership, zoning, and exploitation. And also, it is not time understood in linear terms, from the design to the construction, but it is a time sequence that is negotiated and affected, and thus constructed through specific contingencies; a time that accommodates particular agencies and purposes. It is only through the conscious goal, related to the particular conditions, that we can think about time in those terms; without taking into account those determinants, dune landscape evolution will have been thought from the perspective of a self-referenced linear simulation.

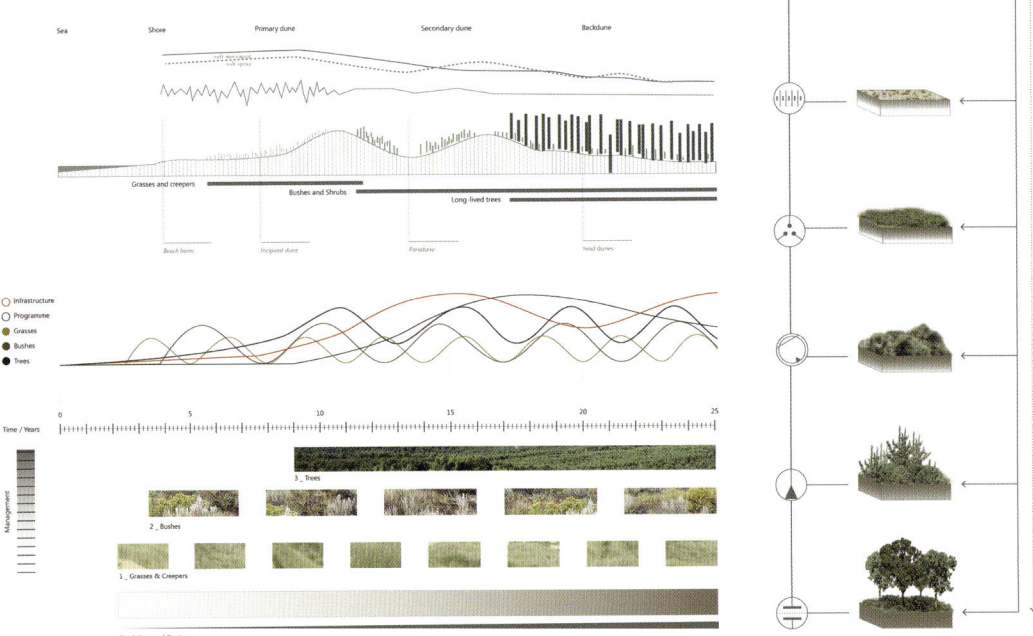

Figure 1.4 Life cycles of each agency involved and intersecting in the development of the Curonian Spit. A series of scripted-digital simulations extract a catalogue of basic configurations, rules and logics pertaining to sand geomorphology. This in turn forms the material ready to be shaped through the negotiation of social formations.

Source: drawn by Anastasia Kotenko and Niki Kakali.

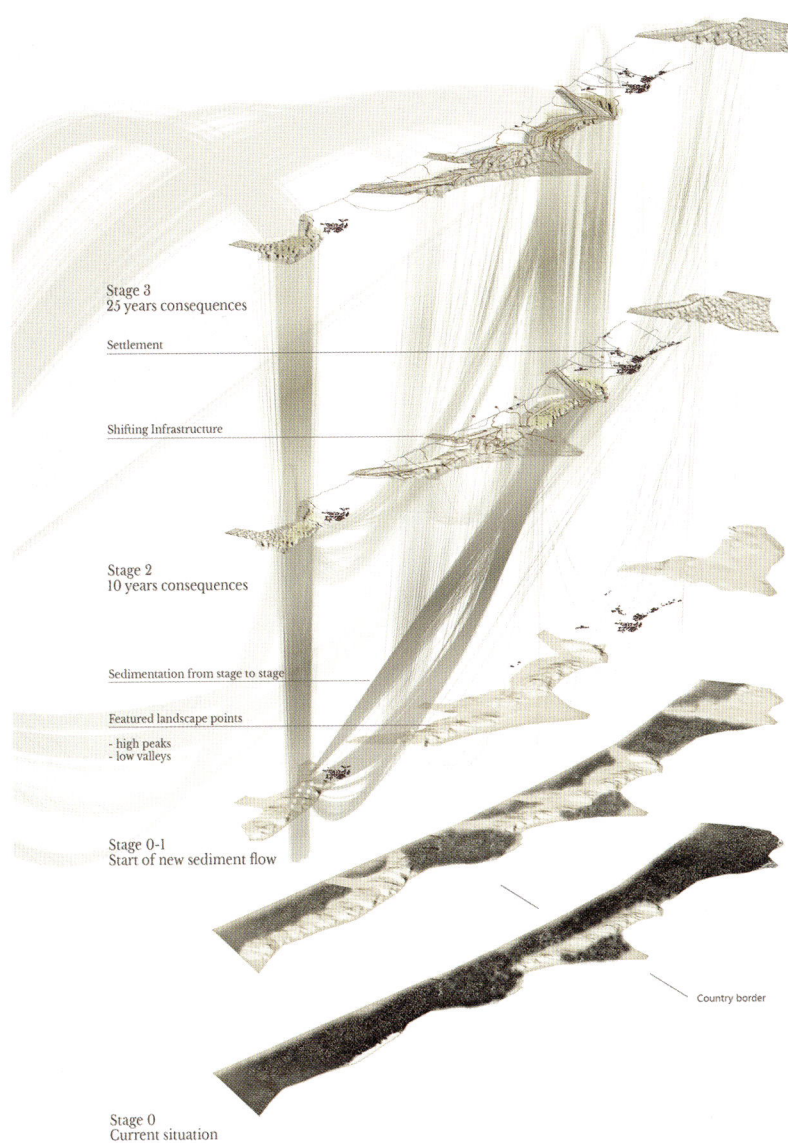

Figure 1.5 Implementation of the strategy through time.

Source: drawn by Anastasia Kotenko and Niki Kakali.

What becomes crucial in this project is the agency of the designer in a decision-making process that establishes priorities and hierarchies among the physical, economic, or political contingencies in the time-based implementation of their project, which would be impossible to formulate, if following a methodological or linear deployment of a digitally run script.

These forms of interaction through time are embodied in a series of material border constructions and control policies that allow the co-existence of conflicting agencies, thus the above-mentioned managerial aspect of digital technologies. The border zone that protects human activities and dunes from each other develops into productive and tourism infrastructure with various time spans (Figure 1.5). Thus, the bordering of this territory is managed through the manipulation of the cycles of the various existing agencies. Added to this, the design of these management strategies and borders entails a constant critical assessment of side implications and the establishment of priorities and hierarchies among the various interests.

On the other hand, through various scales, the constant interaction between general principles and specific purposes, time frames, economic contingencies, and conflicts informs the dynamic formations (Figure 1.6) that allow the materialization of territorial interventions. The indexing of sand dynamics across Europe (Figure 1.7) here is far from an analysis tool, it uncovers political and legal

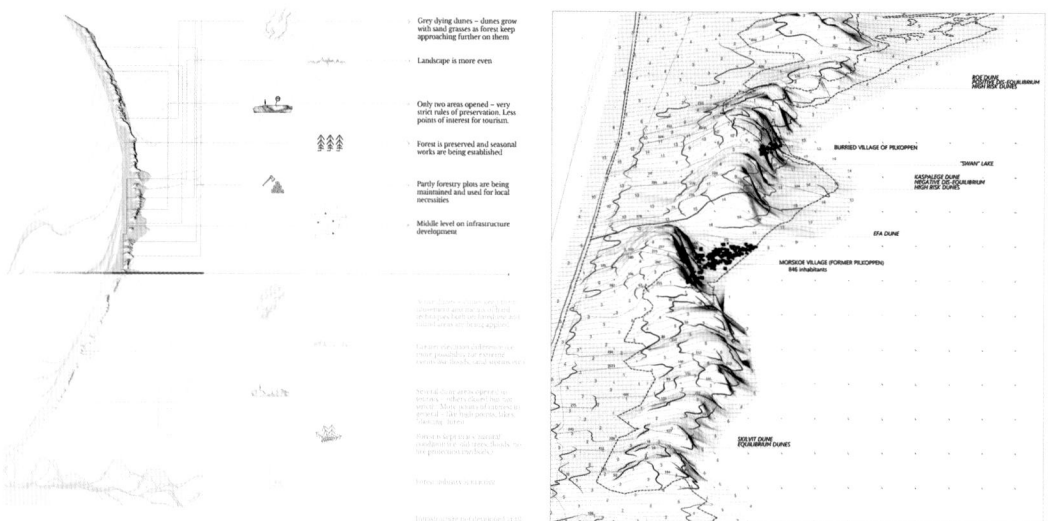

Figure 1.6 Larger scale cartography of the Curonian Spit in Kaliningrad depicting its geomorphological origins and formations in relation to the social patterns in the territory.

Source: drawn by Anastasia Kotenko and Niki Kakali.

LAND script _ data SCAPE

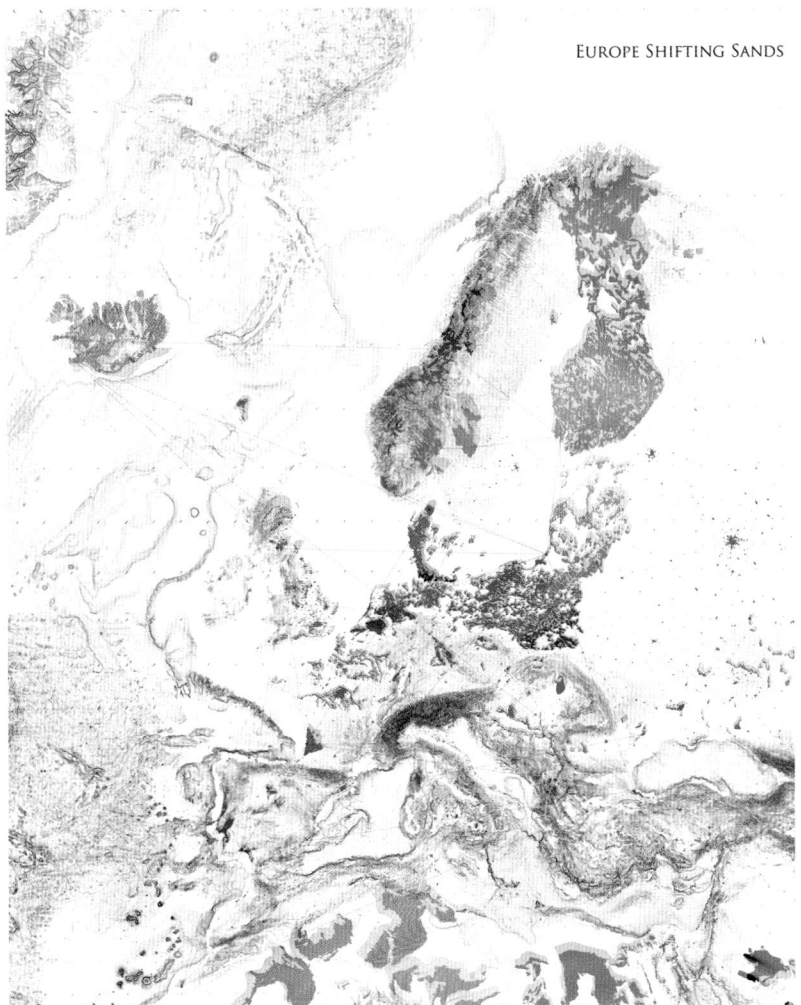

EUROPE SHIFTING SANDS

Figure 1.7 A GIS cartography of a comprehensive understanding of Europe through the dynamics of sand dune landscapes along the entire continental grounds.
Source: drawn by Anastasia Kotenko and Niki Kakali.

issues of sand exchange between countries and a range of approaches across Europe where dune landscapes are protected over existing settlements or where exploitation patterns negate their existence. Moreover, moving away from Cosgrove's depiction of eighteenth-century accuracy (2006, 154), cartography is here used to put forward an argument about the way the designers approach and think about shifting sands as territorial and political conflicts that challenge the conventional stability of land ownership, management and boundaries.

Jose Alfredo Ramirez and Clara Olóriz Sanjuán

TECHNE IN THE DIGITAL AGE

The inherent systematicity implied in the use of simulation and GIS software is a direct consequence of the set of instructions that we use as a language to give commands to a computer. Scripting can be defined as a system of written instructions, in this case, between the computer and ourselves. Methodological and systematic thinking, in its objectiveness, accuracy, and exactness, leads towards the fading of agency and purpose. In our view, some of the previously posed questions related to agency could be derived from the thinking behind the systemic and methodological nature of digital software, as a set of exact and measurable instructions that emphasize its scientific nature.

The previous examples attempt to stress the fact that we should not take for granted the scientific premise in our approach towards technology and digital tools. And it is from there that we can perhaps suggest alternatives to the objectification and validation or methodological fate of digital design in landscape practices and cartography. This assumption may be a consequence of considering technology in its 'narrow sense' in Foucault's terms, like an exact science, hard technology, electricity, fabrication tools, or software, rather than as a rational form of knowledge that brings it closer to its Greek etymology *techne*. When asked by Paul Rabinow about the definition of architecture as a natural science or a dubious 'science', he answers that his interest is not so much on the distinction between exact or inexact sciences but more on the Greek term *techne* (Foucault 1984, 255).

Far from methodologies or recipes, *techne,* as defined by Foucault, is considered as 'a practical rationality governed by a conscious goal' (Foucault 1997, 378). In our case, the 'practical rationality' can be paralleled by what we mean by the agency of the designer or subject in their production of a territorial project that is governed and conditioned by a 'conscious goal'. For us, this means that it is actualized and acquires specificity and meaning through the addressed conditions. In the case of *Coastal Futures* and *Shifting Sands*, the design of creek formations or the scripting of dune corridors is not about a methodological set of guidelines for the generation of these landforms according to 'nature's' rules, but about informing, weaving, and intersecting these dynamics with the existing territorial conditions or purposes through a series of designed negotiation mechanisms.

In similar terms, Shiner defines the English word 'art' from the Latin *ars* and Greek *techne* as 'any human activity performed with skill and grace … human making dedicated to a purpose' (Shiner 2001, 5). The modern split between 'art, craft, and sciences' relegates crafts to skill and rules. In the older art system, before the eighteenth-century division, inventive collaboration, specific place, and purpose were inherent to the work of the artist/artisan, distant from the modern system of art as an end in itself. Alternative to the normative division between art and sciences, several authors describe the relationship between landscape painting and geology in the eighteenth and nineteenth centuries (Cosgrove 1998, 223–252) as a form of interdependence. Marcia Pointon underlines the fact that this unity implied the sharing of language and imagery, empiricism and imagination, documentation and creation, synthesized in 'a new "scientific" attitude to observation with a high degree of intense subjective feeling' (Pointon 1979, 98).

Along these lines, we intend to question these normative distinctions between the scientific or subjective, between art and craft, between digital methods and the designer's decision-making process to build our approach towards the relationship between landscape design and digital technologies. Thus, beyond divisions between exact or inexact sciences, we understand the influence of digital tools in landscape design from *techne*, acknowledging the agency and rationality of the designer together with the role of specificity and purpose or 'conscious goal', embodied in Zeus' artistic veil or landscript. Engaging with today's conditions, we understand the relevance of digital technology and its potential role within landscape and territory to construct an operative framework that challenges methodological assumptions and re-articulates our role as designers.

We seek the application of various techniques, simulation, and GIS software, questioning their principles through a rational understanding, and not as a mere recipe detached from concrete realities. The questioning of given assumptions, methodologies, and conventions is the very ground on which novel approaches, such as territorial alternatives towards shifting sands or coastal defenses, can be thought. So, this stance is intrinsically tied to a conscious goal that makes possible its actualization or materialization in the territory and moves the role of the designer away from narrow conceptions of technology. Therefore, technology here becomes the element of knowledge and the inner forces that inform and reiterate abstract ideas and principles into material reality and particular conditions.

The potential of digital tools within landscape practices cannot simply offer an array of possibilities and variations for a given territory but new forms of production, agency, and operation. Borrowing from what Carpo calls a 'Split Agency' (2011, 123–128), landscript and datascapes can be redefined in a new type of project or territorial praxis from a two fold approach: the generic and the specific, which are intrinsically related and linked. Digital tools allow the design through a generic framework that is defined by means of guidelines. In its process of actualization, decision making, and purpose conditionings, it then acquires and defines specificity which in turn feeds back into the overall framework; thus, in the previous sand atlas, larger questions can be drawn to overarch various territories, where similarities and differences become a constant form of production in the materialization and manipulation of the generic guidelines.

In the case of the *Coastal Futures* project by Valeria and Yunya, the generic project refers to the development of a guideline framework (Figure 1.8) applicable to flooding conditions and territories across coastal areas in the UK and Europe as the given geolocation (Figure 1.9). The understanding of these landscape dynamics generates a set of instructions to design tidal creeks in any territory with similar materiality and land formations. These generic guidelines are then taken into a particular territory, such as Sandwich in the southeast of England where the specific social, cultural, economic, and political dynamics will actualize, inform, and condition the creation of site-specific tidal creeks to design future territories.[4] Similarly, time cycles in sand dune landscapes become a framework that understands conflicting interests and bordering control through time in various sites; that is gradually materialized through the timing of particular social

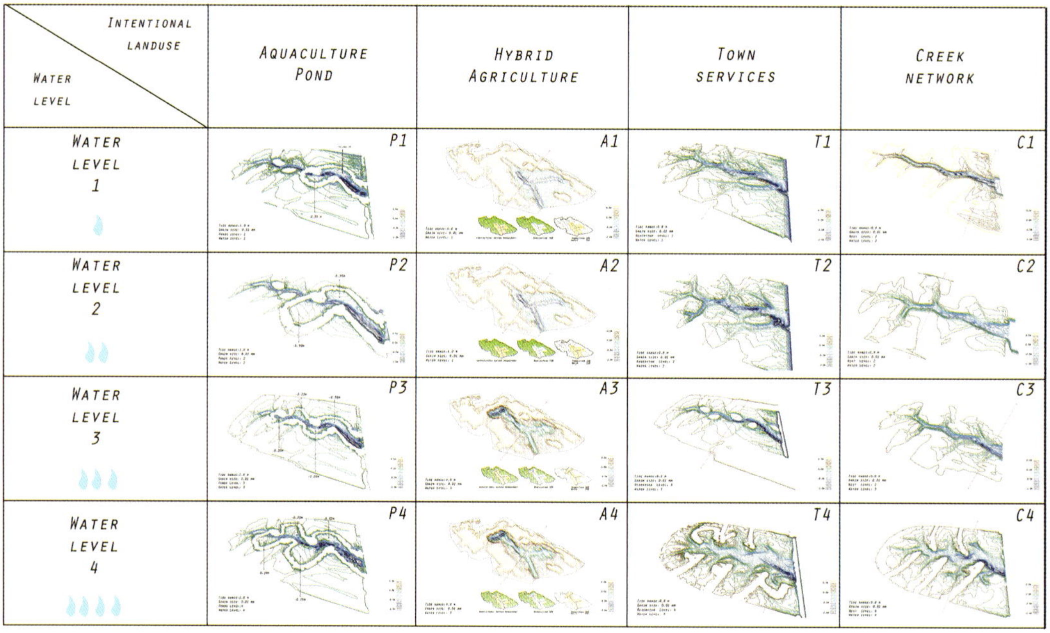

Figure 1.8 Generic guidelines to overlap flooding conditions and productive landforms according to various degrees and types.

Source: drawn by Valeria Garcia and Yunya Tang.

LAND script _ data SCAPE

Figure 1.9 Cartography depicting sites with similar flooding conditions to the site of Sandwich, southeast England.
Source: drawn by Valeria Garcia and Yunya Tang.

formations. In its design process, the unfolding of the generic algorithm is manipulated by the designers' agency, goals, and context, fabricating a landscript.

In this actualization process, technology or *techne* shifts from its scientific, methodological simplification to the engagement with specific conditions through which principles are actualized or informed and design acquires agency. These multi-scalar intersections and negotiations, the draping of the landscript veil, are something that we term manufactured territories in order to emphasize the 'machinic' control of the mutual interactions between landform dynamics and territorial conditions. And it is the place where we find that the production of knowledge through technology in its broadest sense becomes more relevant, not in the division between exact or inexact sciences or in the methodological deployment of software that does not acknowledge a goal-oriented rationality or in other words the agency, specificity, intention, and implication of design decisions.

NOTES

1. The Anthropocene is a term coined by ecologist Eugene F. Stoermer, and made popular by atmospheric chemist Paul Crutzen, in order to describe the present as a new geological age due to influence of human behaviour on Earth's atmosphere. If the international Commission on Stratigraphy (ICS) formalized the term, it would mean the official end of the previous geological epoch and the beginning of the Anthropocene. The Anthropocene Working Group plans to meet in 2016 to take the final decision.
2. For a more extensive argument on agency see Spencer (2014).
3. 'The accuracy of the base map was fundamental to the persuasive power of the statistical information plotted onto it. Rather than celebrating the unity and harmony of urban community, the map's task was to bring into the light of practical reason invisible but all-too-potent urban pathologies' in Cosgrove's 'Carto-City' (2006).
4. For a more extensive reference on Territory please see Stuart Elden's (2010) inflection of the term as Political Technology 'owned, distributed, mapped, calculated, bordered and controlled'.

REFERENCES

Carpo, Mario. 2011. *The Alphabet and the Algorithm.* Cambridge, Mass.: MIT Press.

Corner, James. 1999. 'The Agency of Mapping.' In *Mappings,* edited by Denis Cosgrove, 214–252. London: Reaktion Books.

Cosgrove, Denis. 1998. *Social Formation and Symbolic Landscape*. Wisconsin: University of Wisconsin Press.

Cosgrove, Denis. 2006. 'Carto-City.' In *Else/Where: Mapping – New Cartographies of Networks and Territories,* edited by Janet Abrams and Peter Hall, 148–157. Minneapolis: University of Minnesota Design Institute.

Elden, Stuart. 2010. 'Land, Terrain, Territory.' *Progress in Human Geography* 34: 799–817.

Foucault, Michel. 1984. 'Space, Knowledge and Power. Interview conducted by Paul Rabinow.' In *The Foucault Reader*, edited by Paul Rabinow, 239–256. New York: Pantheon Books.

Foucault, Michel. 1997. 'Space, Knowledge and Power. Interview conducted by Paul Rabinow.' In *Rethinking Architecture: A Reader in Cultural Theory*, edited by Neil Leach, 239–256. London: Routledge.

Gardner, Bob. 2009. 'Euclid's Elements – A 2,500 Year History.' Accessed 5 February 2015. https://faculty.etsu.edu/gardnerr/Geometry-History/before-euclid.htm.

Kakali, Niki and Kotenko, Anastasia. 2014. *Aeolian Sand Odyssey*. Thesis (MA) – Landscape Urbanism. London: Architectural Association.

Letherbarrow, David. 1999. 'Levelling the Land.' In *Recovering Landscape,* edited by James Corner, 171–186. New York: Princeton Architectural Press.

Picon, Antoine. 2013. 'The Digital Culture of Landscape Architecture.' *Harvard Design Magazine* 36: 124–129.

Pointon, Marcia. 1979. 'Geology and Landscape Painting in Nineteenth-century England.' In *Images of the Earth. Essays in the History of Environmental Sciences*, edited by Ludmilla Jordanova and Roy Porter, 84–108. Oxford: The Alden Press.

Sample, Ian. 2014. 'Anthropocene: Is this the New Epoch of Humans?' *The Guardian*, 16 October.

Shiner, Larry. 2001. *The Invention of Art: A Cultural History.* Chicago: The University of Chicago Press.

Spencer, Douglas. 2014. 'Nature is the Dummy: Circulations of the Metabolic.' *New Geographies* 6: 108–113.

An interface for instrumental reconciliation

Alexander Robinson

The landscape architect has always been an agent of reconciliation. The traditional reconciliation was between nature and art: gardens and parks negotiate the space between wilderness and society. In modern times, man is not in need of reconciliation with nature as much as he is with his own cities; today he turns to the wilderness as an agent of reconciliation rather than as a foreign entity. Landscape architecture finds its potency in reconciling our bodies with the machinic urban condition, making our cities 'livable' through the insertion of re-conditioned wilderness and 'green.' In an effort to expand beyond compensatory measures, the profession has sought to escape the 'semantic reserve' of the park and disarm the ubiquitous machinic condition of modern society, (Weller 2006, 71). It asks: can we eliminate this dichotomy? Can we make society's most significant built projects less alienating and more 'human' – places that we relate to, that reflect our values, and that support our health and well-being? How do we reconcile with something that is, ostensibly, of our own making?

In this chapter, I propose that this impulse can be advanced by an instrumental reconciliation: a reinvigorated and idealized relationship between society and the tools which have designed it. Marginalized by the growing influence of specialized methodologies in the authorship of the urban condition and particularly of its infrastructures, landscape architects can find agency by re-fashioning the intermediary between intention and expertise. Defined as the liminal space where human impulse is translated into tools and instruments, the interface becomes a powerful reconciliatory ground by which to re-order design agendas while speaking to dominant agents and their methodologies.

THE INTERFACE

The inadequacy of our interfaces with performance design tools is evident in the shape of our infrastructural landscapes. While multiple factors contribute to their alienating quality, their design interface contributes by skewing design representations to measured performance parameters. Civil engineering relies on synoptic tools that often incidentally eliminate representations of human space and many unmeasurable, seemingly insignificant, irregularities (Scott 1998). With limited or no integration of place representations within the metricized tools, the designer's body and intuition are placed on poor footing during some of the most formative decision processes. While strict adherence to measured function is still considered an advantage and we find satisfaction in an infrastructure's resemblance to performance diagrams, they have as often as not been judged failures of place-making and their stain on the urban condition has become a major reconciliatory project for designers and urban activists.

Nevertheless, we rely on civic infrastructures that are predictable, operational, and efficient. No matter how much we lament their shortcomings, scale and public oversight ensure that the tools that measure and optimize these systems will remain powerful determinants of design. In this context, the interface becomes the site where we recognize and re-calibrate our implicit relationship with these established tools (rather than trying to replace them). According to Branden Hookway, an interface 'describe[s] the ways in which humanness is implicated in relation with technology' (Hookway 2014, 1). This project proposes that building an augmented interface will create a more 'human' relation with these tools and will ultimately produce a more conciliatory built condition.

This pursuit is largely irresistible: we are inevitably drawn to tools that represent and determine our environment with increased accuracy and availability. Properly harnessed, they promise to create operationally competent and phenomenally rich landscapes, legitimized by their relationship to established tools. However, in the approach suggested here, we curate established instrumentations, rather than being the inadequate author of them. Before we can make more 'human worlds, we must build a 'human' interface for world-making tools. In the process, we equip ourselves for a landscape where agency will eventually be defined by the real-time management of landscape processes. Finally, the landscape interface opens up opportunities for increased public engagement, which can re-position the design project in powerful ways.

While the subject warrants a larger, more systematic investigation for landscape architecture, the interface already has 'a familiar albeit indeterminate and even spectral presence,' that is ubiquitous in contemporary society (Hookway 2014, 1). Its exceptional place within landscape architecture practice is exemplified by my lab's project to create an idealized interface for the design of the Owens Lake Dust Control Project. By investigating the development and product of this effort, we can begin to map the design problem and potential of the interface to address the contemporary landscape project.

My lab's project can be divided into three parts, which also represents the chronological development of the work. It began with an impulse to build an improved design interface as a response to the failure for existing tooling in providing place-making values, and specifically state-mandated 'public trust values.' Secondly, by measure of their design agency and place-making value, tools were collected, developed, and integrated into the new design interface, which included a form-making sand modeling system and a multiple value custom analysis software. Finally, following limitations discovered during the development of tooling an interface, the system developed for in-house design was adapted for a broader public engagement to allow user review and play.

IDEAL INTERFACE FOR DESIGNING AN INFRASTRUCTURE

The metrics of cost and resource use loom heavy over the design of the Los Angeles Department of Water and Power's (LADWP) Owens Lake Dust Control Project. The project aims to control dust on an alkaline lake dried by the Los Angeles Aqueduct, which had become the nation's single greatest source of the highly deleterious PM10 particulate pollution. Due to the huge scale of the phased projects to control dust, now covering over 40 square miles of the approximately 100 square mile lake, a single additional dollar per square foot can easily add tens of millions of dollars in cost, and water use can exceed the annual consumption of many cities. As of 2015 the project has cost over one and a half billion dollars with an annual water use equivalent to that of San Francisco. Engineers, under pressure from their managers and constituents in the City of Los Angeles, over 300 miles away from the lake, have therefore been exceedingly motivated to find dust control designs and methods that minimize the use of these resources.

However, tempering the design of a maximally 'efficient' system of dust control is a state-mandated requirement that all navigable bodies of water (and formerly navigable bodies of water) abide by 'Public Trust Doctrine.' This requires the accommodation of 'public' values such as ecological, recreational, aesthetic,

An interface for instrumental reconciliation

scientific, and educational exclusive to this kind of feature. Under the pressure of heavy fines and having few alternatives to meet the doctrine, the LADWP leaned on a straightforward method called 'shallow flooding' (see Figure 2.1). Pouring water into the lake created automatic public trust value. It was the most lake-like method and provided a remarkable bird habitat. It was also cost-effective to implement, and though it used massive amounts of water, it was a resource commitment that the LADWP mistakenly assumed would lessen over time.

The resulting landscape is at once harsh and surreally beautiful. The 'lake' is simultaneously industrial, rural, and wild – a sensorial bath of reflections and wildlife surrounded by a mountain panorama, yet bracketed by berm roads and pierced with plumbing installations. From a designer's perspective there is a sense that the project is a lost opportunity. Defined by its haphazardly shaped polygonal pools and monocultures, it appears un-designed, a purely operational landscape made with little consideration as to how the interventions would become part of the landscape. Now that a landmark legal settlement opens up opportunities for more water-efficient and even waterless dust control techniques, value making can no longer lean on abundant water to compensate for the lack of design.

Figure 2.1 View of the Owens Lake Dust Control Project shallow flooding pond and berm road.

To be fair, there is little consensus about what kind of place this landscape should become. It cannot be restored to its former state, and there is no encompassing historical model for its valuation or design.[1]

Given the scale of the problem, it seems forgivable that the primary concern in its construction and operation was maximum efficiency. Building even the simplest of infrastructures on the fine sediments of the lake was a gargantuan challenge both physically and politically.

However, while the final design must abide by fundamental standards of efficiency and has to manage a complex condition, the process of design need not be thrifted. Advanced tools and simulations tilt the design process deeper into intricate formative territories, allowing more experimentation and manipulation without actual expenditure. While the computational tools to achieve operational efficiency presume greater precision and a narrowing of options, their availability also makes possible a robust engagement within augmented design interfaces.

Thus, the utopian impulse for reconciliation asks: could the modern tools of infrastructure design be re-arranged to discover new possibilities for a *place* within efficient operational models? What would happen if representations and even measurements of a *place* had a footing within the operational design process? These considerations will be marginal relative to concerns for dust control performance, but an appropriate design process could discover a way to maximize public trust values while using less water. By reconciling with our tools, we can discover better ways to reconcile with the dust control landscape. Strategic public trust design could substitute for resource use and allow the use of a more operationally efficient dust control method.

At this point, the project may appear a matter of professional reconciliation between landscape architecture and civil engineering and a tempering of mutual suspicion. Landscape architecture faults civil engineering for failing to make considerations for place within their performance landscapes, while civil engineering can dismiss landscape architecture for its frivolity and deviation from critical parameters of cost, resource use, maintenance, and performance. This impasse calls to mind the classical desire to combine *technic* and *art* – an impetus that has traditionally operated at the core of both practices, but which has become eroded by a methodological collision and displacement between the professions (Corner 2002).

The tools of civil engineering have become increasingly comprehensive and instrumental, reducing opportunities for typical professional collaboration and placing landscape architects at a fatal remove from design agency. Methodologically displaced, in part by aspirations to occupy civil engineering design territory,

An interface for instrumental reconciliation

landscape architects are unprepared to match the multivariate performance efficiency asked of contemporary infrastructure design. They cannot effectively integrate their intuitive, humanistic, or ecological design within the civil engineering design paradigm. Even the LADWP has admitted that the operational requirements they generated for a recent forward-thinking design collaboration with landscape architects on the Owens Lake are impossibly complex and constrained.

At the same time, the growing agency, comprehensive range, and availability of these tools represent an opportune moment for methodological appropriation and synchronization. Now more than ever the expertise and tools of engineering have become externalized and are accessible to generalists. Abundant computational power makes it possible to use these tools to create the long sought-after 'datascape': a virtual design space to explore constrained solutions. 'Datascape' enables design explorations to adhere to parametric determinants, rather than drifting into the territory of impossible, if well-meaning models of place-making (Weller 2006, 71).

In the case of Owens Lake, variably complex and nearly universally constrained in resource and cost, an idealized *interface* would relate the precise agency-defining tools of operational design to the scale and methods necessary for the design of multiple-value place-making. The interface would allow design solutions that engage both representation and a phenomenological consideration of place, as well as efficiency. The resulting design would be distinguished as the product of a careful reconciliation of trans-disciplinary tools and methodologies. Free from professional or theoretical bias, it would reveal its agency through strategic development of tools and playful human engagement with the tools. The interface would harness both our most basic human intuition and our highest and most synthetic expression of expertise.

OWENS LAKE INTERFACE

The Owens Lake Rapid Landscape Prototyping Machine Interface, also known as 'Greetings from the Owens Lake,' is designed as a comprehensive interface to engage the impulses and sensibilities of a designer within the constraints of a specific toolset, resulting in an expanded yet precise exploration of design options. Through its looped engagement with computer simulations and user inputs, the interface informs original impulses and translates them into projective and productive adjustments of the design tools (see Figure 2.2). The feedback loop between impulse and instrumentation defines a new space, an *interfacial gap*

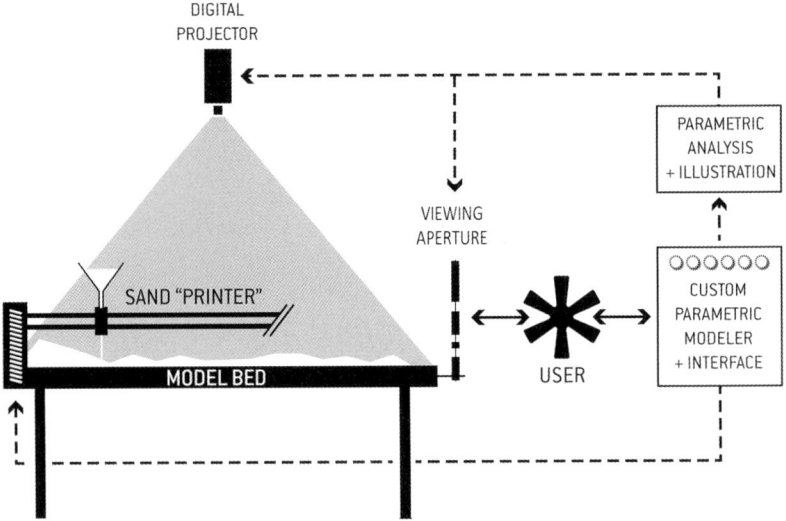

Figure 2.2 Early interface diagram for Owens Lake Rapid Landscape Prototyping Machine ('Greetings from the Owens Lake').

where we can witness cognitive steps or even leaps between our inputs and the resulting actions. An ideal interface in this context creates formative gaps where design is both legitimized by the tools and marked by a sophisticated human sensibility.

My lab's interface for the Owens Lake Dust Control Project consists of two primary parts: a physical drawing system to generate and represent topographical form (important for habitat, dust control, and user experience) and a custom analysis and simulation software model to calibrate the design to particularities of the place. By presenting interactive representations of critical tool building and design outcomes, the system builds an immersive, more 'human' process of exploration and discovery within a design paradigm defined by parameters of machinic efficiency. The interface intertwines consequential engineering parameters with the rich and eccentric qualities of place and ecology. Through this process, the project suggests that we might achieve a more 'human' design process for landscape infrastructures and through this create results that satisfy challenges from both engineers and landscape architects.

An interface for instrumental reconciliation

OWENS LAKE INTERFACE PART I: SIMULATION AND ANALYSIS SOFTWARE

The primary space for reconciliation between instruments and place is a custom experiential and analysis landscape simulation system, developed in the processing programming environment. The software generates and distributes dust control technology on topography based on terrain, user selection, and variables of resource use. From this, the software creates a rendered simulation of the current design selection that can be explored from multiple vantage points. The multivariate generation of dust control systems combined with various analytical visualizations and experiential controls, including adjustable season, time of day, and user movement, overlays a 'datascape' with material landscape to create a dynamically represented solution space.

The selection of instruments that can simulate critical operations is essential to this approach. The tools create agency and define the priorities for any design. As much as possible the established tools and methods are appropriated intact to maintain a legitimized relationship with the original methodology. For example, for the Owens Lake Dust Control Project designs, effective dust control configurations and their resource and capital cost are calculated constantly within the software, using LADWP methods and figures, and represented within a visual graph. An established multivariate habitat suitability analysis is also represented and used to populate the spatio-experiential simulation.

Custom visual analysis tools were designed to align public trust interests and place-making within a paradigm of efficiency. Real-time view-shed, angle of incidence, and fore/middle/back-ground analysis, field-verified, were developed within a custom experiential software suite. The tools do not conclusively measure visual efficiency, but allow for an augmented judgment by the designer. Additionally, they proclaim, within earshot of managing entities, that design responds to both public trust values and measures of efficiency.

OWENS LAKE INTERFACE PART II: SEDIMENTARY MODELING AND DRAWING

Sand modeling was chosen as an ideal medium for developing design form and layering projected visual analysis, as it is both intuitively manipulated and computationally relevant. Although it has been mistakenly perceived as a simulation of dust, sand modeling is a fast, physical, and computational device

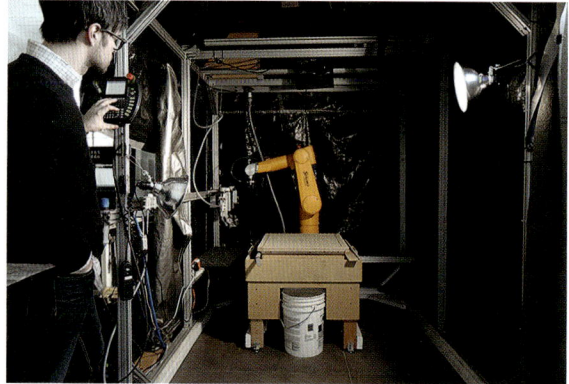

Figure 2.3 Rapid Landscape Prototyping Machine topographic sand modeling system with robotic arm, 3D laser scanner, vacuum-forming sandbox, and digital projection system.

for sedimentary construction, including balanced cut/fill, un-reinforced form, and construction by sequential operations. The process places a designer within a paradigm of logical form-making that is analogous (see Figure 2.3). The physical system is strategically supplemented with the software system, linked via a 3D laser scanning device and digital projector.

The interfacial gap between the sand forms generated and their assessment by the custom software proved vexing. Sand modeling was unexpectedly (and provocatively) challenging and the territory for exploration variably expansive and constrained. Iteratively tuning the sand modeling in dialogue with the software proved ponderous relative to the seductively algorithmic process of modeling the sand alone. Maintaining the shortest iterative loop possible between design action and evaluation (a simple visual assessment of physical model quality) felt necessary and productive. The resulting topographies represent typological scatter shots, covering a territory of algorithmically manipulated sedimentary form, rather than being tuned by the software systems (though we intuited their influence). While this initial setback chastens the impulse for an ideally comprehensive interface, it also provides a lesson in the gravity of playful engagement.

GRAVITY OF PLAY

In this context, play means not the opposite of work but instead takes on a more modern and specific definition. It now commonly describes relations with

An interface for instrumental reconciliation

technologies, many of which barely distinguish between 'work' and the traditional idea of 'play.' To play a video game or perform related activities, such as work training simulation or even operation of drones, is to engage fully with the 'magic circle' (Hookway 2014, 38) of rules and actions within that interface and to become interested and motivated in that world. Play represents a necessary condition for the creation of an interface and is instrumental in determining the nature and quality of the interfacial space and the design exploration that occurs there. Designing interfacial spaces is intricate work, and it is difficult to map out universal strategies for what will induce play *and* design for any given group of users. With practice and experience, however, we can recognize which configurations succeed in which scenarios.

How we define our interfacial site or 'magic circle' is critical to the determination of success. The relationship between play and the boundaries we impose on it recalls the definition of the necessary condition of play as described in Johan Huizinga's book *Homo Ludens* (1955). Seemingly paradoxically, confinement is essential for play and freedom of action. The character of confinement largely defines the character of play. For example, a carefully bounded set of actions allows movement to congregate at the boundaries safely and rambunctiously. Dogs have endless fun by limiting their nibbling to never drawing blood.

While interfacial boundaries of sedimentary modeling were relatively nebulous, the interface for the simulation and analysis software has been designed to operate within a carefully bounded site of parameters and control. Thus, as this critical part of the interface was de-coupled from extensive engagement with the generative sand-based topographic design, there remained a need for the software to validate and assess appropriate dust control treatments. The more confined interfacial site and more controlled arena of play of the software became an opportunity to seek validation and create engagement with the influential site constituents.

THE USER INTERFACE: PUBLIC ENGAGEMENT

Simple controls linked to an enriched feedback system in the software allows a constituent to explore the solution space within its technical constraints. The synoptic interface 'civilizes' diverse impulses into the language of the tools. For large-scale infrastructural projects like the Owens Lake Dust Control Project, the large territory they occupy necessitates engagement with a broad spectrum of constituents and with their social imagination and interests. An interface like the software developed for this project can focus diverse inputs for specific purposes and engage a variety of constituents in an augmented process of design, an action that can produce unforeseen and beneficial tangential effects, as well as the effects it is designed to produce.

To engage with a broader set of actors, the software is embedded within a machine that resembles a stand-up arcade game, but with the physicality of a penny arcade machine and analog components similar to a record player (see Figure 2.4). A familiar arcade-style interface including a set of six large buttons, a dial, and a joystick is positioned before a table where sand models are placed. Robotically sculpted sand models, vacuum-formed and framed, are slid over the top of the machine, and the software automatically loads the appropriate digital model, inserting the user into a first-person landscape simulation. The plan rendering is projected onto the relief topography, along with a set of critical parameters and analyses. Users are encouraged to adjust the landscape parameters for the purpose of creating two 'postcard' views of their preference. As a reward for their participation the machine prints a postcard of their making (see Figure 2.5).

The process of making a postcard for a projective place is a means to motivate and focus the public's judgment of the designs. Though diminished, the postcard maintains a talismanic status as an object signifying a landscape with touristic and other values (Meikle 2000, 267–286). Motivated to receive a free souvenir object, yet responsible for its quality, users have to create a version of the landscape that matched a postcard's familiar, yet subjective, parameters.

While the users express their judgment in searching for their preference, the system precisely maps their sensibility and thus becomes an increasingly powerful tool for legitimizing new landscape models, when constrained parameters, such as cost and resource use, have a large but unresolved impact in terms of providing acceptable values. Rather than reinforcing accepted ideas of place, the machine creates an opportunity to define and validate new typological models of landscape that are aligned to overriding parameters.

The secondary value of the public engagement is harder to measure, but it is likely that this engagement with an experiential representation of a landscape, embedded with opportunities for real agency, engenders a shift in our societal approach to this landscape. The system links citizens with expertise, allowing a legitimate 'crowd sourced' design exploration. The rich environmental representations and postcard reward also consciously propose the construction of a new aesthetic and pictorial sensibility of this landscape that could be instrumental in shifting public perception and motivating political players.

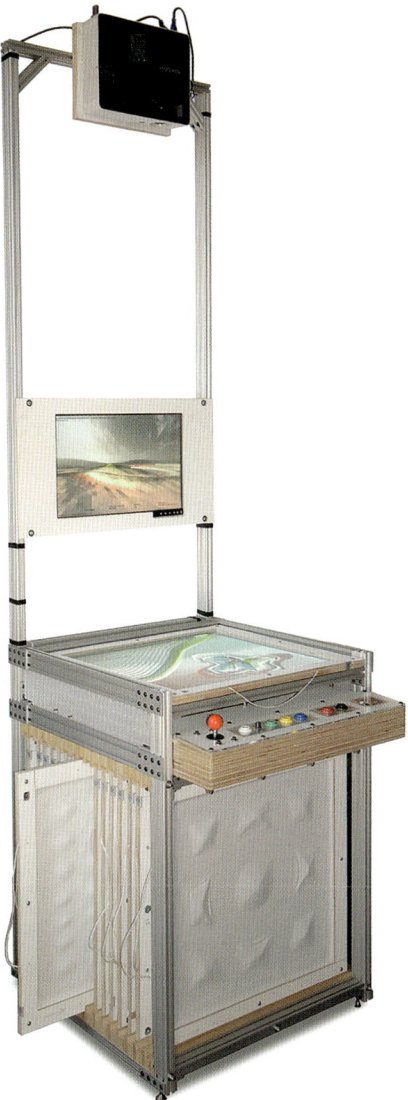

Figure 2.4 'Greetings from the Owens Lake' public interface system with 17 vacuum-formed sand-modeled dust control landscapes, arcade-style controls, first-person display and overhead projection, and embedded postcard printer.

Figure 2.5 User-generated postcards from the 'Greetings from the Owens Lake' public interface.

CONCLUSION

By many measures, the interface does not represent a novel project for landscape architecture. We have long been engaged with complex landscapes and the instruments used to produce them; we have thrived on finding ways to reconcile a human impulse with machinic constructions. The profession is an inherently interfacial practice, and the field's significant cultural contributions are rooted in its synthetic and reconciliatory capacity. For example, landscape architecture's major contribution to New York City's High Line was the addition of a sophisticated public interface to an already picturesque derelict urban rail infrastructure.

However, there is a growing disciplinary crisis as the profession struggles to advance its agendas within broader urban territories, including those traditionally managed and designed by civil engineering. This chapter proposes that rather than attempting to provide a reliable alternate paradigm of engineering, landscape

An interface for instrumental reconciliation

architects can apply our reconciliatory project to the tools that already have an established agency (even as they are partially responsible for the machinic conditions that we seek to reconcile). We can re-frame our project through an explicit relationship with tools and professions, engaging directly with the means that have become technologically more powerful and accessible and re-establishing the agency of ideas and representations of place within these powerful instrumentalities. This project proposes that our role in presenting 'greener' multi-purpose solutions can be advanced by consciously developing the practice and craft of design using the tools and simulations that increasingly represent and control the world.

The Owens Lake case study reveals both the intricacy and promise of developing multi-disciplinary infrastructural design systems. Instrumental interfaces rely on alchemical interactions between disparate bodies whose legitimacy are oft supported by their synoptic exclusions. While this study reveals some of the critical parameters and expanded opportunities of this formative space, there remains a great deal to study and learn of the practice. Even so, this intermediate moment of of the interface begins to manifest a contemporary agenda for landscape architecture in relation to a broader and rapidly growing trans-disciplinary world of instrumentation. The project of the interface suggests that we must not only improve our tools and metrification but must equally seek to empower our human impulse and body within these toolsets. While the profession has long been interested in enhancing its performance through more precise instruments, now that we have access to these tools, the challenge has flipped to harnessing them to the more nebulous and neglected intuitive synthetic power of the individual.

NOTE

1   Re-filling the Owens Lake would take the full flow of the Aqueduct seven years and nearly as much water annually to resist evapotranspiration.

REFERENCES

Corner, James. 2002. 'Origins of Theory.' In *Theory in Landscape Architecture: A Reader,* edited by Simon Swaffield. Philadelphia: University of Pennsylvania Press.

Hookway, Branden. 2014. *The Interface*. Cambridge: Massachusetts Institute of Technology Press.

Huizinga, Johan. 1955. *Homo Ludens: A Study of the Play-Element in Culture*. Boston: Beacon.

Meikle, Jeffrey L. 2000. 'A Paper Atlantis: Postcards, Mass Art, and the American Scene: The Eleventh Reyner Banham Memorial Lecture.' *Journal of Design History*, 13(4): 267–286.

Scott, James C. 1998. *Seeing Like a State: How Certain Schemes to Improve the Human Condition Have Failed*. New Haven: Yale University Press.

Weller, Richard. 2006. 'An Art of Instrumentality: Thinking Through Landscape Urbanism.' In *Landscape Urbanism Reader,* edited by Charles Waldheim. New York: Princeton Architectural Press.

3

Computational landscape architecture

Procedural, tangible, and open landscapes

Brendan Harmon, Anna Petrasova, Helena Mitasova, and Vaclav Petras

With emerging technologies, we can begin to model intuitively and creatively design dynamic, evolving landscapes. Advances in geospatial modeling, remote sensing, rapid prototyping, and 3D scanning are changing the way that landscapes are modeled. Now we can generate dynamic landscape form with process-based scientific models. We can build precise physical models using remote sensing and rapid prototyping. And we can link physical and digital models with real-time 3D scanning. Our new technology – Tangible Landscape – enables designers to intuitively sculpt a physical model of a landscape coupled with a digital model in a real-time feedback loop of 3D scanning, geospatial modeling, and projection. This bridges the digital-analog divide by combining the embodied, kinæsthetic creativity of traditional modes of design with the analytics and procedural dynamism of geospatial modeling. Since Tangible Landscape seamlessly integrates geospatial modeling, analysis, and simulation into the design process, designers can assess the performance of landscapes and quantitatively explore the impact of their designs. Tangible Landscape's real-time analytics enable designers to iterate rapidly through design ideas while rigorously testing their ideas.

INTRODUCTION

Landscapes are dynamic – their forms, the shape of the land and pattern of plants, continues to evolve, generated by geomorphological processes like erosion and deposition and ecological processes like disturbance and succession. The form of the landscape directs processes and processes simultaneously shape the form of the land; landscapes are the result of the interaction of ecological and geomorphological processes and forms (Huggett 2011). Humanity also transforms the landscape. Anthropogenic processes such as land degradation and accelerated erosion regimes and built forms such as structures, excavations, dams, and channels shape geomorphic systems (Goudie and Viles 2010). The scale and extent of anthropogenic impacts have led some scientists to claim, controversially, that we have entered a new geological epoch, dubbing it the Anthropocene (Steffen et al. 2007; Ellis 2011).

The form of the land is contingent on its history, upon for example the evolutionary pathway of the landforms, the structure of the bedrock, pedogenesis, and any construction and excavation. And likewise the pattern of life in a landscape is determined by its past, by its memory nested across spatiotemporal scales, be it the adaptive radiation of species (Whittaker and Fernández-Palacios 2008), the genetic memory stored in banks of seeds (Bengtsson et al. 2003), or the cultural memory of places. The potential structure of the landscape is inherited from the past, but the future trajectory of the landscape is conditional upon human choices, upon the chance, type, and magnitude of disturbance, upon the possible responses of the landscape to a disturbance, its memory of disturbance, and upon the dynamic instability inherent in the landscape. Thus, every landscape is irreversible and unique; each landscape is the result of a highly improbable set of events unfolding across time and space (Phillips 2007). Our actions generate novel patterns and processes.

While landscapes are dynamic, landscape architects have typically designed landscapes as relatively static artifacts, at best designing for the phenomenological character of the landscape, harnessing ecological processes to remediate or restore ecosystems, or planning the landscape in phases. Even though landscape is such a dynamic medium, dynamics have played a relatively minor role in the discipline for landscape architects, who have been stymied by the challenge of modeling landscape dynamics and the even greater challenge of designing with such modeling.

Landscape architects are beginning to assess and evaluate the performance – the ecological function, the health of the plantings and soils, the integrity, and social benefits – of built designs. This will help the discipline to learn, adapt to social and environmental change, and prove its value to society. Designing performance landscapes, however, requires more than monitoring, assessment, and evaluation. Rather than waiting to assess the impact of a design once built, landscape architects should integrate performance into every stage of the design process by continuously, rigorously modeling the impact and effectiveness of their design as it develops.

To creatively design dynamic, evolving landscapes, landscape architects need to model processes and not just form, model intuitively and strive for a culture and poetics of openness. With procedural modeling, landscape architects can use geomorphological and ecological processes to generate the form of the landscape. With Tangible Landscape designers can intuitively interact with a procedural model of a landscape, coupling the creativity, intuition, and kinaesthetics of traditional modes of design with the analytics, dynamism, efficiency, and precision of digital design. Finally, landscape architects should develop a new poetics of the open landscape as evolving processes and inchoate forms that invites interaction, improvisation, and expression and inspires engagement and stewardship (Figure 3.1).

PROCEDURAL LANDSCAPES

Procedures and algorithms are now used extensively by the architectural avant-garde to generate complex architectonic forms. By changing the seeds or the parameters of a procedural architectural model, architects can computationally generate alternative forms and thus explore a greater number of formal variations on a design theme of greater complexity than would be possible using more typical analog or computer-aided design methods. As an iterative process procedural modeling can be used to analyze and test alternative forms or build upon past forms.

The architectural avant-garde is using parametric and procedural modeling to try to move beyond the paradigm of building as static form. Architects like Zaha Hadid have sought to express a sense of dynamism in static structures with sculptural, often procedurally generated forms, presenting form as frozen motion (Picon 2010). Furthermore, architects are experimenting with mass customization, and procedurally generated families of form as a means to create variations on a static form (Carpo 2011; Cache 2010), albeit static variations on a static form. While the architectural avant-garde is exploring dynamism through sculptural

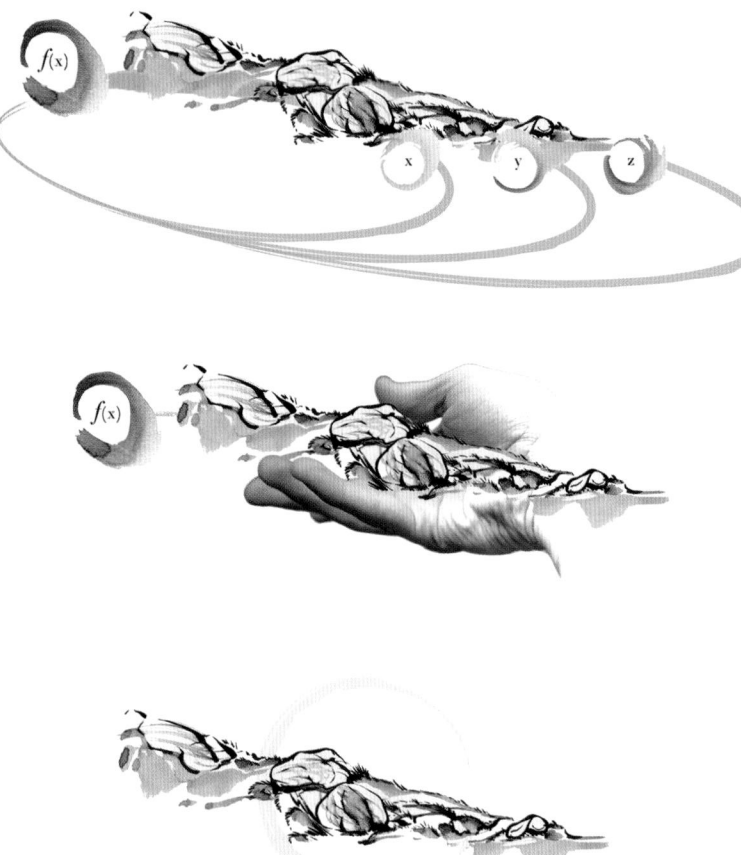

Figure 3.1 In *procedural landscapes* the form of the landscape is procedurally generated by the landscape process $f(x)$. The parameters x, y, and z of the new landscape in turn shape the process. With Tangible Landscape, as a model of the landscape is sculpted by hand, the parameters and thus the processes change. Designers can intuitively experiment and learn how they will impact landscape processes by changing the form of the land. By designing landscapes that are driven by processes and are in a constant state of becoming, designers can express the dynamism of landscape. To fully express this dynamism a new strategy for expression – a poetics of the *open landscape* – is needed. This poetics would be open to natural processes, it would invite interaction and free expression, and it would give rise to an aesthetics of change.

forms, mass customization, and families of form, landscape architects have a highly dynamic, living medium with which to work; with procedural landscapes, landscape architects can begin to model and design for the natural processes that make landscapes so dynamic.

There is a great, as yet unrealized potential to procedurally model landscapes since landscape process shapes form and form guides the process. By procedurally modeling this process, landscape architects can study landscape dynamics and begin to work with the landscape as a dynamic medium rather than a static form. While architects vary the parameters of a procedural architecture model to generate new forms, landscape architects can vary the parameters of a procedural landscape model to change ecological and geomorphological processes and generate new landscapes so that they can explore how these scenarios evolve over time. By modeling processes landscape architects can more deeply understand and take fuller advantage of their medium, finding new ways to explore and express the poetry of a medium that unfolds through time – constantly shifting, never the same – along an unstable, uncertain trajectory contingent upon its history, upon its natural and human legacies.

Landscapes can be procedurally modeled in a geographic information system using scripting or visual programming to scientifically model, analyze, and simulate how processes and forms interact in multidimensional geographic space. Geographic information systems have the tools that scientists need to study landscape; by using geographic information systems in a procedural modeling paradigm designers can adapt these tools to a design process, begin to realize landscape as a dynamic medium, design for performance, and ground design in science. There are growing repositories of open source scientific models for landscape processes such as the Community Surface Dynamics Modeling System. While scientific models for spatial simulations were once static, empirical, and spatially averaged there are now dynamic, process-based models that are spatially distributed and scalable (Mitasova and Mitas 2000). With these process-based geospatial models, designers can procedurally generate dynamic form and simulate how a landscape might evolve.

With emerging remote sensing technologies like airborne lidar and stereoscopic imagery from unmanned aerial systems, we can 3D scan entire landscapes and compute very precise, high-resolution models of bare earth topography, structures, and vegetation. 3D data can be fused with hyperspectral imagery to precisely classify vegetation types and identify structures. These remote sensing technologies have the resolution we need to model ecological and geomorphological processes

Brendan Harmon et al.

at a site scale. Furthermore, with repeat aerial surveys we can collect a timed series of data that we can use to evaluate designs.

With process-based simulations, we have procedurally modeled how a landscape could evolve as the flow of water erodes the landscape surface and shapes its terrain (Figure 3.2). We have used a path sampling method to solve the water and sediment flow equations (Mitasova et al., 2004) and model mass flows over complex topographies based on topographic, land cover, soil, and rainfall parameters. The modeled flow of sediment – a function of the flow of water, soil detachment, and transport parameters – was then used to estimate the net erosion and deposition rates and the associated short-term evolution of the topography (equation 1; Mitasova et al. 2013). In our example, we have simulated the impact of large storms in a detachment limited soil erosion regime leading to net erosion over the entire landscape and the evolution of gullies in areas with a concentrated flow.

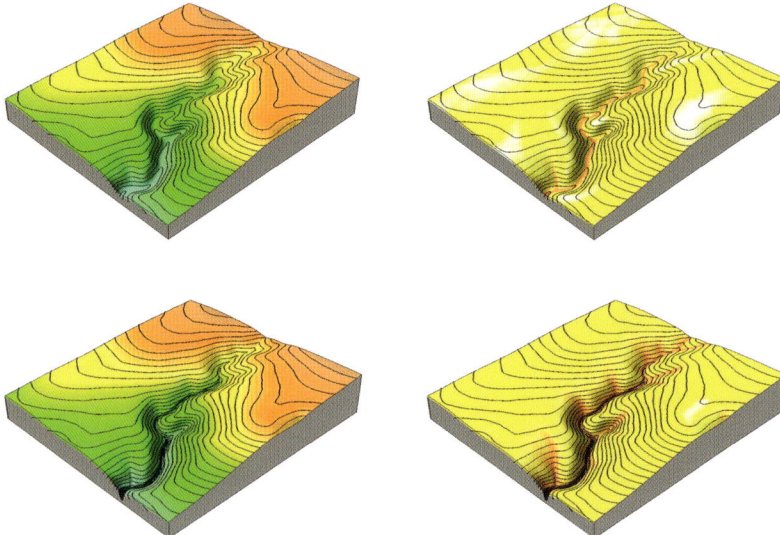

Figure 3.2 Gully evolution. A simulation of how this hillside landscape could evolve over the next decade. In this short-term landscape evolution model, runoff flows across the terrain, detaching sediment and carrying it downslope. The flow of water concentrates in ephemeral streams in the valleys of the hillside, carving gullies. As the stream channels deepen into gullies during large storms, the increasing force of water accelerates erosion in a positive feedback loop. Much of the detached sediment is deposited in the lake below.

Equation 1: Gully evolution

$$\Delta z(x,y,t) = \Delta t \cdot q_s(x,y,t) \cdot \varrho(r)^{-1}$$

where

Δz = change in elevation (m)

Δt = change in time (s)

q_s = sediment flux (kg $\cdot$ m^{-1}s^{-1})

ϱ = mass of water carried sediment per unit area (kg $\cdot$ m^{-2})

While procedural modeling has been used to design some revolutionary works of architecture, furniture, and art such as Greg Lynn's teapots for Alessi, Neri Oxman's experiments in material ecology, and Nervous System's 3D printed jewelry, it has serious limitations. Digital design – procedural modeling included – requires a high level of abstraction, for a concept must be translated many times from human to computer and back. With a graphical user interface, multiple dense layers of abstraction separate ideation and expression; a concept is translated from the mind to the hand, from the hand to the mouse and keyboard, into machine language, into programming language, from the display to the eyes. So many layers of abstraction, of translation, separate human and computer. This high level of abstraction, lacking in kinaesthetic experience, inhibits intuition (Ishii 2008) and constrains or transforms creativity, perhaps giving rise to a new, very different mode of creative thinking.

When design is unintuitive, we lose the immediacy of coupled ideation and creation that is so characteristic of certain highly expressive modes of analog art and design such as poetry, sketching, and calligraphy. By coupling ideation and creation artists and designers can interrogate and critique their thoughts as they form, using their kinaesthetic intelligence to continually, automatically, and immediately imagine, express, critique, and reimagine. This immediacy has given rise to maxims like drawing is thinking. By decoupling kinaesthetics and creative thinking, digital design has lost an expressive and critical immediacy, trading it, perhaps, for computational creativity and analytics (Figure 3.3).

Thinking procedurally, through code rather than visually, fundamentally transforms the way designers think. This is also true of visual programming but is obfuscated by an added layer of graphical abstraction. The logical, conceptual, and syntactical constraints of the chosen programming language are not necessarily an obstacle to creativity but unquestionably change the design process.

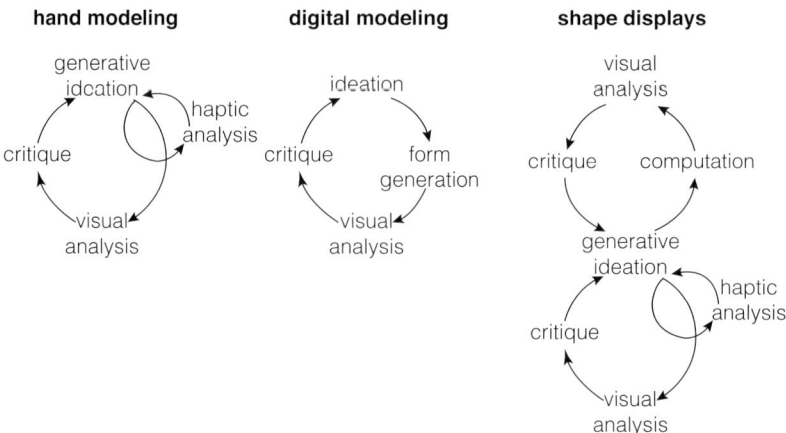

Figure 3.3 Analog, digital, and hybrid creative processes. When modeling by hand, ideas are generated through action. An idea is continuously developed through both immediate kinaesthetic intuitions derived from tactile feedback and critical judgments derived from visual feedback. In digital modeling ideas are first conceived abstractly and then given digital form. Ideas are developed in iterations – in cycles of ideation, computational form generation, visualization, and critical judgment. With shape displays like Tangible Landscape, the analog creative process informs the digital creative process and vice versa.

TANGIBLE LANDSCAPES

With tangible landscape designers draw upon both the intuitive, creative nature of drawing and modeling by hand and the analytics, precision, and dynamism of geospatial procedural modeling. Tangible Landscape is a continuous shape display that couples a malleable physical model of a landscape with a digital landscape through a cycle of real-time scanning, analysis, and projection (Figure 3.4). As designers change the physical model – sculpting landforms in polymeric sand – the changes are 3D scanned into an open source geographic information system in which landscape processes are then simulated and projected back onto the physical model, all in real-time (Figure 3.5) (Mitasova et al. 2015; Petrasova et al. 2014; Petrasova et al. 2016). Thus designers can directly, intuitively shape and interact with their coupled physical–digital model in an iterative design process informed by geospatial analytics (Harmon et al. 2014).

Computational landscape architecture

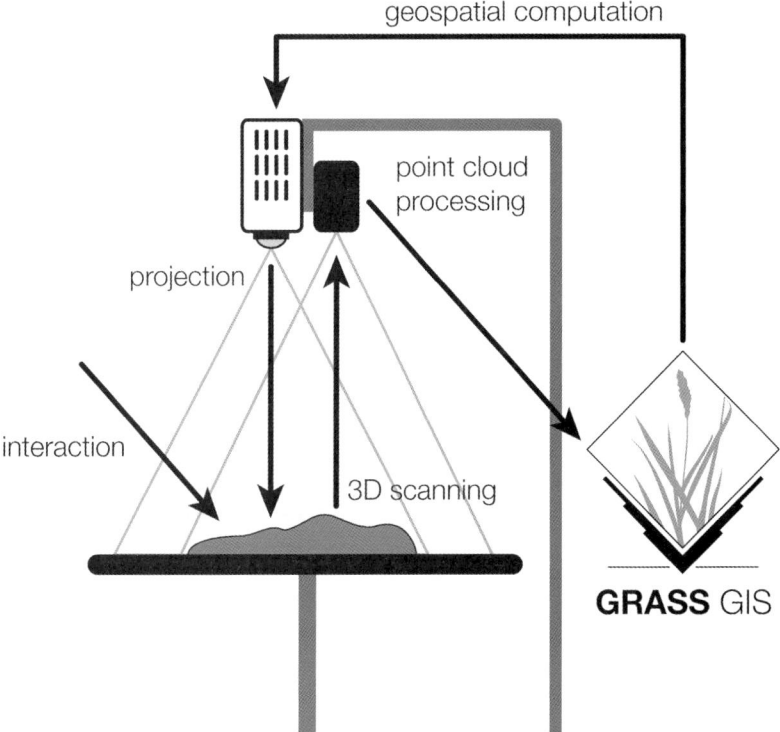

Figure 3.4 System setup. In Tangible Landscape a projector and a 3D scanner are mounted above a malleable physical model of a landscape. The scanner continually captures the 3D form of the physical model as a point cloud. The point cloud is automatically imported into GRASS GIS and interpolated as a digital elevation model. The digital elevation model and derived analyses and simulations are then projected back onto the physical model in near real-time.

To build precise yet malleable physical models for Tangible Landscape we use 3D printed, CNC milled, or vacuum formed molds to cast polymeric sand. The sand model can be cast precisely, sculpted with ease, and recast. As a design is developed or the scale of a study changes, new models can be rapidly prototyped. Airborne lidar data can be used to generate digital terrain models of the bare earth topography, the tree canopy, and buildings for fabrication by 3D printing or CNC milling (Figure 3.6).

Traditionally, design projects are developed in a relatively linear process – in phases from conceptual to schematic to detail design and finally construction.

Brendan Harmon et al.

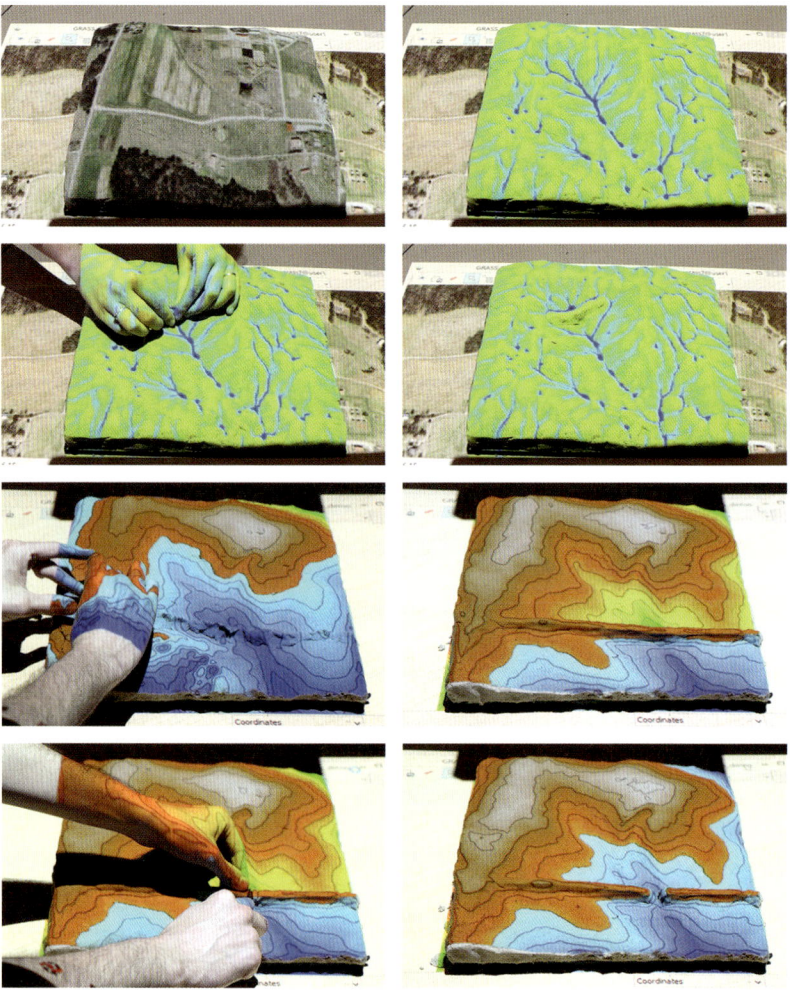

Figure 3.5 Natural human–computer interaction. With Tangible Landscape designers can intuitively sculpt a model with their hands and see how simulations like water flow and flooding change in response.

Analyzable digital models typically emerge in the later phases of design. Therefore, designs are often only rigorously analyzed too late in the process to change the creative direction. With Tangible Landscape, however, designers can rapidly explore and test ideas rigorously and yet creatively from conceptual design onwards.

With Tangible Landscape designers can not only experiment more rapidly but also begin to design with and for dynamics. As they shape the terrain, designers are interacting with geophysical process models such as erosion–deposition,

Computational landscape architecture

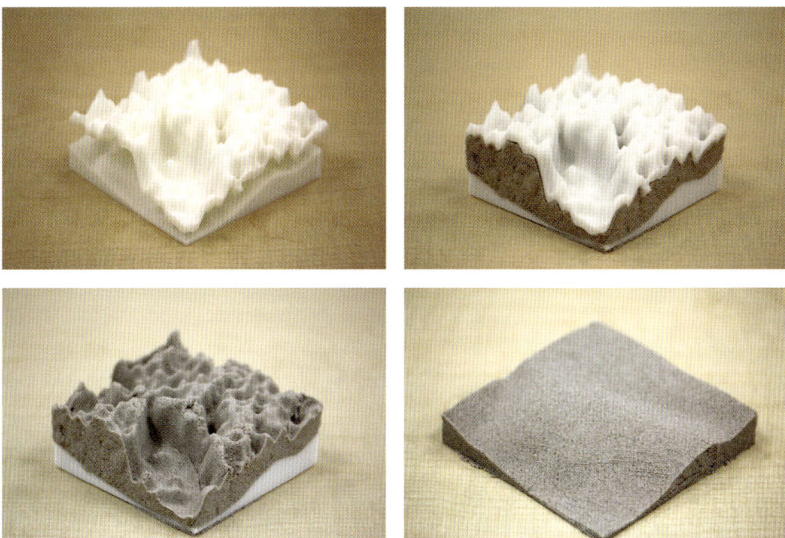

Figure 3.6 Casting polymer-enriched sand in 3D printed molds. We used 3D prints of the digital elevation model and digital surface model as molds to cast polymer-enriched sand as the forest canopy and the terrain.

surface water flow, and solar irradiation, with ecological process models such as wildfire and disease spread, and with anthropogenic process models like urbanization. Designers can, for example, use geophysical process models to dynamically study and analyze a site, grade topography, and manage storm water (Figure 3.5). Tangible Landscape can also be used to rapidly and dynamically plan routes such as trail networks across a landscape – combining the ease of sketching or modeling by hand with the power of network analysis. With a paper map, one can easily sketch a route, but it is hard to quantitatively compare routes, much less optimize one. With digital maps, on the other hand, digitizing points can be laborious, but one can compute optimal routes. With Tangible Landscape, designers can place markers such as wooden blocks by hand to simultaneously mark trailheads, viewpoints, and other waypoints on both the physical and digital models. As the markers are continually scanned into a geospatial model, designers can site and digitize points without mouse and keyboard. As designers place markers to designate waypoints, the optimal route across the landscape between these waypoints is computed in near real-time. First, the least cost paths between all of the waypoints are automatically computed, based on walking energetics across the terrain and a cost surface such as suitability. Potential costs could include aesthetics and views, cultural heritage, the risk of soil erosion or compaction, and ecological sensitivity. Then the traveling salesman problem is solved to find the optimal route through this network of least cost paths.

By quickly and intuitively exploring different trail scenarios in Tangible Landscape designers can combine creative exploration with the rigor of geospatial analytics. If, for example, a path skirts around a stream then the designers can sculpt a bridge for the path to cross. As the new terrain is scanned, the trail automatically reroutes over the bridge (Figure 3.7). As they design a trail, designers can study the impact of the trail on geophysical processes such as erosion. To reduce erosion around the trail designers can procedurally model the optimal pattern for erosion control measures such as planting and installing live willow fascines.

Tangible Landscape encourages collaboration and interdisciplinary exchange as multiple users can shape a physical model simultaneously – interacting, sharing knowledge, and designing together. Architects, landscape architects, urban planners, scientists, geospatial analysts, decision-makers, and stakeholders can all gather around the same model and experiment together, exploring potentially conflicting ideas and seeing the modeled impact of their design decisions. Thus, Tangible Landscape encourages engagement and consensus decision-making, guided by geospatial analytics and the collective knowledge. Due to its ease of interaction and analytic rigor, Tangible Landscape can help open the design process, enabling the public to play a greater, more informed role in the design of their landscape.

OPEN LANDSCAPES

Humans leave their mark indelibly in the history of a landscape, but the cultural and artistic intent of our designs, our built artifacts is inexorably distorted or lost in time. As landscape architects, we impress our ego upon the land, imbuing it with a specific, static meaning, a meaning that will not last. If any designed landscape is transient, and it must be, for landscapes are inevitably changing, then we should design for change. In time, everything built or planted in the landscape will weather, erode, decay, die, or become something else. As landscape architects we should embrace this; we have a medium that is uniquely alive and dynamic. Rather than designing all landscapes as artifacts, we could design landscape as process. Let us try to design landscapes to become something else, to design openly, to design with nature, with others. Embrace change; embrace the land's constant state of becoming. Design meaning that is never fixed, that is always becoming. Express yourself – not as the illusion of yourself, alone, ego writ on the

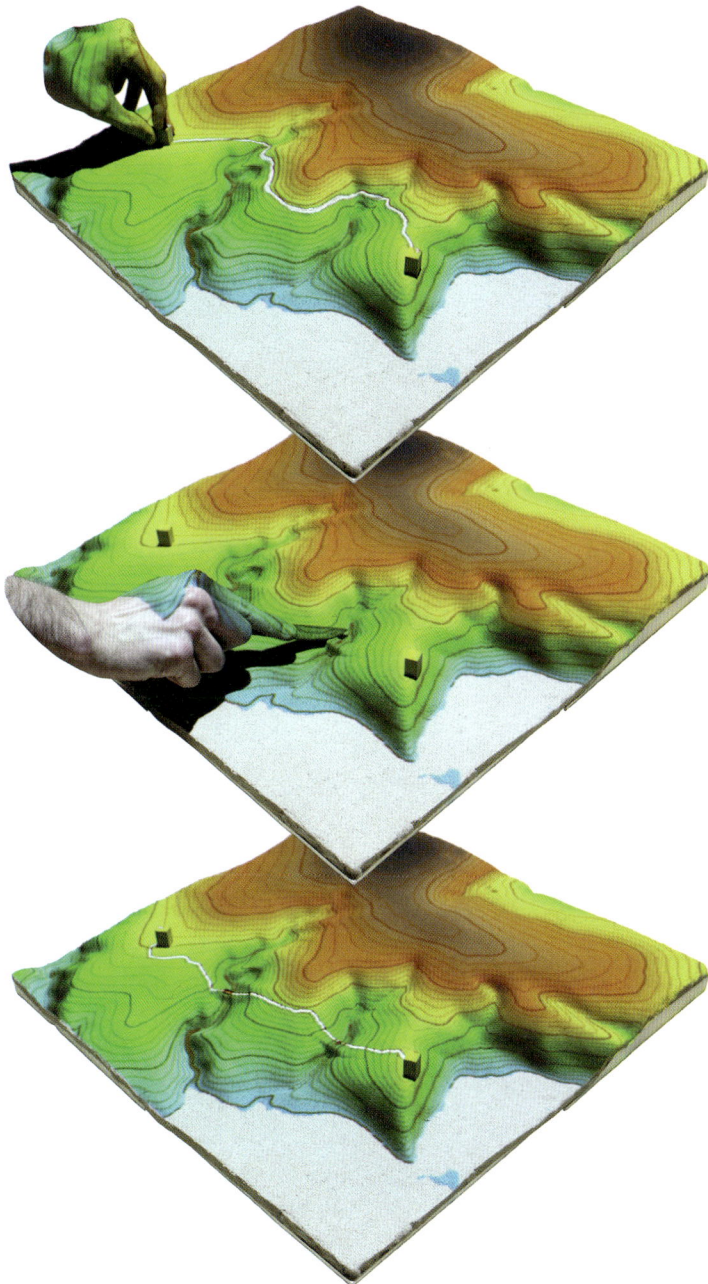

Figure 3.7 Tangible trails. With Tangible Landscape designers can site trailheads to automatically generate optimal routes and sculpt bridges to reroute trails. Routes can be optimized for walking energetics and suitability.

land – but as an invitation, a catalyst: as the start of a movement, the opening phrase in a work, in a landscape that will have a life of its own unfolding in unknowable ways along a trajectory you set in motion.

Procedural landscapes and tangible landscapes – these new paradigms of landscape modeling could help us design more dynamic landscapes, but they are just a start; we also need to make these landscapes mean dynamism, to evoke it. If we design landscapes to change, then we will need a new aesthetics; not just an aesthetics of the phenomenological, but an aesthetics of impermanence, imperfection, and open-endedness. To realize such an aesthetics, we need a strategy for expression, a poetics.

We need an open poetics (Eco 1989), a poetics in which form and meaning are not fixed, a poetics in which meaning transcends initial intent and art arises not from ego, but from interaction. An art that arises from an opening statement, from the seed of a design through evolving process, through a constant transformation by others, by chance, by nature. Such a poetics would evoke an experiential aesthetics of change, an aesthetics of interaction to be experienced directly. This would synergistically link landscape aesthetics with ecological theory and conservation ethics thus spreading awareness, encouraging engagement, and inspiring cultural change. This new poetics of the open landscape as evolving processes and inchoate form would invite interaction, improvisation, and expression. By being open, to interpretation and collaboration, this poetics would invite participation and the co-construction of meaning of place and identity. Always improvisational, there would be freedom within its narrative structure. The open landscape, driven not only by geomorphological, ecological, and climatic processes but also by us, would be in a constant, shifting state of becoming.

How can we design open landscapes? Form is easily grasped; process is more intangible, its visible, embodied form fleeting if even recognizable. To move beyond a poetics of form to a poetics of process we will need new design strategies. We should seek to express dynamism in our designs – artistically exposing and evoking sociocultural and environmental processes. And we should seek to express dynamism in ways beyond mere metaphor – experientially: by interacting with the landscape, with its processes we can experience dynamics and intuitively grasp them. Beyond that, we should attempt to open these processes by treating design as an ongoing experiment and encouraging others to take part in it or in the ongoing making of the landscape.

To learn more about landscapes, to advance the science of landscape dynamics we should make the design and management of landscapes actively experimental, and we should share open source code so that our results are reproducible and testable (Ince et al. 2012; Rocchini and Neteler 2012). If the procedural models are to be reproduced, tested, and verified or more likely critiqued, then the models and data must be openly available. Furthermore, by opening both the modeling and design process, we can contribute to and learn from communities, co-producing knowledge and nurturing involvement (Landström et al. 2011). Open source blueprints (Ratti et al. 2010) could be shared to encourage reproducibility, customizability, flexibility, transparency, and free expression. With open landscapes, we may be able to plant the seeds of new vernaculars for the digital age. By looking to local culture, harnessing processes, and opening the design and creation of the landscape, we may be able to nurture new vernaculars that empower the public and foster diversity in cultural landscapes.

CODE

Landscape evolution – *https://github.com/baharmon/landscape_evolution*
Tangible Landscape – *https://github.com/ncsu-osgeorel/grass-tangible-landscape*

SOFTWARE

GRASS GIS – *http://grass.osgeo.org/*

GRASS MODULES

r.sim.water – *http://grass.osgeo.org/grass70/manuals/r.sim.water.html*
r.sim.sediment – *http://grass.osgeo.org/grass70/manuals/r.sim.sediment.html*
r.walk – *http://grass.osgeo.org/grass70/manuals/r.walk.html*

REFERENCES

Bengtsson, Janne, Per Angelstam, Thomas Elmqvist, Urban Emanuelsson, Carl Folke, Margareta Ihse, Fredrik Moberg, and Magnus Nyström. 2003. 'Reserves, Resilience and Dynamic Landscapes.' *Ambio* 32 (6): 389–396.

Cache, Bernard. 2010. *Projectiles*. London: Architectural Association.

Carpo, Mario. 2011. *The Alphabet and the Algorithm*. Cambridge, MA: MIT Press.

Eco, Umberto. 1989. *The Open Work*. Cambridge, MA: Harvard University Press.

Ellis, Erle C. 2011. 'Anthropogenic Transformation of the Terrestrial Biosphere.' *Philosophical Transactions of the Royal Society* 369: 1010–1035.

Goudie, Andrew and Heather A. Viles. 2010. *Landscape and Geomorphology: A Very Short Introduction.* Oxford: Oxford University Press.

Harmon, Brendan A., Helena Mitasova, and Anna Petrasova. 2014. 'Tangible Geospatial Modeling for Landscape Architects.' In *2014 Geodesign Summit*. Redlands, California: Esri. http://video.esri.com/watch/3170/tangible-geospatial-modeling-for-landscape-architects (accessed December 10, 2015).

Huggett, Richard. 2011. 'Process and Form.' In *The SAGE Handbook of Geomorphology*, edited by Kenneth J. Gregory and Andrew Goudie, 174–191. London: SAGE Publications Ltd.

Ince, Darrel C., Leslie Hatton, and John Graham-Cumming. 2012. 'The Case for Open Computer Programs.' *Nature* 482: 485–488. doi: 10.1038/nature10836. http://dx.doi.org/10.1038/nature10836.

Ishii, Hiroshi. 2008. 'Tangible Bits: Beyond Pixels.' In *Proceedings of the 2nd International Conference on Tangible and Embedded Interaction – TEI '08*, xv. New York: ACM Press. doi: 10.1145/1347390.1347392. http://dl.acm.org/citation.cfm?id=1347390.1347392.

Landström, Catharina, Sarah J. Whatmore, Stuart N. Lane, Nicholas A. Odoni, Neil Ward, and Susan Bradley. 2011. 'Coproducing Flood Risk Knowledge: Redistributing Expertise in Critical "Participatory Modelling."' *Environment and Planning A* 43: 1617–1633.

Mitasova, Helena and Lubos Mitas. 2000. 'Modeling Spatial Processes in Multiscale Framework: Exploring Duality between Particles and Fields.' In Plenary Talk at *GIScience2000 Conference*. Savannah, GA. www4.ncsu.edu/~hmitaso/gmslab/gisc00/duality.html (accessed December 10, 2015).

Mitasova, H., M. Barton, I. Ullah, J. Hofierka, and R.S. Harmon. 2013. '3.9 GIS-Based Soil Erosion Modeling.' In *Treatise on Geomorphology*, edited by John F. Shroder, 228–258. San Diego, California, USA: Elsevier. doi: 10.1016/B978-0-12-374739-6.00052-X. www.sciencedirect.com/science/article/pii/B978012374739600052X (accessed December 10, 2015).

Mitasova, Helena, Vaclav Petras, Anna Petrasova, and Brendan A. Harmon. 2015. 'Tangible Landscape.' http://geospatial.ncsu.edu/osgeorel/tangeoms.html (accessed December 10, 2015).

Mitasova, Helena, Chris Thaxton, Jaroslav Hofierka, Richard McLaughlin, Amber Moore, and Lubos Mitas. 2004. 'Path Sampling Method for Modeling Overland Water Flow, Sediment Transport, and Short Term Terrain Evolution in Open Source GIS.' *Developments in Water Science* 55: 1479–1490. doi: 10.1016/S0167-5648(04)80159-X.

Mori, Akira S. 2011. 'Ecosystem Management Based on Natural Disturbances: Hierarchical Context and Non-Equilibrium Paradigm.' *Journal of Applied Ecology* 48: 280–292.

Petrasova, Anna, Brendan A. Harmon, Vaclav Petras, and Helena Mitasova. 2014. 'GIS-Based Environmental Modeling with Tangible Interaction and Dynamic Visualization.' In *7th International Congress on Environmental Modelling and Software*, edited by D.P. Ames and N. Quinn. San Diego, California, USA: International Environmental Modelling and Software Society. www.iemss.org/sites/iemss2014/papers/iemss2014_submission_131.pdf (accessed December 10, 2015).

Petrasova, Anna, Brendan Harmon, Vaclav Petras, and Helena Mitasova. 2015. *Tangible Modeling with Open Source GIS*. Springer. doi:10.1007/978-3-319-25775-4.

Phillips, Jonathan D. 2007. 'The Perfect Landscape.' *Geomorphology* 84: 159–169.

Picon, Antoine. 2010. *Digital Culture in Architecture : An Introduction for the Design Professions*. Boston, MA: Birkhauser.

Ratti, Carlo, Paola Antonelli, Adam Bly, Lucas Dietrich, Joseph Grima, Dan Hill, John Habraken, et al. 2010. 'Open Source Architecture (OSArc).' *Domus* 948 (June).

Rocchini, Duccio and Markus Neteler. 2012. 'Let the Four Freedoms Paradigm Apply to Ecology.' *Trends in Ecology and Evolution* 27(6): 310–311. doi: 10.1016/j.tree.2012.03.009. http://dx.doi.org/10.1016/j.tree.2012.03.009.

Steffen, Will, Paul J. Crutzen, and John R. McNeill. 2007. 'The Anthropocene: Are Humans Overwhelming the Great Forces of Nature?' *Ambio* 36(8) (December): 614–621.

Whittaker, Robert J. and José María Fernández-Palacios. 2008. *Island Biogeography: Ecology, Evolution, and Conservation*. 2nd edn. Oxford: Oxford University Press.

4

Get animated!

Dynamic visualization and the site analysis process

Ken McCown and Phil Zawarus

Digital tools may help landscape architects rethink the site analysis process, allowing them to model sites and communicate how they work to stakeholders. The result of a site analysis should positively impact the capacity for design teams to deliver ecologically sensitive design. Designers, professional collaborators, contractors, clients and users should all be able to understand site analysis information. Digital tools may reshape the site analysis process so that site-planning guidelines can affect ecological change in the development of lands for human uses.

In this chapter, the authors will explain the landscape architecture site analysis process, and suggest a new workflow using digital tools. The authors will use a case study project done in Haiti to illustrate how to use dynamic visualization in the site analysis process.

Get animated!

SITE ANALYSIS

Site analysis is important. It is an essential method to optimize the relationship between land development and ecological function. James LaGro, in his book on site analysis, writes that designers and planners need to 'understand a site's past and present, within its spatial and temporal context, to effectively design the site's sustainable future' (2013, 24). Planning and design responding to information from good site analysis can help make places more sustainable for people, economically sound and ecologically functional. A site analysis is a critical document that helps stakeholders establish a set of ecological guidelines and the analysis shows how to proceed with development.

Site analysis and development can be classified into two conditions. The first condition is a client with a program looking for a site that is suitable. The other condition is using site analysis to find a program that might best fit the site. In either scenario, designers must account for the physical, biological and cultural attributes of the places they seek to design.

Landscape architects lead site analysis. They are the most qualified professionals to lead site analysis, due to their training in both urban and natural systems, including training in site analysis methods. While not leading experts in either urban design or ecological science, landscape architects have enough fluency in both to be specialists in the art of integrating site designs within ecological contexts. Their use of the site analysis method gives them an applied means to discover the unique traits of place, often unseen by others. Site analysis is different from site inventory, the analysis, done by the theoretical discourse in landscape architecture, assigns value and insight to critical issues related to site ecology and development.

Landscape architects Phil Lewis and Ian McHarg were leaders in the development of replicable methods of site analysis. They based their methods upon the creation of an inventory of site information. These designers made maps for each site factor, then overlaid them upon one another. By laying maps over one another, people using this method were able to generate scoring systems for development. This scoring system identified landscape areas best suited for development and necessary to preserve. This method was ostensibly replicable, and this reliability of projected similar outcomes was a large part of the appeal of this method.

Layered maps with ecologically sensitive areas occurring in the same place on each map steered planners away from development in a certain area, while overlaid maps with a confluence of areas not as sensitive to disturbance showed where development might occur. These layers included climate, slope, soils, and vegetation, among other environmental factors. The drawing created for each layer was an abstracted diagram of the site in plan, axonometric, or section view. This abstraction often came through tonal maps, and the layering of tones helped landscape architects visually see what areas of the site were more and less suitable for development.

This method of mapping was germane to landscape architecture and is a standard practice in the profession. These abstracted maps from overlays simplify the places. This method of separating ecological systems into layers can remove the complex, interdependent and synergistic relationships existing within environmental systems, including peoples' interdependence with them. Instead of viewing environmental systems separately and in layers only, environments can and should be integrated to be understood holistically.

In addition to the layered method, landscape architects will often use a single, summative site analysis presented in one image, or perhaps in just a few images. These brief analyses can leave out important information and also frequently rely on plan views and symbolic notation. Even small sites can be too complex to communicate necessary analysis information with a small set of drawings, and symbols used on the drawings can often cover large areas of the page or image. We propose that digital tools and methods now offer the opportunity for integrative, holistic narratives grounding sites within their global, regional, local, and site contexts in space and time. These stories should be told through dynamic visualization with digital tools.

It has been hard for landscape architects to convey the dynamic information about landscapes within the profession using the overlay and diagrammatic methods of representation, principally in plan views. These methods may not be effective in getting people outside of the profession to see the relationship of the real places to the site analysis drawings. Landscape architects, as leaders of site analysis, should be teachers to the stakeholders involved in projects. Kevin Lynch and Gary Hack note, in their book *Site Planning*, the role of site analysis in the decision-making process: 'this ring of decisions is fashioned according to the limits and the possibilities which the initiator of the project sees before her, but the designer can enter the ring and affect its shape' (1984, 5). Landscape architects' capacity to see a project ecologically and holistically, even in the analysis phase, allows them to get to the critical issues and reveal the potential of the site clearly. Site analysis is thus an important method to establish an ecological vision for a project shared among stakeholders and collaborators.

Get animated!

Lynch and Hack also note that the 'actors' in the site analysis, planning, design and construction phases of the project are 'numerous and often in conflict' (1984, 135). They note the designer is a teacher, one who allows clients and users to see their needs and possibilities. The responsibility to teach others places an obligation upon the designer to reveal hidden factors. Ecological process, changes in weather patterns, and sounds are just a few of the panoply of factors that may go unseen both by the non-professional and professional collaborator. Traditional communication through drawings usually missed these unseen matters of how landscapes operate over time – be it a day, season or year.

Clear information to the 'actors' in the process about ecologies of a site can help reduce conflict in the design process. Accessible information presented to laypersons in the site analysis process may enable a common understanding among all of the stakeholders. Landscape architects need to develop and maintain rigor in representation and communication on issues related to sustainable site development. The site analysis documentation is the foundation for sustainable development, and it must be clear and accessible to anyone involved in the project.

Lynch and Hack state this point by noting that information must be presented in 'an open and explicit process that non-specialists can penetrate' (1984, 375). Digital tools afford the possibility for designers to tell clear and dynamic stories to help people see the ecological processes impacting site development. As the American Society of Landscape Architects and kindred professional groups lead the members of the design professions to become advocates for sustainable development, the impetus for clarity and inclusion has never been more important than it is now. To be successful, advocates must have clear and accessible information to carry their message. Professionally, landscape architects need to use clear site analysis stories to gain consensus for sustainable and regenerative planning and design.

Landscapes are dynamic, and drawings are static. Traditional methods of site analysis were done using static images, and most of the time these images were cognitive, not perceptual. Cognitive drawings are ones that must be constructed in the mind, such as plans and sections. We cannot see the world in a straight plan or section view. These cognitive drawings require users to construct information in their minds about what the reality of a site is. Perceptual drawings, such as perspectives, reveal the world as it appears, without abstraction. Opportunities exist now for a combination of perceptual and conceptual drawings in methods like 'smart photography' which enables the ability to overlay information about ecological processes not seen by the human eye on a photo, as well as animated imagery to show people these processes.

What we see and share is what we talk about and design. It should not be a stretch to say all of us in the design profession sat in design reviews where 'the view' was a driving force in design decision-making when someone presented a project. A big part of site analysis historically has been to locate users in a design to take advantage of the best available view out of a proposed building. This shows the power of the perceptual image to impact design. The photographs a designer takes on-site are easily accessible to the people involved in the project. These perceptual images allow the non-specialist to penetrate the concept of the design. 'The view' shown by the designer in a presentation is easy to see, and therefore these images of the view enable consensus among stakeholders and collaborators due to the common ground: it lets them find a vision for the future of the site. More complex factors shown in cognitive drawings and diagrams are much harder for the group to see and therefore minimized in the design process.

Cognitive drawings, such as plans and sections, sometimes clustered with axonometric drawings, are used to convey information to stakeholders and collaborators in the site analysis process. These conceptual images often do not clearly convey the dynamics of sites and the ecological processes happening in them, and *through* them. As noted above, there are opportunities for digital tools to remove this abstraction from the site analysis process. Digital tools create possibilities for animated drawings; movies and other perceptual image types that let people see the living landscape.

Before we get into the site analysis and dynamic visualization, there are new and upcoming issues within the practice of landscape architecture, adding further layers of landscape dynamics that compel the designer to use dynamic visualization. LEED, process-based design, 'Sustainable Sites,' and 'Landscape Performance' all require the capacity to model the dynamics of a landscape for sustainability in the analysis and design process.

Process-based design is becoming increasingly important and compulsory. Ecological processes are now increasing in importance for site design. There are greater land areas of landscapes developed globally as populations rise, creating the need to be more efficient than ever with the resources used on these developments. Processes involving air, water, energy, and habitat are factors of increasing importance to design and planning.

Scoring and rating systems can affect site analysis and design, and make it imperative for the designer to be able to model sites dynamically. Ecologies and nature are no longer being valued for only environmental benefits and aesthetic quality. Their social value, and their 'ecosystems services' translated into economic value is part of the site analysis, design and monitoring process. The Sustainable

Sites Initiative, LEED, and Landscape Performance require a capacity for planners and designers to embrace ecological systems and flows as part of not only site analysis, but also planning and design to monitor projected performances in ecological systems. These systems and flows are too complex to be communicated clearly through static imagery. Many of these rating systems are performance-based, requiring site monitoring. The use of digital tools in the site analysis process may enable dynamic models that can be used for analysis, predictive modeling, and later for site monitoring to see if the analysis and scenarios were accurate regarding performance metrics. Digital tools and dynamic visualization can help the designer see the implications of their projected plans.

The growth of practice into a global economy may also prompt the efficacy of dynamic visualization. Practice is now more global and interdisciplinary than it has ever been. Landscape architects work in tandem with planners, architects, and ecologists. These groups increasingly use digital tools to deliver site analysis and design in compressed project delivery times. Dynamic visualization methods may enable groups working from a distance to more quickly see the potential ecological implications of projects. By harnessing the power of digital tools to create stories about sites in site analysis, landscape architects may not only establish leadership with respect to sustainability but may be able to change how a project gets built.

This capacity for change is perhaps best seen in flows and systems. Water flow, such as runoff from building roofs on to sites, or heat gain are issues that affect architects and landscape architects. In the past, site analysis drawings by a landscape architect, or even plans from these designers, held little information about the buildings. Now, perceptual images of buildings and landscapes together should enable interdisciplinary teams to see water flow and thermal gain, and how buildings and sites can work in tandem ecologically.

This global method of interdisciplinary practice may negatively impact the quality of the design response to site factors simply due to designers working from a distance. A professional team working on one continent and designing a place on another is a challenging situation. An important part of site analysis involves being on-site to gain insight. Can digital tools help designers understand distant places? We argue they can. Accurate models, immersive panoramas, and movies can help designers, especially the young 'digital natives', see sites in more detail than ever. These methods should be used with rigor to help designers, collaborators, and stakeholders see the ecologies of sites.

Another key factor related to global practice is data sets. Teams working from a distance typically use predeveloped data sets about the site. This information typically comes from different sources, especially when spanning scales from a region to a site. A federal jurisdiction may have regional data, and a local government may have other data that does not fit the information on the larger scale. This can further fragment understanding of the site by the stakeholders. Digital tools and methods often enable designers to fill the gaps in the information across scales by using dynamic visualization.

DYNAMIC VISUALIZATION AND THE SITE ANALYSIS METHODS

As noted earlier, the predominant mode of representation in site analysis by landscape architects has been through static images, such as plans, sections, axonometrics, and other drawn images – plus photographs. The easy accessibility of digital tools and the arrival of 'digital natives' into the schools of landscape architecture and the profession have made digital tools feasible for landscape architects to use in site analysis. Can the model of investigation be reconsidered? We argue it can, and we encourage harnessing the power of dynamic visualization with digital tools to incorporate them into the traditional site analysis process.

Dynamic visualization may make site analysis dynamic in two ways. One, it is relatively easy to animate information now. Programs that animate drawn diagrams, time-lapse images, and video can relate information about ecological processes to professional collaborators and stakeholders so the complexities of sites can be understood with minimal abstraction.

Second, information can become dynamic through integrating narratives about sites. Information no longer has to be solely categorized into soils, climate, topography, et al., this information can be combined into scripted presentations that tell people a story. The interactions between site factors can be revealed, and quantitative and qualitative information integrated. As an example, an immersive 360-degree panorama can have overlays showing the data behind what people see, or in the case of ecological processes, don't see. A panorama taken in dry conditions in an area subject to flooding could be animated to show flood levels during a major storm event. What may be difficult to understand on a black and white (and blue) topography map showing one moment could be taken away from the paper, shown as people would see it, and animated to describe different hydrological conditions.

Figure 4.1 shows the traditional site analysis categories, the information needed in those categories, and the means of representation typically used in that

Site Analysis	Evaluative Visualization Used (usual practice)	
Climate • Temperature • Precipitation • Wind direction and speed	Wind	Wind rose displays direction and speed. It can reveal change throughout the month, day, or hour.
	Precipitation	Use of charts and graphs to show yearly and monthly precipitation amounts. These charts can reveal yearly wet and dry seasons.
	Temperature	Charts and graphs display air temperature by month, day, hour, or any other designated time frame necessary.
Vegetation • Canopy cover and major trees • Understory/plant communities	Tree canopy	Photography and base maps as key plans – together can show establishing and mature vegetation.
	Understory	Plans and sections can be used with photographs to reveal plant communities and their habitat zones.
Hydrology • Drainage: major and minor • Stormwater runoff	Drainage	In plan, diagrams drawn over landform show primary, secondary and tertiary runoff areas from a fixed perspective.
	Runoff	Site runoff information includes quantitative and qualitative values, these being volume and velocity of water, as well as pollution and sediment loads.
Soils • Topsoil texture • Subsoil infiltration	Topsoil	Collection of topsoil samples help determine soil texture, which is a factor relating to stormwater surface flow. This information can be combined in layers with topography maps and runoff calculations.
	Subsoil	Infiltration rates of water levels at designated points on a site will indicate the subsoil type. This information is likely in a report from a consultant.
Topography • Contour lines and terrain	Contour lines	The designer uses contour lines from survey maps or civic databases. Traditionally, plans and sections were most common. Where time and budget allow, a physical model may be used.
Wildlife • Avian and amphibious wildlife • Domesticated and livestock	Wildlife	Information is likely in reports, usually from consultants. These reports contain information on sensitive species or communities and areas of importance may be in text only or plan diagram.
	Parasitic	Reports, likely from consultants, noting any potential parasites, pests, or invasive species that may be harmful to the natural conditions of a habitat or proposed users of the site.
	Livestock	Information in reports, likely from consultants, noting the presence of domesticated wildlife or livestock and potential impacts on the natural environment or proposed programming.
Spatial Quality • Unique spaces and conditions	Intangibles	Intangibles are the combination of site conditions providing attractive or unattractive qualitative values that may include light quality, lush vegetation, noise or comfort. Qualitative aspects of site have been communicated through photographs, including panoramas, videos, and sketches.

Figure 4.1 The matrix shows site analysis factors, normative practices of representation, issues and opportunities related to visualization, and suggests new methods of dynamic visualization for site analysis.

Issues and Opportunities	Dynamic Visualization Methods
Discrepancies resulting from compiling of different data sets may prevent consistency in matching of various layers and information.	Programs such as Rhino, Grasshopper, and Ecotect can be used to integrate information and unique data sets for dynamic representation of temporal site conditions, setting up a platform for visualizations in climate factors.
Issue – Climate analysis is often an independent component of generalized data in the site analysis process. The relationship between climate data and other site variables may not be considered.	Integrated information can be made illustrative and animated to communicate how climate impacts a site; especially how climate changes over time. As an example, showing how a rainy or dry season works, can help clarify an analysis to help with water harvesting calculation.
Opportunity – Integrating the climate data (temperature, precipitation, wind, sky conditions) with other conditions (vegetation zones and surface types) can create descriptive and informative visualization. These dynamic visualizations can be temporal in nature, communicating through the span of months, days, and even hours, specifically from day to night.	Integrated data sets can create analysis 'contours' or 'clouds' for dynamic climate data representation over designated time frames.
Opportunity – The interactive data layers above can be used to determine meaningful takeaways from the information. As climate information such as heat gain, or human comfort zones cannot be seen visually, computing can help designers and stakeholders see these forces that can determine design.	'Contour' and 'cloud' maps can reveal unseen built and outdoor conditions including such as thermal heat gain of buildings, and human comfort zones in outdoor spaces. 'Smart photographs' including those that might show light levels or heat can expand the image beyond the range of the human eye.
Issue – Accurate descriptions of vegetation cover are crucial to being able to calculate stormwater runoff volume and soil erosion.	Canopy cover can be modeled accurately over time, and growth can be projected as a multifactor analysis including water runoff and soil erosion.
Opportunity – Dynamic visualization of vegetative cover on site can show succession over time. This imagery may let designers and others see the plant growth of various canopy trees and shrubs or grasses. With these qualitative visualizations, designers may be able to evaluate and quantify the environmental benefits related to increased shade cover, diverse ecosystems, soil nutrition, and runoff infiltration.	Through layering the physical locations of a region or site, and adding a temporal element by iterative site layers, site areas can be prioritized regarding preservation or development. of vegetation along with determining adequate vegetation needs to address shade, soil stabilization, and runoff interception or infiltration.
Issue – Drainage calculations rarely account for soil properties or the effect of soil saturation levels. Both factors will influence the volume of sheet flow and soil erosion.	Site drainage systems and watersheds can be accurately animated through digital models, allowing people to see the hydrological forces upon sites. The animated diagrams can be used to create time-lapse images of runoff.
Opportunity – Use dynamic visualization and analysis to connect hydrologic flow and soil properties. Digital tools may make it easy to calculate the storage capacity of basins to minimize flooding. Water quality data sets may be formatted to align with information on pollution sources from other data sets. This correlated information may help people to understand impact upon a site's vegetation, wildlife, and soil types.	Progressive time-lapse drawings can be animated to represent storm intensity for infiltration and runoff volume, including critical moments to design such as the time of concentration.
	Digital databases provide information upon location of pollution sources, enabling more precise mapping of pollutant flow, load and direction. Thus, site analyses, and therefore site designs, can be performative to respond to specific pollutants with efficacy.
Issue – Identification of soil types on-site will help decode areas of flooding, erosion, and suitability for building foundations; but these risk areas may have a confluence with other areas including vegetation and hydrology.	Digital models with algorithms from soil types, runoff, and vegetation can be animated to examine potential development impacts upon soil erosion from new planning and design.
Opportunity: Correlate soil analysis, vegetation analysis and hydrology.	Assign values from soils, vegetation and hydrology to determine different infiltration rates and saturation levels within an algorithmic model tied to a physical model to see how hydrology and infiltration operates on-site.
Issue – Land surveys and contour maps cannot capture the details of micro conditions of contours. A designer or planner may not get the most accuracy of the topography of the site.	Use global positioning system (GPS) to record points for quick interpolation to refine the topographic models of the site. Software can take the specific tracks and points logged from the GPS investigation to create a more precise digital model. It is also possible for the designer to gather elevation data points to create accurate digital terrain.
Opportunity – Collection of precise elevation points in critical areas for site development may provide detail where drainage and specific conditions are not available on given maps.	
Opportunity – Vegetation type and climate conditions define wildlife habitat areas. Connecting existing habitat maps, with vegetation analyses and climate may aid in maintaining and protecting sensitive ecosystems. Additionally, disturbances to the structure and function of plant communities can be modeled to study impacts of invasive and parasitic species.	The wildlife inventory, modeled with species preferences, vegetation and climate can support the creation of animated diagrams showing migration patterns of species over daily and season time periods. These diagrams can help stakeholders 'see' how species live in the landscape over time.
	Domesticated animals may have different impacts than wildlife, but they can also be modeled in their migration and waste patterns. Domestic and invasive species can be modeled in disturbance scenarios to test impacts of invasive species.
Opportunity – The rise of data about regions and sites, with the prevalence of photography and video (along with sharing platforms) allows for an unprecedented ability to integrate qualitative and quantitative data. This integration can provide information that collective stakeholders share, such as raw temperature, but can also express subjective feelings such as how that temperature might feel.	Animation, video, gif-making software, coding and other apps enable designers and even laypersons to create accessible presentations of the unseen forces in landscapes. Immersion formats include 360 degree panoramas and where accessible, virtual environments people can enter into through head gear or large screens.

Figure 4.1 continued

site factor. In the traditional representation through static imagery, there are issues acting as a barrier to understanding by stakeholders. There are also opportunities offered by dynamic visualization methods to clarify ecological processes and see typically unseen factors such as heat gain, or air flows. In the last column of the chart, we suggest dynamic visualization methods to analyze the site.

CASE STUDY

A case study by co-author Phil Zawarus may reveal the importance of narrative to the design process. After the latest earthquake, a resettlement of people to rural areas of Haiti was necessary. The case study development was in a region stressed by the lack of water supply and stricken by poor water quality. Water quality and quantity is a problem. With the arrival of new people to the town in the case study, Fond-des-Blancs, these problems were likely to be chronic. An interdisciplinary team of designers from the United States brought architecture, engineering, design, and landscape architecture expertise to the project, and were at first unfamiliar with the local landscape. The project the team delivered was a school, housing, and food and water infrastructure on the site.

The narrative tying the site analysis together was water. The scarcity of clean water made it the critical factor defining all design decisions. In the warm, tropical climate, people needed to be kept cool so as to minimize perspiration; the site design needed to have an infrastructure able to maximize water capture and reuse. The local water would support drinking, everyday use, and irrigation for growing food to feed the locals.

Figures 4.2–4.7 (stills from animations) describe the water story, from the mega-region of the tropics, down to the site. Dynamic visualization allows the landscape architect to link scales, helping the stakeholders of a project locate themselves within the ecological context of a site. The landscape architect was able to tell the story of wet and dry seasons, how the land formed and created a rain shadow on the site locale, and how hydrology worked on-site. By being able to visualize how water flowed on-site, how sun heated buildings, and how the site looked, the landscape architect led the design team and clients on building siting, orientation, and construction of site infrastructure.

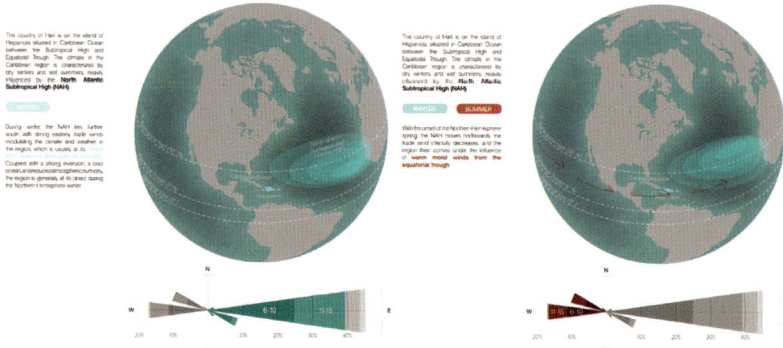

Figure 4.2 Snapshots of an animated diagram showing the trade winds in global tropical zones related to the project site in Haiti. The design team, volunteers from the United States of America, was having trouble understanding why the region was so dry even though it was located in the tropics. This animated diagram by the landscape architect showed how global air and water currents led to wet and dry seasons. This animation helped the design team to see months where there could be water scarcity, helping them to size the water harvesting units to potentially supply water on-site during the dry season.

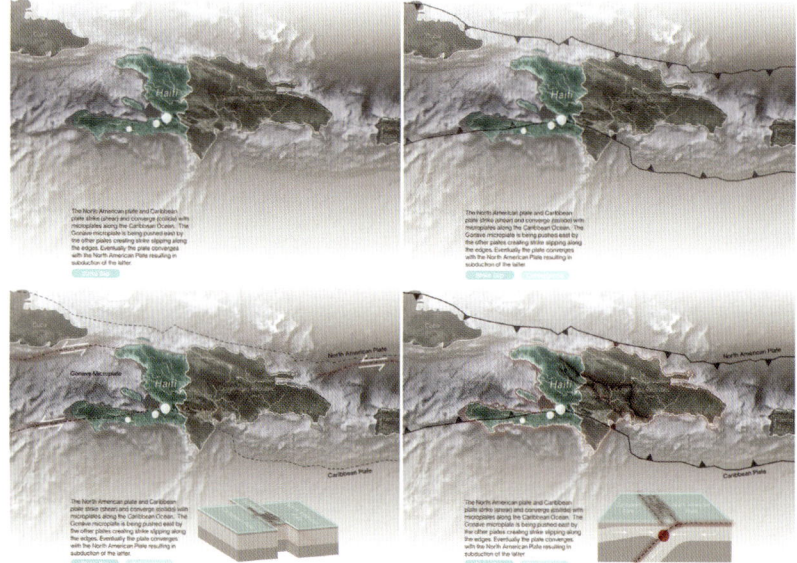

Figure 4.3 The design team was still surprised about how relatively dry the project site and surrounding area appeared, even in the wet season. The geomorphology impacted the amount of rainfall on the site even in the wet season. These still shots from the animation of the land movement not only created a foundation for talking about the local impacts of the land on rainfall among the stakeholders, but also showed the reasons behind the powerful earthquakes that can occur on the island and where they may occur along the fault lines.

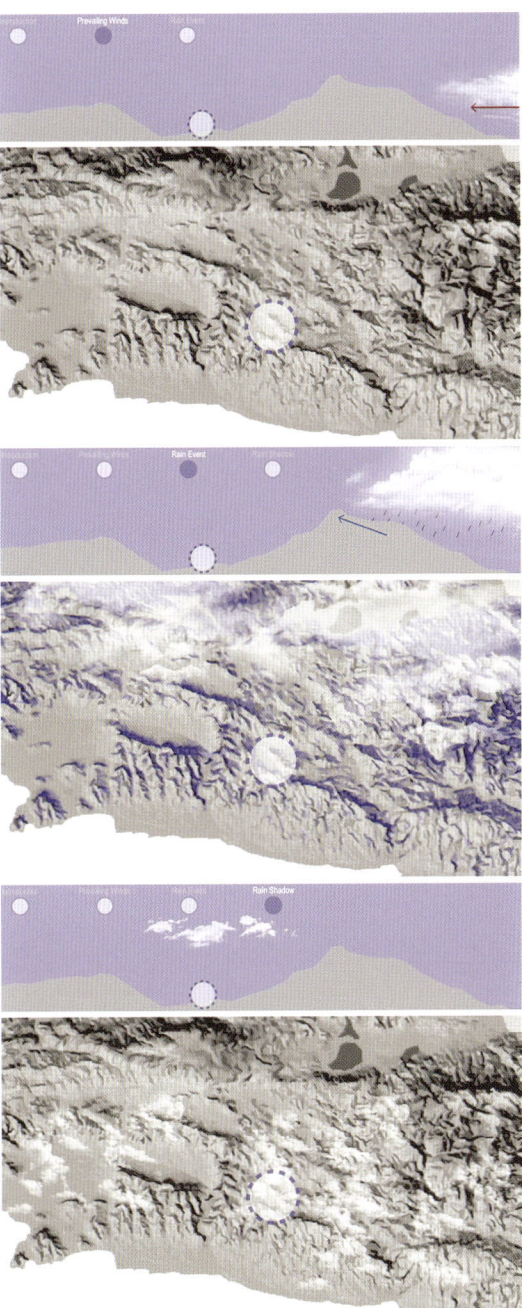

Figure 4.4 Still images from an animation showing the rain shadow effect on the area of the project site. The tectonic collision of the plates created mountains that caught the storms in the rainy season, leaving a rain shadow where the design site was. This set of images allowed the designers to finally understand why the area the project site was set within had such a paucity of water relative to locations nearby.

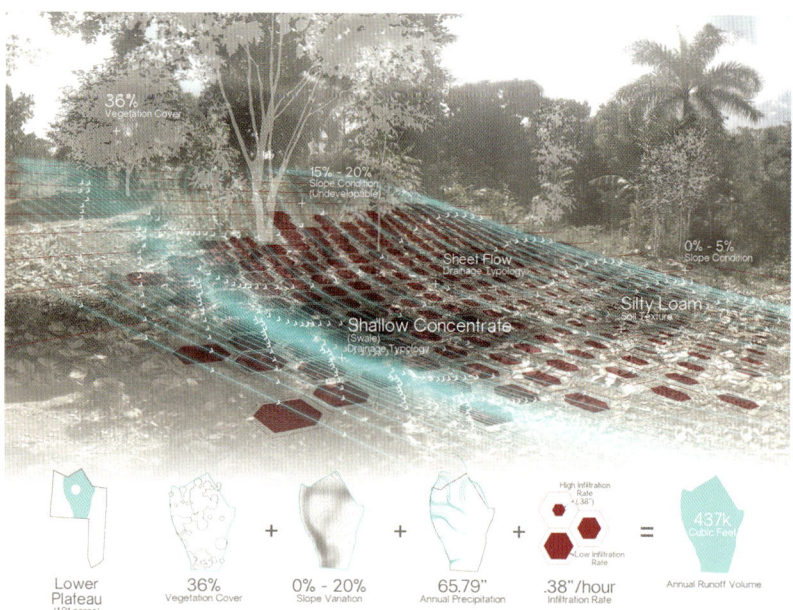

Figure 4.5 A still of parts of an animation illustrating the site hydrology. This set of animations and images enabled design team members to see water collect and increase in amount (noted by arrow thickness) on the topography lines. These visualizations helped the designers establish water catchment areas and place buildings. The combination of hydrology with soils data revealed areas on-site prone to erosion. Healthy soil on-site was essential to growing crops.

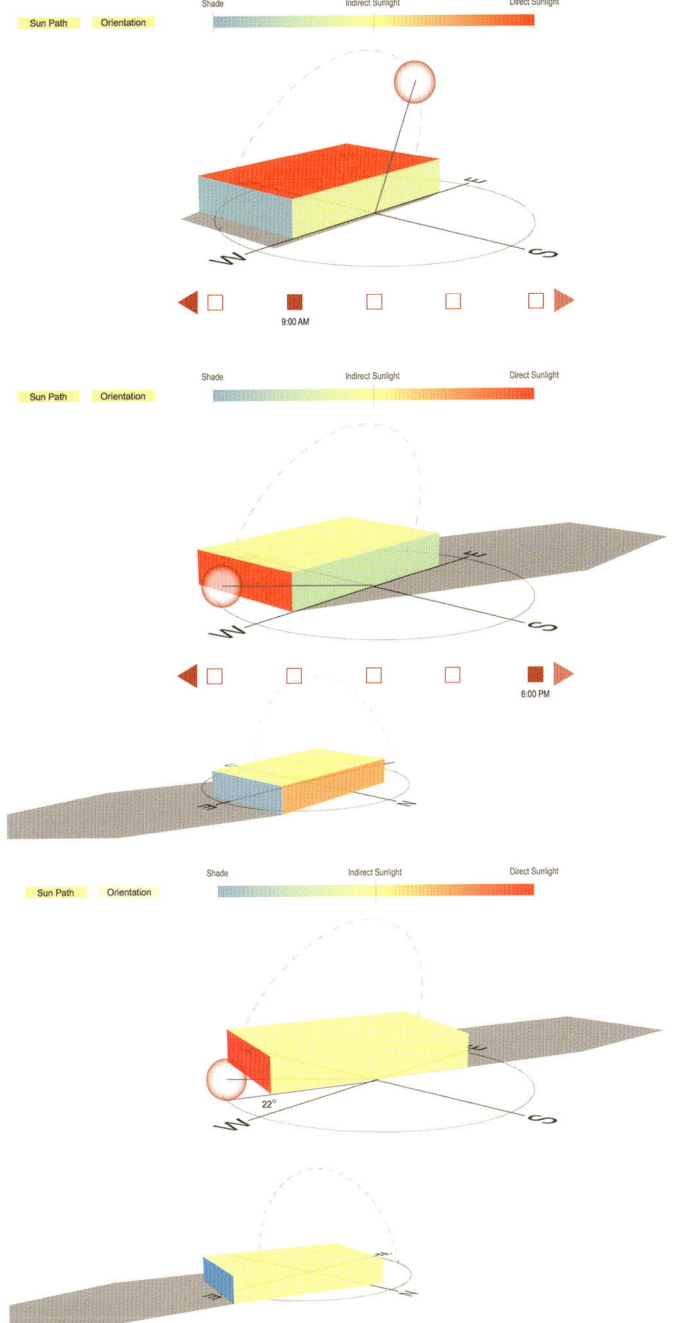

Figure 4.6 In this image, the landscape architect on the design team illustrated thermal loading on the building. A simple rotation of the building minimized the heat gain to only one side of the building. The hottest time of day in this environment was close to and during sunset. In the final snapshot of the story, the red color shows the thermal gain on this west side, the gain is high relative to the other building sides but minimizes the amount of facade area on the building needing insulation.

Without air conditioning in this environment, maintaining cool temperatures inside was essential. The design team wanted to make the most comfortable indoor environment that minimized sweating in an area where clean water can be scarce. The rotation of the building enabled them to do this by reducing direct heat gain.

Ken McCown and Phil Zawarus

Figure 4.7 The project was built by local and volunteer labor; therefore, construction drawings might not have been the best method for describing the project's construction. The landscape architect created immersive, 360-degree panoramas of the site, and used stills from this animation to create before and after images to be used for design and construction.

The landscape architecture representative on the team tested methods of dynamic visualization on this project, to see if the digital means of representation could help explain the ecological processes, as well as impact the design decisions made by the collaborators on the project. The results showed that dynamic visualization did enable collaborators and stakeholders to see ecological factors better, and raised their awareness of them. It helped everyone see the opportunities to change the design to make it more sustainable.

Dynamic visualization, incorporated into the traditional site analysis process, does have the capability to weave together accessible stories to help the landscape architect advocate to allied professions, clients, and other stakeholders how to develop sites sustainably. Digital tools offer an unprecedented capacity to clarify ecological processes, and should be harnessed to help landscape architects lead in getting sustainable, performance-based designs built.

REFERENCES

LaGro, James. 2013. *Site Analysis: Informing Context-Sensitive and Sustainable Site Planning and Design.* 3rd edn. Hoboken, NJ: Wiley & Sons.

Lynch, Kevin and Gary Hack. 1984. *Site Planning.* 3rd edn. Cambridge, MA: MIT Press.

5

The landscape as database

*Chris Speed and
Duncan Shingleton*

The advent of smart phones equipped with GPS technologies and constant connection to the internet has fostered a suite of applications allowing developers and owners to associate data and information with physical locations. Longitudinal and latitudinal coordinates create instances of physical locations that then populate a database for use by others to support navigation, addressing and mapping.

This chapter explores the conditions of the landscape as a database and the possibilities that this holds for reconfiguring both the representation of the landscape and the practices that can occur within it. A paradigm in which data points become the primary material that describes the landscape means that any 'thing' can become a landmark. Whilst we are used to buildings, monuments and trees having a datum, the streaming condition of cars, people, animals and all variety of objects within the internet of things, means that the landscape is no longer described through architectures with fixed points of longitude and latitude. Instead, the landscape is fluid, a non-static database in which all and any correlations can be made to represent the landscape. In support of their theoretical premise, the authors present three funded research projects that introduce the application of geofences to moving things: people, buses, clouds, and base maps.

The landscape as database

THE DATABASE IS THE TERRITORY

At some point in the last five years the information about the landscape as we know it tipped from being something that we knew as landmarks in personal cognitive maps, to a collection of instances within databases. No longer navigated through paper road based atlases, or by asking people in the street where a particular destination might be, spaces are also now traversed via the database accessed through the smart phones that we hold in our hands.

In his 2004 paper, Nigel Thrift argued for an update of de Certeau's romantic idea that the walker is the primary agent within the city. Thrift identified digital technologies as offering a more complex substrate for enabling communications to become part of a negotiation with space (Thrift 2004). The car complemented with satellite navigation, air conditioning, musical soundtracks, and a figure-hugging seat provides a very personal interface with a city, one that predisposes the driver to allow the car to become an extension of his/her body. Once driving, we find ourselves expressing a series of characteristics that indicate a deep embodiment of the car including: the charged emotional state in which we engage with others, communication techniques using lights and movement, and the 'tactics' that allow us to navigate spaces by reading the 'gestures' and actions of others (Katz 2000).

> *The advent of a mixture of geographical information systems, global positioning and wireless communications means that getting lost will no longer be an option and, equally, that increasingly it will be possible to track all cars, wherever they may be. The result is that both surveying and being surveyed will increasingly become a norm: it is even possible that, through the new informational and communicational conduits that are now being opened up, some of the social cues that have been missing from the experience of driving will be re-inserted (for example, who is driving a particular car), making the whole process more akin to walking again, but with a new informationally boosted hybrid body, a new incarnation.*
>
> (Thrift 2004)

Thrift explored the potential for digital systems to extend the social negotiation with space through the car. Published in 2004, over ten years later the widespread adoption of smart phones means pedestrians now far extend the technology that Thrift identified in the car. As the smart phone has gained popularity, on-board mapping applications have developed in different ways to provide us with access to the databases that describe and represent where we are and the places around us.

Described as locative media services, the competition to provide the best app with the most accurate maps, the biggest database of landmarks, the most up-to-date information on venues and social places has required a number of interesting strategies. In 2004, following the acquisition of Where 2 Technologies, Google began systematically equipping themselves with further procurements to complement their own mapping and georeferencing technologies to create what we now know to be Google Maps. Available through a browser and as a smart phone app, Google Maps offers detailed location-based information in the form of satellite imagery, street maps, and Street View perspectives, as well as functions such as a route planner for traveling by foot, car, bicycle, or with public transport. Through a combination of databases, Google provides an extensive database for the landscape. However, along their path toward domination they failed to recognize the potential for crowd derived location-based information.

In 2003, Dennis Crowley and Alex Rainert launched Dodgeball. A location-based social networking platform for mobile phones, Dodgeball allowed users to use SMS messages to send details about their location to friends including interesting venues nearby. In 2005, Google bought Dodgeball and shut it down in 2009, replacing it with their form of social media/location service Google Latitude that was later withdrawn in 2013. Once released from his 'golden handcuffs' at Google, Crowley worked with Naveen Selvadurai to recast Dodgeball as Foursquare and offer highly personalized recommendations of the best places to visit around a user's current location. Launched in 2009, the application used a highly effective form of gamification that encouraged users to 'check-in' to locations that they valued. Multiple check-ins at one location could result in being awarded the position of 'Mayor' of an establishment. The platform became extremely popular and by December 2013, Foursquare boasted 45 million registered users. Since then the business model has changed, and the user experience has now split into two applications that critics feel dilutes the performance. However, at the peak of their success in 2012, Foursquare signed a partnership deal with Apple to provide access to its database of 50 million venues in 220 countries that had been generated by members of the public.

Constituted upon a wide range of location-based databases, Apple Maps pulls from a host of services to provide its mapping app. As well as data derived from Foursquare's databases that were generated through the actions of individuals checking-in to their favourite bar/café/store, Apple Maps include data from the travel app Waze, that provides real-time data from people as they drive their cars. Waze was founded in 2008 and allows users to see real-time road conditions (traffic congestion, road works, and even police activity) in return for pushing data

The landscape as database

about the speed of their car back to the database. This form of crowd-sourced data depends upon having many members within the transport network, all of whom are streaming data about the progress of their vehicle to Waze. Users can choose to leave their phone to push data, or add additional comments about the conditions of the road. As well as relaying real-time data back to its users, Waze is collecting vast amounts of data about the conditions of our roads, the average speeds during specific periods of the day, and the experiences of drivers on them. The acquisition of Waze by Google in 2013 makes the entanglement between mapping apps such as Apple Maps and Google's own smart phone app complete, as the range of databases to describe the landscape combines top down and bottom up data to provide larger and more detailed information about the landscape.

Of particular interest to the authors is the combination of inputs to these databases. No longer is it the just role of the geographer and cartographer to input data, everyone who is using mapping applications is now involved in feeding data back, and the mobility of the smart phone means that this data does not only describe the static landscape, but also the things that are moving through it. The much used term 'internet of things' refers to the technical and cultural shift that is anticipated as society moves to a ubiquitous form of computing in which a significant amount of the objects in our lives are connected in some way to the internet. While the specific reference to 'things' typically refers to physical devices, the data available from many of the elements found in urban and rural contexts constitute Landscapes across the Internet of Things, things ranging from cars to buses, buildings to animals, and lampposts to drains.

The following three projects highlight different design strategies that extend the premise that the landscape is now a database. Each project uses data sets in novel ways to offer experiences or representations that reconfigure how we understand the rural and urban landscapes as databases.

FLOWS

A critical dimension to achieving an Internet of Things is for individual artifacts to be able to be identified within a database. Described as Universally Unique Identifiers (UUIDs) they come in many shapes and forms including barcodes, RFID tags, IP addresses, and phone numbers (see Figure 5.1). Whilst we have become used to the common barcode that associates an entire product line with one number, and the concept that our smart phones and computers have IP addresses, Internet of Things developers often overlook one of the oldest, most visible and more common UUIDs in the landscape: the car number plate.

Figure 5.1 IoT: Barcodes, QR codes, RFID, and registration plates.

Cars are the single most visual form of actual moving data that we know, and yet they are often overlooked as packets of data that interface with humans, businesses, and the environment. Car registration plates can be used as unique identifiers in the same way as barcodes and offer a platform for people to store data onto them, use them as interfaces to social networks, pass messages between people, and connect to data.

Dynamic, fluid, and representing individual packets of information within a UK-wide network, cars could be critical components within the emerging phenomenon known as the Internet of Things. Each one tagged with a unique identifier that is scannable with smart phones, as well as the highly sophisticated roadside cameras, cars with their number plates have been the equivalent of barcodes on supermarket products for many years. Visible in the street, cars that are linked through a common web platform offer a fluid interface to the Internet of Things that will make visible the flow of products and services that could change the way we inhabit cities in the twenty-first century. Able to 'see' where things have come from and where they are going, cars have the potential to become the next web browser (Speed and Shingleton 2012). The ability to tag a vehicle's registration plate with information to allow others to read at various points in the future offers a potentially new way of disseminating not only traffic information (journey times, congestion/incident hotspots), but data on weather/road conditions, special events, and user relevant offers.

The *Flows* art installation explores the experimental use of cars as a manifestation of flow across social networks. Manuel Castells first proposed the theory of the Space of Flows, in *The Rise of the Network Society* (1996), and it relates to network society and technologies' role in a new type of space (Figure 5.2). *Flows* bring things and people into synchronous, real-time interrelationships made up of purposeful, repetitive, programmable sequences of exchange and interaction. Therefore, we can define flows as consisting of three elements – the medium through which things flow, the things that flow, and the nodes among which the flows circulate. *Flows* interprets these three elements through vehicles, CO_2 emission rating data, and the A354's ANPR cameras.

Approximately 40,000 cars are recorded every day on the A354 between Dorchester and Weymouth. Through the use of a vehicle look-up enquiry, a service

The landscape as database

Figure 5.2 Flows CO_2 emissions representation.

you might use when purchasing a car, one can ascertain detailed information about the vehicle including make, model, fuel type, engine size, and CO_2 output. *Flows* as an artwork uses the information held on the CO_2 output of each vehicle passing through one of six Automatic Number Plate Recognition sites on the A354, and converts the total amount of carbon dioxide being emitted on the stretch of road into a physical data representation. Each one of the acrylic tubes represents a position along the A354, and drawing reference from the Emissions Ratings Charts, they are lit to correspond to the heaviest polluting site. As CO_2 is invisible to the naked eye, fans at the base of each tube blow particles in to the light, with a higher velocity indicating a greater output of CO_2 at that site. All of these calculations are done in real-time, and the output is a live representation of the material traffic flow along the A354, and the corresponding immaterial environmental impact.

TREASURE TRAPPER

Flows established a critical methodology within our studio's works, that of developing correlations between otherwise disparate databases to form new representations. However, while *Flows* manifests an invisible dimension to a landscape, the representation is fed to a gallery and is not able to affect the behaviour of drivers. The Treasure Trapper project was developed in such a way as to directly affect tourists' behaviour across the cultural landscape of Edinburgh.

The tourists' city is defined by two extremes: the static cultural centers, including museums and galleries, and the dynamic flow of people and traffic. Digital technology has the potential to connect the flow of traffic that passes cultural centers with the tourists who are interested in seeking out all that a city has to offer.

As a popular tourist destination, Edinburgh's museums are of particular interest; however, the large national museums and galleries dominate the tourist trails, eclipsing the smaller venues, leaving the smaller venues with a smaller proportion of the market. The top three most popular attractions listed, through a visitor survey by Edinburgh Tourist Attraction Group, are currently Edinburgh Castle (72 percent), National Museum of Scotland (32 percent), and National Gallery of Scotland (30 percent). Although City of Edinburgh Museums and Galleries Service manage eight visitor attractions across the city, including the iconic Scott Monument and the home to the capital's history, Museum of Edinburgh, the only venue mentioned throughout in a recent survey was the Museum of Childhood (10 percent). Edinburgh Museums and Galleries have a wealth of stories, objects, collections, events, and authentic experiences to offer the visitors and residents of Edinburgh that can be lost in the shadow of their complementary counterparts listed above.

The solution to make these overshadowed cultural venues more 'visible' was to develop a game that would mobilize these otherwise hidden treasures by bringing them out of the museums and galleries. Interested in the opportunities of correlating different data sets that are available in places such as cities, the authors struck upon the idea of using the flow of buses that passed by museums to move objects around the city.

The Treasure Trapper project was a seven-month project developed by the authors for Edinburgh Museums and Art Galleries, The Assembly Rooms, and Edinburgh Bus Tours (part of Lothian Buses and Transport for Edinburgh). Interested in better understanding how location-based services and gaming could be used to boost footfall, Edinburgh Museums and Art Galleries approached us to develop a creative solution. In response the authors developed a game in the form of mobile applications for iOS and Android platforms that brought together data derived from the Lothian Buses open API which describes the time of arrival of buses to bus stops across the city with cultural information about artifacts held within the museum collections (Figure 5.3).

The landscape as database

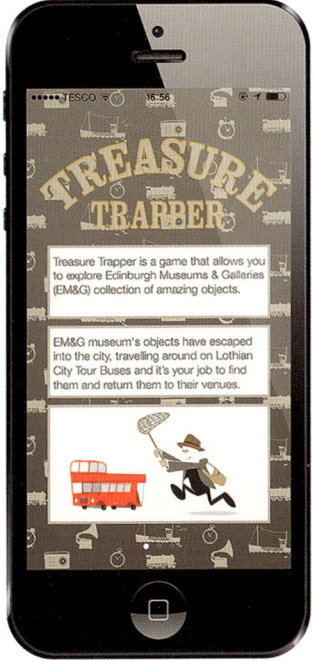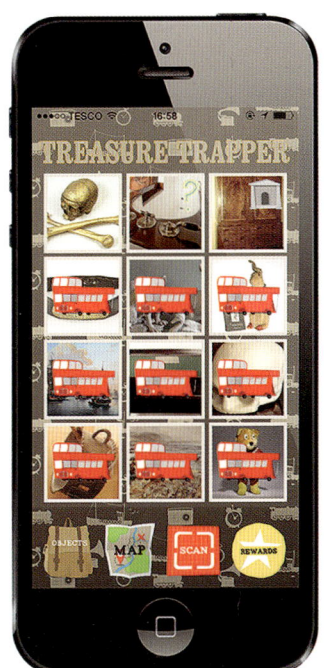

Figure 5.3 Treasure Trapper iOS interface.

The applications integrate data to form a simple but compelling game. Simply put, as the tourist buses that are operated by Lothian Buses pass by a registered museum or cultural venue, they 'steal' an object from the museum's collections. The buses drop the objects off at bus stops around the city, and if a child spots one with the App, they have a short amount of time to capture it (Figure 5.4). When a child has collected all of the objects within a level of the game they can 'level up' by returning the virtual objects to a museum and redeem a prize. The more levels the child completes, the more lucrative the prize.

Developed as a trial for Summer 2014 the challenge of developing user experiences that rely upon interoperability between different city databases and location-based data was successful, and the project received good coverage in the local and Scottish press.

Understanding how to 'lace' together city services is a particular challenge for the near future and what some describe as the smart city. Evidently there are significant challenges in designing across services when the details of how each operates are unavailable until deeper inquiry. Nevertheless, the project demonstrates the potential for creative technologists and programmers to ideate across services and open up potential markets for multiple stakeholders.

Chris Speed and Duncan Shingleton

Figure 5.4 Participants in the Treasure Trapper game. At this point the players are picking up a virtual artefact dropped by the bus.

COGET

Treasure Trapper combined data from two separate databases that previously had little to do with each other, and in doing so created an experience that affected the behavior of tourists within Edinburgh. Using a gaming methodology, including incentives to encourage use, the platform demonstrated the marketing opportunities for representing the landscape in a different way. CoGet, the final design case study, looks further into the future and posits an entirely different representation of the urban landscape, one in which people become coordinates for exchange rather than the postcodes and buildings.

Across the connected city, small things play a large part in sustaining the flow between people and places. Cups of tea, bottles of water, books, four-way plug adaptors, bicycles, computers, and many more objects are the 'things' that support the meeting of people and the jobs that they do. However, sometimes these things aren't where we need them, and flow is halted. If things knew where they were likely to be needed, perhaps they could ask passers-by to move them there.

The landscape as database

The CoGet software and experiments reveal where things want to go, and asks the public to move them on their behalf. Connected to the internet, and able to read the social complexity of a local area, CoGet lets objects control people's movements by predicting where they need to be and borrowing the legs of a human to move them.

In March 2014 the authors ran a series of workshops at the Future Everything festival in Manchester to better understand what it might be like to allow objects to 'piggy back' the urban routines that we perform on a daily basis so that they may move across the city.

The iPhone app (Figure 5.5) requires a critical mass of people running the application that visualizes the speed and bearing of participants on a map, allowing everyone to see the direction of where people are going, and predicts where they might be based on their current movements. At any point, somebody in the network can request something and members can choose to accept to 'Take the object' along a part of its journey. In fact, the object can remain with any one person until someone offers to take it a little further toward the person who requested it. But for the sake of participants and to foster a dynamic sense of flow, the workshops at Future Everything tried to move things across an area within 20 minutes.

On reflection, the app presents many challenges to new users. While many were enthusiastic, it was clear that using a new app in an urban landscape (familiar or unfamiliar) presents a significant cognitive load to participants.

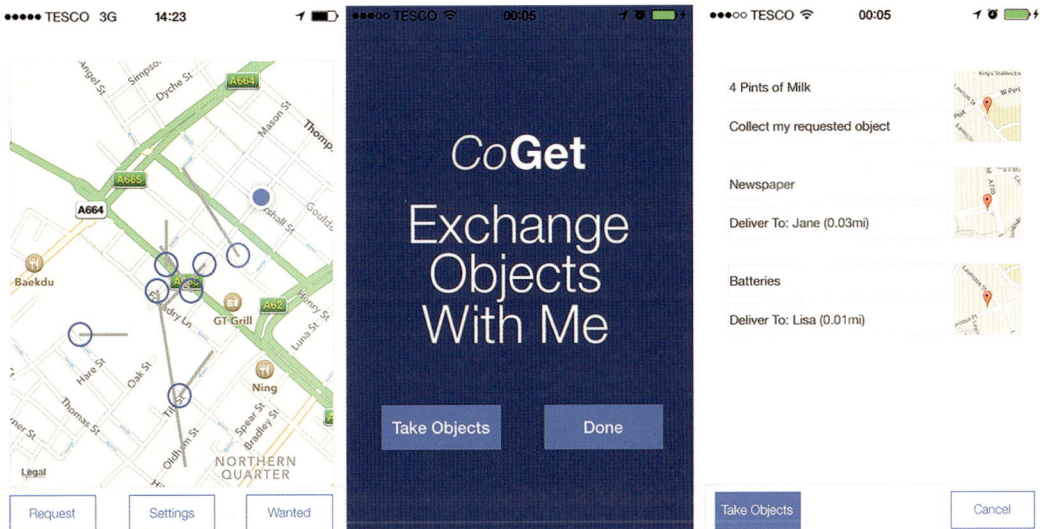

Figure 5.5 The CoGet interface on iOS. The image to the left describes the location, bearing and speed of participants. The image to the right describes the objects that are in need of movement.

Figure 5.6 Participants exchanging items during the workshop at Future Everything, Manchester 2014.

Although the workshops only had a few people within them compared to the mass users within a city, the workshop allowed participants to anticipate its potential as an exchange platform (Figure 5.6). Perhaps most interesting and unexpected to the authors was how the phenomenon of exchanging objects with strangers appeared so tantalizing and interesting in transforming daily routines. The experiences of participants seem to suggest that a connected landscape, that was made up of data points, reconfigured the street into a space of potential rather than a space of traditional social behaviour that was passive and less networked.

REFLECTIONS

In many ways, the landscape was always a database, and its data was a complex mixture of the qualitative and quantitative, of stories and datums. In her exploration of how Raymond Williams described how space is not a flat surface that we walk across, the geographer Doreen Massey described how space is 'like a pincushion of a million stories: if you stop at any point in that walk there will be a house with a story' (Massey 2013). Maps, as we know them, shift from being printed representations of databases that are snapshots in time, and instead become dynamic representations in which the 'image' of the map is personalized; the landscape will increasingly become a contingent concept that is relative to the data profile of the viewer. Consisting of a mixture of open and closed data sets that are accessed and updated from a huge variety of sources, the landscape continues its movement away from being something that is consensual that can be represented on traditional paper-based maps on which we can all point to the same landmarks. Instead, we can assume that everybody sees the map differently, and depending upon what streams of data we are plugged into, the landscape will be described in different ways.

This condition presents both positive and negative opportunities for how we conceive, represent, and experience the landscape. From a positive perspective, the recombination of data from different databases allows for new experiences to be constructed to challenge habits and actions within the landscape. Both CoGet and Treasure Trapper demonstrate how new social practices can emerge from an interoperability between different data sets. *Flows* take otherwise disparate data sets and uses them in an integrated installation to manifest a unique insight into CO_2 emissions on a single road in the UK.

In contrast, the condition also presents issues about inclusion, exclusion, and privacy. The user-experiences that are designed to engage us in the use of smart phone apps have become increasingly more creative. The use of incentives within the gamification models that attract users is complex. If successful, in the case of Foursquare and Waze, vast amounts of data can be captured and used to inform other services. However, if the data is only gathered from people who value the incentives, then any representation of that landscape is limited. These limitations construct landscapes for types of people and cannot reflect or provide insight into the broader concerns of the landscape. For example, if users of Foursquare are limited to the 'young and tech savvy' (Emerging-Advertising-Media 2010) then the maps that it constructs only provide a limited interpretation of the city. Likewise, if Waze is predominantly used by private car drivers, their data cannot describe the experience of traveling in the city from the perspective of a cyclist or bus user. As data continues to become a currency, data sets that can boast large amounts of users will sell their data to third parties and be used to describe the conditions and characteristics of the landscape. Consequently, the complex range of sources that inform the representation of landscapes on handheld or desk-based platforms is only subject to the contractual relationships within the business model of that provider.

Equally as problematic as the questions of an inclusion of particular groups within data sets, the data sets cannot tell us about who is being excluded from the representation of landscapes. If data is beginning to inform government and policy (Kitchin 2014), then people require access to devices to produce data that represents their stake in the city or rural landscape. So long as data is only taken from selected data sets it could be said that individuals have no representation in the landscape; if you're not in the database you don't have a voice.

Finally, data gatherers don't always provide a clear model for the opting in and opting out of providing data. The incentives that we are attracted to within the gamification methods behind smart phone apps can be wildly disconnected from the uses of our data that are exchanged. Agreeing to the pages of terms and conditions that flash up on screen, or worse are buried within the 'about' pages of a platform, can hardly be considered as offering informed consent to the user. By clicking on 'agree' or linking an app with our social networking profiles enables the flow of personal data between databases and it becomes quickly possible for any relevant or irrelevant data to be extracted, mined, and the wildest assumptions to be made that in turn produce any 'mixture of extraordinary insights and monstrous lies' (after Harvey 1996).

Located between ethical dilemmas surrounding the production of data and a will toward new opportunities for social interaction, the authors remain wedded to the critical design of data that challenges the prevailing models of landscape in which authorship is in the hands of those with power and data is selective. Acknowledging the landscape as a database is a preliminary step toward the design of new configurations of practice and representations.

ACKNOWLEDGMENTS

Treasure Trapper was funded through a Smart Tourism award funded by The Scottish Informatics and Computer Science Alliance (SICSA). Additional credits go to the wider Treasure Trapper team: J. Macdonald, R. Baxter, N. Tyack, H. Adams, B. Johnston, E. Gouni, and J. Oberlander.

Flows and CoGet were funded through the Sixth Sense Transport project and supported by an Energy/Digital Economy UK Research Councils grant. Additional credits go to the wider 6ST team: T. Cherrett, J. Dickinson, N. Davies, S. Norgate, S. Box, V. Filimonau, K. Ghali, M. Harding, T. Kubitza, M. Lau, F.N. Mcleod, and L. Smith.

REFERENCES

Castells, Manuel. 1996. *The Rise of the Network Society*. Oxford: Blackwell Publishing.

Emerging-Advertising-Media. 2010. 'Foursquare.' Accessed April 20, 2015. http://emerging-advertising-media.wikispaces.com/Foursquare.

Harvey, David. 1996. *Justice, Nature and the Geography of Difference*. Oxford: Blackwell.

Katz, Jack. 2000. *How Emotions Work*. Chicago, IL: University of Chicago Press.

Kitchin, Rob. 2014. *The Data Revolution: Big Data, Open Data, Data Infrastructures and their Consequences*. London: Sage.

Massey, Doreen. 2013. 'Doreen Massey On Space.' *Social Science Space*, February 1. Accessed April 20, 2015. www.socialsciencespace.com/2013/02/podcastdoreen-massey-on-space/.

Speed, Chris and Shingleton, Duncan. 2012. *An Internet of Cars: Connecting the Flow of Things to People, Artefacts, Environments and Businesses*. Mobisys 2012: International Workshop Sense Transport '12. Proceedings of the 6th ACM workshop on Next Generation Mobile Computing for Dynamic Personalised Travel Planning. New York: ACM.

Thrift, Nigel. 2004. 'Driving in the City.' *Theory, Culture & Society,* 21(4–5): 41–59. London: SAGE.

Discovering landform processes through creative 3D mapping and diagramming of form, pattern, and arrangement

Nadia Amoroso and Nadia D'Agnone

This chapter illustrates aspects of the ground and the understanding of its visual forms, patterns, and processes as perceived and interpreted from the ground within the contemporary city. The ground is constantly changing even if we cannot directly see it; creative mapping visualization and processes are applied in an attempt to manifest geographic data to reveal the hidden elements of the ground through its visual form. This chapter will also examine the question, 'do the forms, patterns and processes of the ground have a visible presence within the contemporary city?'

Discovering landform processes

Over the past ten years, the power of mapping has transformed the way landscape architects 'see' and 'assess' landscapes. Leveraging new technologies, the power of geo-data and high-quality representations, sophisticated mapping processes and outcomes, go well beyond the analytical stage and are part of the 'formal' expression of design.

In the 1960s, Ian McHarg turned his scientific approach to examining sites and geo-data by overlaying a series of site conditions from hydrology to soil types to vegetation. By superimposing all the layers of data, one began to see the connection, constraints, and opportunities for design and the overall relationship between various site conditions and elements to make more informed design decisions. This became known as the *McHargian overlay mapping*. He pioneered the overlay mapping systems that paved the way for Geographic Information Systems (GIS) today used in landscape architecture and planning.

In the 1990s, James Corner transformed the notion of mapping as part of an empowering and creative process in design – it is poetic, artistic, and beautiful. In 1996, he released his seminal book, *Taking Measures Across the American Landscape*, which showcases stunning aerial photos (captured by Alex S. MacLean) of residual and relic landscapes to farmland fields, industrial sites, desert lands, and more, and showcased the natural beauty of each landscape. The aerial photos are accompanied by Corner's interpretations of these views as 'creative map-drawings,' that, in essence, reveal the visible and often invisible elements that compose the site. These graphic interpretations transform mapping beyond the scientific realm but are seen as works of art and yet still informative pieces that represent both a 'quantitative measure' and 'qualitative' character of the site. Corner also speaks about the importance of the aerial view in 'Aerial Representation and the Making of Landscape,' stating that

> *the power of the aerial image lies less in its descriptive capacity, compelling as that is, than in its conditioning of how one sees and acts within the built environment. Like other instruments and methods of representation, the aerial view reflects and constructs the world; it has enormous landscape agency, in real and imaginary ways.*
>
> *(Corner 1996, 16)*

The aerial view fundamentally changed not only the way we think about the ground and the landscape – but how we act upon it and interpret it.

In Corner's seminal article 'The Agency of Mapping: Speculation, Critique and Invention' in Denis Cosgrove's *Mappings* book (1999b), Corner emphasizes the mapping process as creative and empowering. He states:

> As a creative practice, mapping precipitates its most productive effects through a finding that is also a founding; its agency lies in neither reproduction nor imposition but rather in uncovering realities previously unseen or unimagined, even across seemingly exhausted grounds. Thus, mapping unfolds potential; it re-makes territory over and over again, each time with new and diverse consequences.
>
> (Corner 1999b, 213)

James Corner claims that mappings have dual characteristics – 'analogous and abstractness.'

'Their surfaces are directly analogous to actual ground conditions; as horizontal planes, they record the surface of the earth as direct impressions' (Corner 1999b, 214). This involves a literal projection of the site via geometrical measures and plotted points and lines drawn on a paper plane. This is more of a true and objective reading. Mappings also inherit a level of abstractness. This means that the visual result is based on 'selection, omission, isolation, distance and codification' (Corner 1999b, 215). There is a level of interpretation of the site and its condition. The mapping process operates with rules and procedures. The mapmaker sets these rules, and graphic notations are critical to the mapping process and visual outcome.

Is there a deeper understanding of the site based on the visual dissection of the ground through mapping? The creative process of mapping allows one to uncover new findings hidden deep within or on the surface of the ground. To manifest a revealing of the ground, one can draw upon Corner's modern take on cartography including fields, extracts, and quantities. (Corner 1999b, 229). This would include the landing of geographic coordinates, positioning of the site, quantifiable data, and the graphic projection and visual forms of relationship between ground and data. Figure 6.1 is a visual expression of the level of toxicity mapped around the Great Lakes Region. The field selected was a simple base map of the Great Lakes Region set as its field, and the plotting (coordinates) of towns and major cities in the area including Chicago. This includes the indexing of data readings (toxicity levels) at its geographic positioning. The toxicity levels, including benzene, are extracted from the center point of each city or town. The higher the levels of toxicity, the larger the inflation of the bubble space becomes in terms of the visual representation. Composed using a combination of software from AutoCAD and

Discovering landform processes

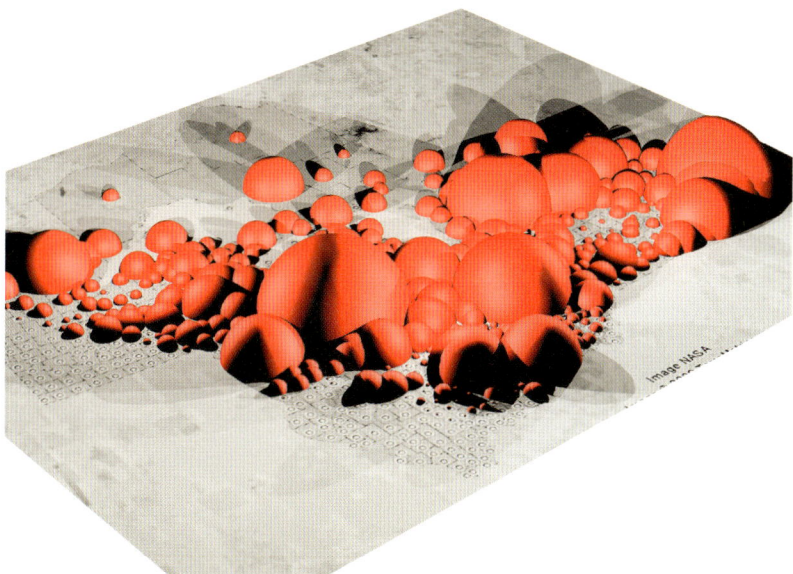

Figure 6.1 Ground toxicity level of the Great Lakes Region visually expressed and red invasive bubbles emerging from the ground. The higher the level of toxicity, the larger the bubbles.

3DS MAX, digital tools have drastically changed the way we analyze and visualize site and the understanding of its ground. The visualization allows us to make sense of the hidden or invisible site conditions or elements within the grounds or its surface and, in turn, foster a better understanding of site through this newly exposed visual information, and allow us to make wiser interventions.

With sophisticated software and digital tools, we can digitally dissect the ground and formulate an understanding of its visual forms, patterns, and processes, as perceived and interpreted from within the contemporary city. Using various software programs that include ESRI ArcGIS, ArcMap, CityEngine, AutoCAD, 3DS MAX, and Rhino we can begin to test, assess and discover new 'ground' information through advanced mapping. The ground and its landforms as we see them presently are a mere instant of a much larger geomorphological material process that has evolved over the 4.6-billion-year history of Earth. As a direct part of the geologic morphology of Earth's strata, the contemporary urban ground is a complex palimpsest of its deep past, and present forms, patterns, and processes that are in constant change and interacting with one another in various scales of time.

The principles of landscape ecology explain to us that the spatial forms, patterns, and arrangements found on a site in the present are a direct result of processes of the past. Landscapes are therefore considered to be the result of the processes acting upon them. As explained by D'Arcy Wentworth Thompson in *On Growth and Form* (1917), 'form is the diagram of force' (quoted in Forman 1995, 5). This means that the formal composition of elements found on a site can tell us about the forces and conditions that have shaped them. This is important because it can help us gain a better understanding of the natural environmental conditions of a site prior to intervention, even those conditions hidden deep within geological time. From this perspective, the ground can be therefore understood as an autonomous, heterogeneous, and formative material process consisting of overlapped, intertwined, and interacting layers functioning together on various scales of time and space, and which possess an implicit structural logic that can be visually read through form.

The vertical dimension of mosaics is what Richard T.T. Forman calls *the third dimension* (Forman 1995, 302). By introducing height, the third dimension begins to allude to the topographic complexity of landforms. In a way to delineate a series of predicted ecological processes and patterns associated with the development of landform types, Forman explains how landforms can be measured and quantified. Topographic variation is formed by two main processes, erosion and deposition caused by water, wind, and ice. Each of these processes produces very different landforms but is predictable in its formation of size and shape (Forman 1995, 307). Water-formed landforms are caused by the fluvial deposits from streams and rivers that are eroded upstream until they are carried and deposited downriver. Aeolian landforms are those caused by the erosion and sedimentation of rocks and sediments carried by the wind. Lastly, glacial landforms are those caused by the freezing of ice.

Since the invention of the aerial view, a modern airborne subjectivity (Waldheim 1999, 124) has emerged in design and planning that has produced a new way of seeing from above which has fundamentally transformed how we think, interpret, and subsequently act on the ground. The aerial view, and later the overlay method so omnipresent and ubiquitous in design and planning today, disembody us from the ground and radically flatten its spatial, formal, and temporal complexity. While the diagrams, maps and images this tool produces reveal and visualize important regional, territorial, and environmental processes otherwise hidden from the ground level view, they do so in an incorporeal and abstract way as displaced from it. The aerial view brought us the modern airborne subject and the disembodied, scaleless, spaceless, timeless, and placeless ground.

Discovering landform processes

This chapter also questions the role of the ground level view in the obtaining of knowledge and information of the material processes that have formed and continue to shape the contemporary urban ground today. It asks the question, *can the forms, patterns and processes of the ground be interpreted and studied from the ground level view? What can be seen and how can this help us in the contemporary practice of landscape architecture?* Raising questions about appearance and reality, and imagination and knowledge, the hypothesis is that the forms, patterns, and processes of the geologic ground have a visual presence within the contemporary city but that they are anamorphic. The strata on the surface are incomplete, fragmented, overlapped, and intertwined with one another and can therefore only be seen if looked at in the right way – through space, time, and the intertwined connections in-between. Through the aid of creative cartographic techniques, mapping and diagramming, with a specific focus on 3D modeling and rendering, this chapter will explain how we can discover more about imbricated landform processes simply by analyzing its form.

The methodological tool is that of the anamorphic view that traces over the otherwise unseen, invisible, or unperceivable formal visual elements of the ground's forms, patterns, and processes. The anamorphic view aims to incorporate the information as presented to us in the aerial view and confront it anamorphically with the ground-borne view. The anamorphic view is, therefore, a critical investigation and 're-evaluation of the picture-making process itself, together with contemporary understandings of vision and their relationship to perception in the making of visual representations' (Waldheim 1999, 128). With the cartographic tools of creative mapping, diagramming, and modeling, the visual elements of form, position, scale, composition, value, color, texture, depth, change, pattern, and movement are marked out in the aerial view, projected on top of a digital topographic model, and then presented in perspective as seen from the ground level view. These projections are then confronted in perspective with a series of panoramic views taken on strategically chosen existing sites to determine which, if any, of the elements are actually directly visible in the contemporary urban ground from the perspective of actual space. The above stated operations are enabled by the eidetic (Corner 1999a, 153) visualization techniques that rely on various contemporary digital mapping and modeling technologies. A software palette of programs including Google Earth, ESRI ArcGIS, ArcGIS Pro and CityEngine, Rhinoceros, RhinoTerrain plugin for Rhino, Autodesk 3DS Max, and AutoCAD are used along with other physical modeling technologies such as laser cutting, CNC milling, and 3D printing. These technologies have revolutionized the understanding of the ground and have permitted sophisticated and precise visualizations of terrain that would be otherwise incomprehensible and are explained step by step here.

The case study is Catania, Sicily. Catania is the largest commune and capital city of the Province of Catania, located on the east coast of the Mediterranean island of Sicily, Italy. The city of Catania is situated at the foot of Mount Etna in the Plain of Catania facing the Gulf of Catania and the Ionian Sea. Located near the boundary of the Eurasian and African tectonic plates, a zone of subduction, and the largest active volcano in Europe, the Etnean region where Catania lies is one of the most seismically active areas in all of Italy. It is changing both rapidly and slowly, and thus is an interesting case study for this research.

On a regional level, the Plain of Catania has had an important geological history and relationship to the terrestrial ground, being subject to both the alluvial deposits of the Dittaino, Gornalunga, and Simeto rivers and their tributaries and the volcanic eruptions of Mount Etna. Mount Etna is a stratovolcano, being composed of various composite layers of its hardened lava that form the layers of the contemporary urban ground of Catania today. The contemporary constructed ground of Catania is thus a palimpsest of prehistorical, historical, and contemporary archaeology, with many strata hidden within the sedimentation and residual traces of the ground. What is visible today is but one layer of a much larger succession of strata superimposed on top of one another from various periods of time.

Testing is initiated with the practical task of modeling out the existing topographic relief of the entire region of the case study, the Province of Catania. New developments in three-dimensional visualization technologies have helped reveal and render visible and invisible forces hidden within a territory. Modeling here refers to both physical and digital three-dimensional modeling of the natural landforms and topographic relief of the province of the case study region. This step is fundamental to the study of the ground in both urban and rural areas and is the primary tool for studying its geology, geomorphology, and urbanization patterns. Like a territorial skin or membrane, the surface produced by a terrain model gives primary information data linking regions and territories into a measurable, observational, and morphological datum for further study.

A digital elevation model, DEM is a three-dimensional representation of a part of Earth's surface. There are two types, a digital surface model (DSM) that represents the surface and the objects on top of it, and a digital terrain model (DTM), showing only the ground surface. However, even when not including information such as streets, buildings, or infrastructure, the topographic relief of the surface produced does include the topographic base where all these elements

Discovering landform processes

are placed. The surface, therefore, implies these structures, even if they are not directly presented in the model. The model therefore can be understood as an imbrication of various geologic, morphologic, infrastructural, and urban processes.

The modeling process is started with a digital elevation model (DEM), usually presented as an *asc* text file. These datasets resemble scripts or codes that withhold spatial information in numbers and letters translating to space on a three-dimensional grid. This spatial information can also be held within an image, for example a *GeoTIFF* (which is essentially an image file with embedded geo-referencing data) or *jpg,* etc. which are considered 'raster' DEMs and are made from a series of 'pixels' which withhold data within a given area. This is also known as a height map and is also made of a raster grid of square pixels. The precision of the resulting model is associated with the 'resolution' or the amount of pixels in the image. The data required to obtain this model are acquired through photogrammetry, LiDAR scanning, and land surveying. DEM data is normally obtained through remote sensing techniques using LiDAR satellite images.

The digital elevation model for the specific case study site was obtained by the INGV, *Istituto Nazionale di Geofisica e Vulcanologia.* The INGV was established in 1999 as a research, monitoring, and surveillance unit aimed at uniting the scientific and technical institutions in Italy, Europe and internationally operating in Geophysics and Volcanology (INGV 2015). A high-resolution digital elevation model of the whole Italian territory on a 10 m cell grid, named TINITALY/01, was presented in 2007 (Tarquini et al. 2007, 407–425). Italy is administratively partitioned into 20 regions and each regional territory into several sub-territorial authorities. This means that the data needed to construct a high-resolution digital elevation model came from many different sources in various formats. The TINITALY/01 project created a DEM of the Italian territory combining disparate data obtained from heterogeneous database sources including contour lines and spot elevations deriving from Italian regional topographic maps, satellite-based global positioning system points, and ground-based and radar altimetry data into a seamless Delaunay-based *Triangular Irregular Network* (TIN) (Tarquini et al. 2007, 407–425).

The digital elevation model data is processed with GIS software in ArcGIS and then converted into a series of points on a Cartesian grid in the x, y, and z axis to what is called a *point cloud*. A digital point cloud model is essentially a series of spot elevations that indicate a prescribed x, y, and z coordinate for each point. The data is obtained using the DEM should it be available, or can be produced through remote sensing methods with digital scanners attached to airplanes, helicopters, or other types of manual drones or low-flying devices should this information not be available. The data can withhold any information including those relating to the terrain surface itself, but also the objects found above and within the surface as well. The point cloud model is then translated into a triangulated surface mesh for further modeling and rendering purposes.

The mesh surface is cut at regular intervals and is prepared as a layered laser cutter file for physical modeling and output. The contours can be cut in either negative or positive, producing either a final output or a negative mold. A negative mold is useful should multiple copies of the model need processing, but also because it gives you a solid block of your surface topography. Should the technology be available, this can be easily done also using the CNC-milling or 3D printing process. Figure 6.2 showcases the image processing of ground and its elevation.

The anamorphic view consists of a tracing of elements as seen from the orthographic aerial view and then projects them onto the three-dimensional topographic surface to then present them in perspective from the ground level view. To do this, both the digital and physical topographic relief model produced are further analyzed and studied visually. The various types of landforms found are established, marked out, and projected three-dimensionally on top of the digital and physical model. The landform typologies that are established create an inventory of sites used for further detailed study and analysis (Figure 6.3). From this, an inventory of the 'landform patch' typologies found within the region determines the location of a series of strategic sites on which to conduct further research.

The chosen sites are analyzed in further detail. The otherwise unseen visual elements of landform processes including form, position, scale, composition, value, color, texture, depth, change, pattern, and movement are marked out on each site from the aerial orthographic view and organized into a hierarchical taxonomy using a series of interpretive images, models, and exploratory drawings of the strategically selected landform typologies described above (Figure 6.4).

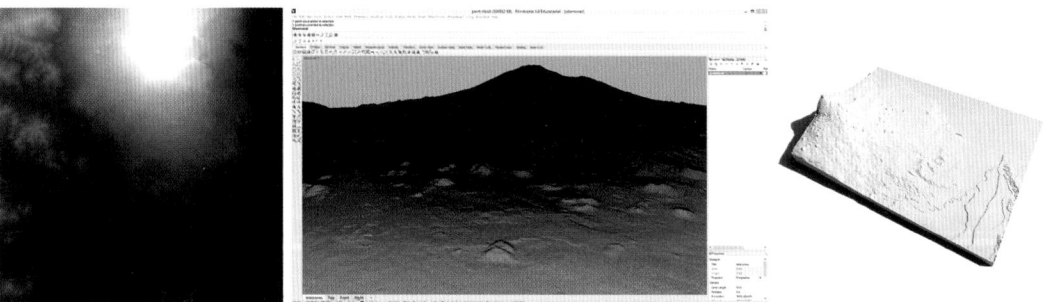

Figure 6.2 This showcases the digital elevation model and raster using CityEngine (a); point cloud model using RhinoTerrain plugin for Rhino (b); contour physical model (c).

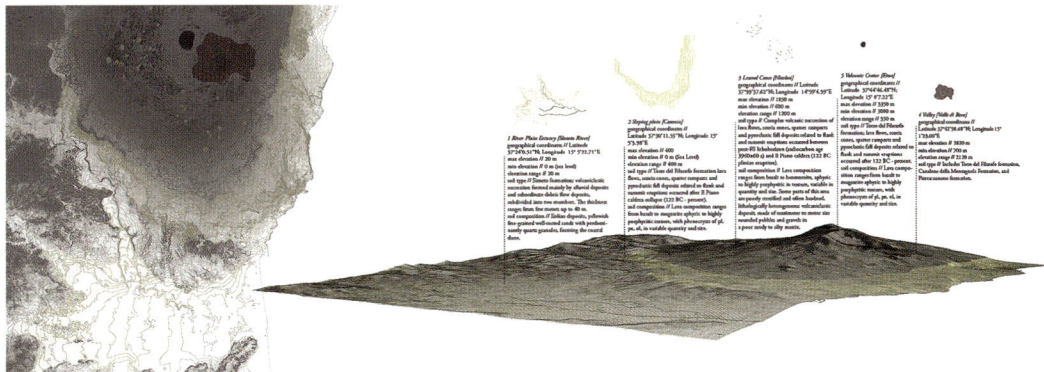

Figure 6.3 Landform typology inventory identified through interpretive surfacing.

Figure 6.4 Landform elements rendering – Simeto River Plain (a); lateral cones (b); Etna volcanic crater (c).

These images illustrate the visual presence of the spatial forms, patterns, and arrangements that are visible from the ground level view. Some elements are more obvious than others while some are less so. The formal elements that are most evidently visible and telling about landform processes are those that are associated with the greatest topographic variation, including both changes in elevation and slope gradient. Movement is also one of the elements that are most visibly understood but less frequently occurring than other elements. Other elements that are less conspicuous include surface texture and patterns that are read on a much smaller scale from the ground level view.

The way we see and perceive the world radically changes the way we understand, interpret, and intervene upon it. It is through the mapping process, and the new visual representations, that deeper understanding of the ground are formulated. Through the link between the anamorphic ground level view, the goal is to physically engage human processes within the non-human processes of the physical, biological, and geological environments they inhabit, and thereby emphasize the relevance and importance of the physical world to the sociological, political, economic, and cultural world that occupy it.

REFERENCES

Corner, James. 1996. 'Aerial Representation and the Making of Landscape.' In *Taking Measures across the American Landscape,* James Corner and Alex MacLean. New Haven: Yale University Press.

Corner, James. 1999a. 'Eidetic Operations and New Landscapes.' In *Recovering Landscape: Essays in Contemporary Landscape Architecture*, ed. James Corner, 153–170. New York: Princeton Architectural Press.

Corner, James. 1999b. 'The Agency of Mapping: Speculation, Critique and Invention.' In *Mappings,* ed. Denis Cosgrove, 213–300. London: Reaction Books.

Forman, Richard T.T. 1995. *Land Mosaics: The Ecology of Regions.* Cambridge: Cambridge University Press.

INGV – Istituto Nazionale di Geofisica e Vulcanologia. 2015. 'The Institute.' Accessed July 1, 2015. www.ingv.it/.

Tarquini, Simone, Ilaria Isola, Massimiliano Favalli, Francesco Mazzarini, Marina Bisson, Maria Teresa Pareschi and Enzo Boschi. 2007. 'TINITALY/01: A New Triangular Irregular Network of Italy.' *Annals of Geophysics* 50: 407–425.

Waldheim, Charles. 1999. 'Aerial Representation and the Recovery of Landscape.' In *Landscape: Essays in Contemporary Landscape Architecture*, ed. James Corner, 120–139. New York: Princeton Architectural Press.

7

Data-driven landscape

Ming Tang

This chapter presents a study investigating the emerging data-driven processing related to urban design and landscape design. Unlike conventional design procedures, the new data-driven model considers quantifiable geospatial and time-based data as input parameters. A data-driven design is defined as a hybrid method, which seeks logical landscape forms and analyzes its importance through various advanced computational methods including scripting, mathematical models, and quantitative analysis. We extended these methods by exploring, collecting, analyzing, and visualizing geospatial data and representing it through 2D, 3D, 4D, fabrication, and various simulation technologies.

Data-driven landscape

GEOSPATIAL DATA SET

For architects, urban designers, and landscape designers, a design process usually starts with data mining. It is essential to collect geospatial information and visualize it in a meaningful way to stimulate the design process. Although the data format might be different, the nature of various geospatial data at this stage is usually a statistical distribution across a physical environment. The statistical features such as mean, median, and outliers can be computed on the associated elements such as parcel, block, and county. Typically multiple possible distributions are compared by graphing quantities against each other and then studying the generated patterns. For instance, the Geograph Information System (GIS) allows the viewer to measure whether the plot values are similar and if the two distributions are related in a map format (Figure 7.1).

There are a variety of conventional methods for data representation and infographics techniques such as tables, histograms, pie charts, and bar graphs. However, designers are always interested in finding alternative ways to visualize data from a designer's mindset. But at first, we must understand that two primary components of a geospatial dataset are geometric representations, and the associated information stored in the database.

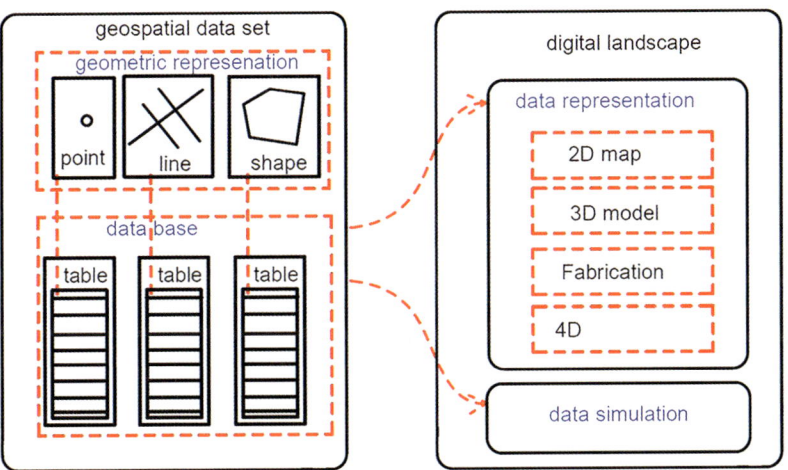

Figure 7.1 Left: data set contains geometric representation (point, line, shape) as well as the database. Right: various data representation and simulation methods.

Geometric representation

Point, line, shape are the basic geometries representing geospatial features such as the landmark, river, parcels, blocks, county, and land use in GIS. There are many methods that can be used to visualize landscape data within a geometric representation. For instance, point, lines, and shapes can be used to generate a diagrammatic map. These thematic maps contain GIS data such as zoning, population, transportation, and other spatial information. Emerging parametric modeling tools can read the geometries extracted from the GIS data set and execute a corresponding modeling operation to analyze and manipulate the geometries. The resultant model inherits all the geometric information from the initial GIS data set.

Database

Besides GIS, there are other emerging methods that involve using scripts to connect to the database directly. The imported values from a database can dictate geometric operations automatically and thus replace the most labor-intensive modeling. Designers can stream values from the Excel or dbf format database, and generate new values by combining some existing values.

There are many creative and design related methods to integrate space–time data with the emerging parametric modeling tools in the design industry today. Many of these new data collections, representations, and analysis methods are established by directly feeding the statistical data into the emerging digital modeling process to produce 2D, 3D, 4D, and simulations.

DIGITAL LANDSCAPE

Inspired by the data-driven modeling techniques, many computational methods have been developed since the 1980s. Digital modeling is increasingly implemented in computing to create digital landscapes with a high degree of complexity, such as the agent-based urban modeling by Michael Batty, parametric urbanism by Patrick Schumacher, and City Engine by Pascal Mueller. These methods utilize a set of computational principles to generate diagrammatic landscape models driven by a variety of data sets. One of the objectives of

Data-driven landscape

connecting abstract data to a geometric form is to create an engaging experience that allows designers to investigate the data through a dynamically changing interface. The new process permits designers to create a large number of representation options and explore unique design concepts. It is advantageous for the designers to be aware of the following essential categories of a data-driven process. We defined digital landscape into two major categories, data representation and data simulation, based on its objective and computational techniques.

Data representation as a 2D map

Geospatial data can be organized into point-based, polygon-based, or line-based hierarchies. For instance, states, counties, tracts, blocks, and parcels are typically represented as polygons. Streams and transportation networks are typically represented as lines. Simple lines with added values can be interpreted as different spatial features such as transportation networks or social connections, depending on their representations in the context. In GIS, a standard map uses point, lines, shapes, colors, symbols, and space-filling variants to represent the geospatial data. Instead of simply representing the physical environment, the abstract analytical data can be projected and superimposed on the map. For instance, a color map can be constructed based on the circulation analysis and spatial integration values with space syntax method. The new data can then be added on top of the existing street network to represent its spatial linkages. Spatial integration values associated with the streets can be perceived visually with color (Figure 7.2).

Ming Tang

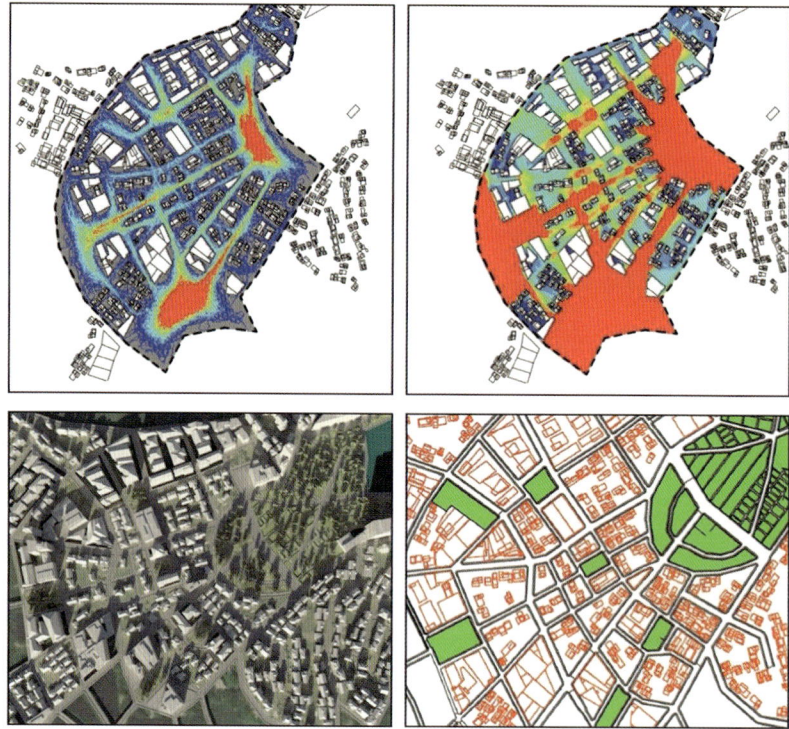

Figure 7.2 The color value is projected onto a 2D map to represent the spatial integration value. Silicon Valley of China. Tools: Space Syntax, ESRI City Engine. Autodesk Maya.
Source: Ming Tang (2014).

Data representation as a 3D model

One of the goals of constructing a 3D landscape is to represent the statistical information, such as demographic data from the Census Bureau. This process can explore the relationships among landscape elements and other social and economic parameters. For instance, the spatial integration values can be defined as the rule to control the height of a 3D surface. Although the generated model does not reflect any real typology in this area due to its singular parameter, it does allow the viewer to observe complex 3D urban patterns that communicate the information clearly. This process is similar to how contour lines and digital elevation images are used to represent 3D topography. These types of translations deliver meanings by manipulating data in various formats and structures, which allow points, lines, surfaces, and masses to be interpreted as diagrammatic objects (Figure 7.3).

Data-driven landscape

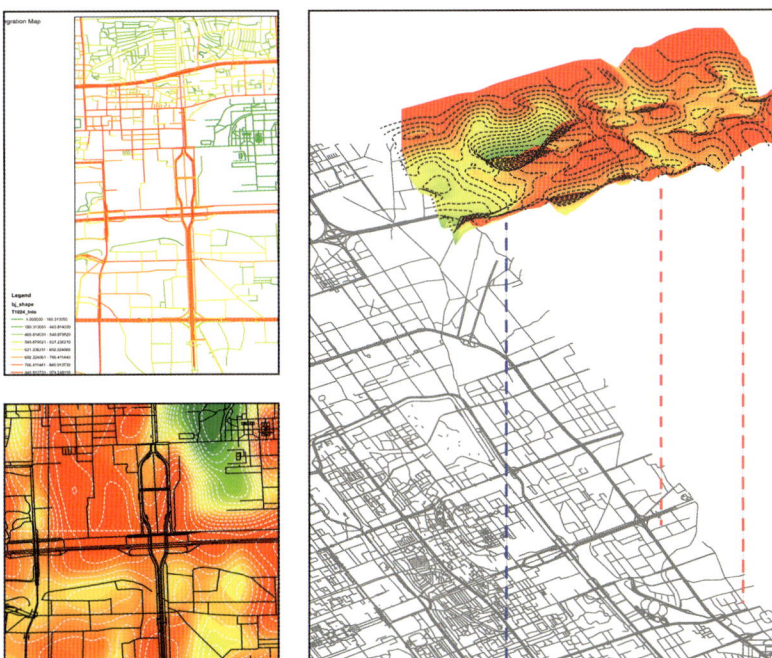

Figure 7.3 In order to integrate space syntax into parametric modeling tools, the spatial integration value is visualized by the height of the digital landscape in the DSL district of Beijing, China. Tools: Space Syntax, Rhino, Grasshopper, ESRI ArcMap.

Source: Ming Tang.

PROJECT: 3D DIAGRAMIC URBAN MODEL, YIZHUANG, BEIJING

Three-dimensional data representation is also a powerful tool as an adaptable method of large-scale site design that can work to produce a responsive working system of distributed site programs and activities. The Yizhuang industrial district in Beijing was used as a target area to test the capabilities of this data-driven system. Developed in the digital 3D modeling programs Rhinoceros and Grasshopper, the data-driven system applies measurable parameters such as population density, residential population, and means of travel to a set of building footprints. The goal is establishing the corresponding programmatic volumes.

A group of variables and parameters formed the responsive 3D model. A set of values worked together to integrate flexibility into the design process. Driving this flexibility were adjustable Grasshopper parameters that related calculated values back to the 3D program and adjusted building heights based on the proportion of programmatic volume required. The most important parameter of this process was the population density as it was the first parameter of the script that could be adjusted. Subsequent parameters were based on population percentage and the space needed per person for specific design focuses. Based on these two variables in the script, Grasshopper was able to calculate the total residential program square footage needed. Furthermore, this square footage was related back to the 3D model in that the required square footage was divided over the total building footprints allocated towards residential programming, producing corresponding building heights.

Ultimately, this allowed the design team to update and model the entire urban model based on changing assumptions and calculations. After the 3D building mass were made in Rhino, they could be adjusted and moved around. If a building was unrealistically tall, the building floor print could be multiplied, lowering the height because the necessary space could be distributed among more buildings. The buildings were then moved to appropriately zoned blocks and monitored by the Floor Area Ratio (FAR) of the blocks.

Throughout the 15 work weeks, the parameters were adjusted constantly, and more parameters were added based on the interaction with local planners. Using this type of parametric design process made updating the urban model very efficient. Figure 7.4 depicts the possible layout of various buildings and green space.

The process was robust and easily adjusted when changes of the urban model were desired. The design team focused on the 3D modeling and scripting process, the relationship between various building types and their occupancy, parking, as well as the agricultural options. The types of agricultural options described included a brief mention of traditional field crops in the periphery of the site. The research on agriculture focused more so on vertical farming and green roofs. The vertical farms are represented as 3D building blocks. The final urban model became an interactive system controlled by the complex relationship between population, land use, FAR, agriculture infrastructure and other parameters.

Data-driven landscape

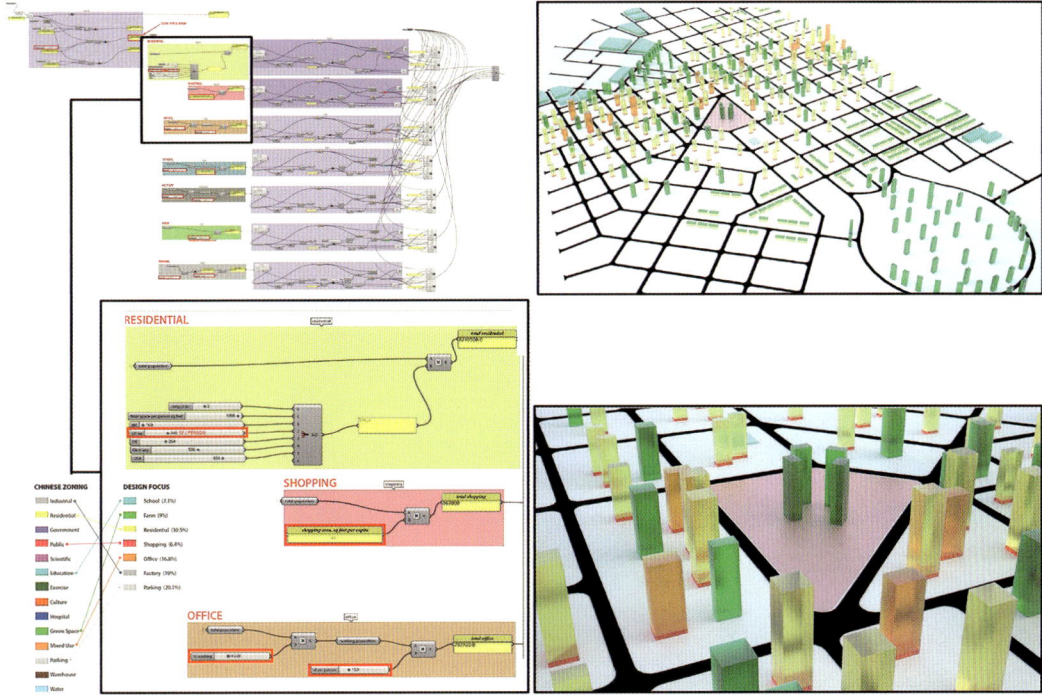

Figure 7.4 Parametric urban model of Yizhuang District, Beijing, China. Students: Ellen Crawford, Kelsey Reichenbach, Connor Borchardt, David Schaengold, Yinan Wu, Kyle Zook, Lydia Yen. University of Cincinnati.

Data representation with digital fabrication

With the newly generated data, the creation of physical models through 3D printing, CNC milling, and laser cutting is a powerful representation method. Designers can stream geospatial data into a 3D modeling program, which allows them to manipulate and control the representational geometry and generate the appropriate file for digital fabrication. As a result, designers can translate the abstract information into cutting patterns, tool paths, and 3D forms for digital fabrication. These artifacts were informed by the non-geometric data and not designed arbitrarily by the fabricators. During this process, designers had to take into account material property and machine processes. Fabricating, assembling, and interacting with a 3D physical model are the unique experiences that designers will never be able to achieve by viewing an abstract data set or thematic map. The physical model became a representation of the dynamic

Ming Tang

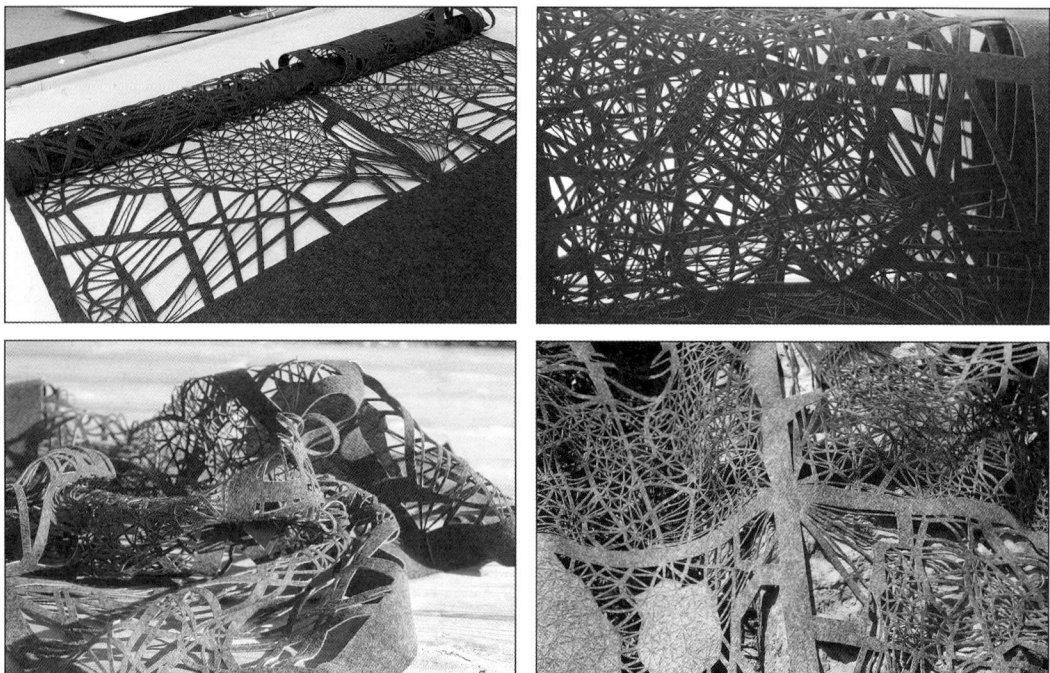

Figure 7.5 A tessellated city pattern is laser cut on felt and deformed based on various operations. By Enrique Sanchez. University of Cincinnati.

Source: photograph by Ming Tang.

relationship between various data sets. 'The marriage between abstract data and fabrication technologies stimulates a different mindset and design thinking process. The dimensional and physical model becomes an object that represents the combination of various geospatial data sets' (Tang and Anderson 2011). The physical model also displays the hidden spatial pattern and sparks unique design solutions (Figure 7.5).

Data representation with animation and scenario (4D)

The computational method is extended by exploring and visualizing time-based data and scenario-based data, and interactively representing data through digital technologies. A sequence of static models allows complex conditions to be described in an animated sequence so that it might be more easily understood and managed. For instance, by constructing an animated digital landscape, the

Data-driven landscape

designers would be able to read certain correlation patterns over a period of time. Time-series data is frequently used in data processing. Index charts and stacked graphs are the conventional ways to illustrate the relative changes over time. However, it is hard to interpret trends graphically over a complex spatial pattern.

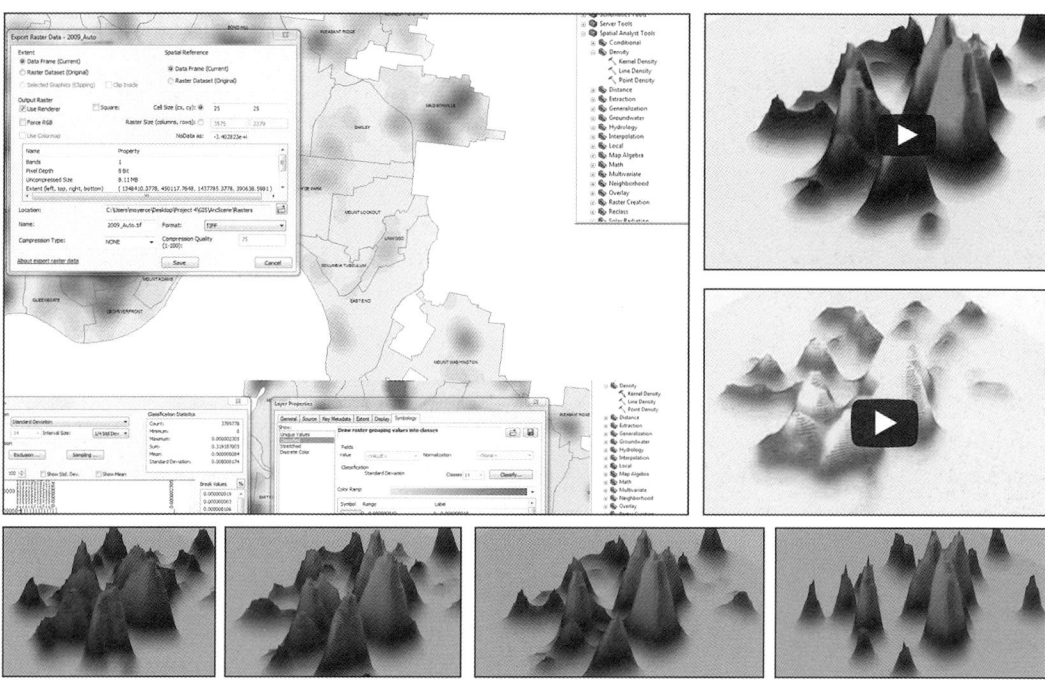

Figure 7.6 Animation based on urban crime data 2007–2009, City of Cincinnati. By Craig Moyer. Tools: ESRI ArcMap, Rhino, Grasshopper. We first collected point-based crime data for the city of Cincinnati. Data from 2007, 2008, and 2009 at Hamilton County was downloaded as Excel files. Then the data was compiled and prepared to be geocoded in Excel. Geocoding is the process of assigning each instance of reported crime to a point in space. This was done through a custom address locator, based on the GIS street grid layer, which matches the street, house number, city, and zip code in the original crime table with a physical, real address existing in Hamilton County. After only the points occurring within the city had been plotted, their respective crimes and densities of occurrence were analyzed. We chose to perform an essential kernel density analysis. This process examined and charted statistically significant clustering patterns of point-based data. To ensure an accurate and unbiased analysis of the clustering patterns, the ¼ standard deviations settings were used, which resulted in 14 classes of clustering. The resulting raster images were exported and brought into Rhino and Grasshopper to construct a 3D morphing surface to represent changes in crime over time and space. This 3D surface was animated and effectively displayed spatial changes in crime over the years. The final result was rendered as several videos.

Source: Craig Moyer, University of Cincinnati.

An alternative way is to use morphing 3D forms, and the overall trends are more easily interpreted. 3D animation can become very powerful when it is used to illustrate geospatial data within a defined coordinate system. The animated objects can be constructed based on geographical geometries such as parcels, blocks, counties, or states. Animation becomes a natural way to represent the changing data. Designers can depict time and space through the use of lines, shapes, colors, and other visual elements. For instance, the animated geometry encodes crime-related data through its changing location, size, color. or shape (Figure 7.6). Using a variety of data, either from a map sequence or multi-column Excel database, the resulting animation allows for a larger number of changing values to be represented.

4D data representation can also be understood as changing scenarios over time. Similar to the 4D representation in building construction sequence, a large-scale urban model can be constructed with various parameters. By changing values through the slider, an urban model can simulate the growth from a low-density scenario to a high-density scenario.

PROJECT: SCENARIO-BASED 4D MODEL, LOW CARBON CITY, SHENZHEN, CHINA

PINGDI, the low carbon city's project area, is located 30 km east of Shenzhen. It is part of the strategic Ping-Qing-Xin ECO-2-ZONE. It is surrounded by mountains on three sides and has much more land reserve than Shenzhen. Industry and services have been less developed and, therefore, offer ample opportunity for transformation into low carbon technologies/practices. While developing the vision of a low carbon city, various entities (government, research institutes, and companies) in Shenzhen have done a very thorough review of low carbon cities around the world.

Based on the already established research, the goal of this research is to construct a relationship model, a '3D model and changing scenarios.' The model allows developers to understand the complex relationships among various urban parameters such as population, density, carbon emission, car usage, development intensity, zoning, and energy consumption. The focus of Shenzhen Low Carbon City project is to formulate relational dynamic variables and parameters of which a low carbon city would be comprised. We created three scenario variables, named low-density, medium-density and high-density development. A shift in any of the scenarios will result in a change in connected parameters. The use of dynamic modeling has allowed us to compare the advantages and disadvantages of underground, surface, and vertical development, as well as different transportation and building densities and coverages. The model helps us to propose an optimal strategy for new infrastructure development and land use. We believe the objective for the low carbon city project is to create evaluation systems that can quantify various parameters of the urban built environment, and ensure a low carbon life to all residents through various scenarios including iterative proposals on urban infrastructure, land use, building programs, waste management, renewable energy, and transportation systems (Figure 7.7).

Step 1: Construct measurable low carbon indicators

Low carbon indicators from various aspects were proposed. These indicators are very helpful in establishing an eco-city performance monitoring system for the low carbon city.

- Building-based
- Transportation-based
- Infrastructure
- Greenspace
- Electric power/renewable energy
- Recycling.

Step 2: Construct assumptions

Quantifiable relationships were established based on the following assumptions of the PINGDI low carbon city starting zone.

- Population density
- Industrial space requirement
- Carbon emission per employee by industry (ton/person)
- Energy consumption rates per area by industry sector (J/sq. m)
- Commercial/office space requirement (square meters per employee)
- Residential
- Energy consumption rate per residential area (J/sq. m)

- Carbon emission rate per residential area (ton/sq. m)
- Water consumption
- Wastewater generation
- Municipal waste generation
- Stormwater runoff
- Proportion impervious area
- Automobile carbon emission rate (ton/km)
- Assumption of surface parking
- Transit carbon emission rate (ton/km)
- Percentage by travel modes
- Total distance traveled per person (km)
- Carbon sequestration rates (ton/sq. m).

Step 3: Construct site database

A digital 3D model of PINGDI site is constructed using advanced parametric modeling tools in Rhino and Grasshopper, which includes blocks and buildings. Street network, land use, FAR, building height, building program, and other parameters will be coded into a database allowing further computing. Three scenarios named as high-density development, mid-density development, and low-density development were constructed.

Step 4: Scenario-based 4D analysis

Using advanced 3D and scenario analysis software, the parametric modeling results are analyzed based on low-carbon city criteria related to various services including zoning, transportation, renewable energy with a solar panel, green infrastructure with green roof and trees. We have constructed various analysis models to discuss its impact on carbon emissions. The conclusions are made based on the analysis of different scenarios that are generated from the GIS scenario 360 programs in relation to the low carbon planning methods. The estimated population reached 15,000, 7,500, and 5,000 based on high-, mid-, and low-density development. As a consequence, the total carbon footprint is decreased from a high value to lower value.

This 4D analysis examined approaches where assumptions and indicators were set and integrated into the quantitative analysis pipeline to explore the

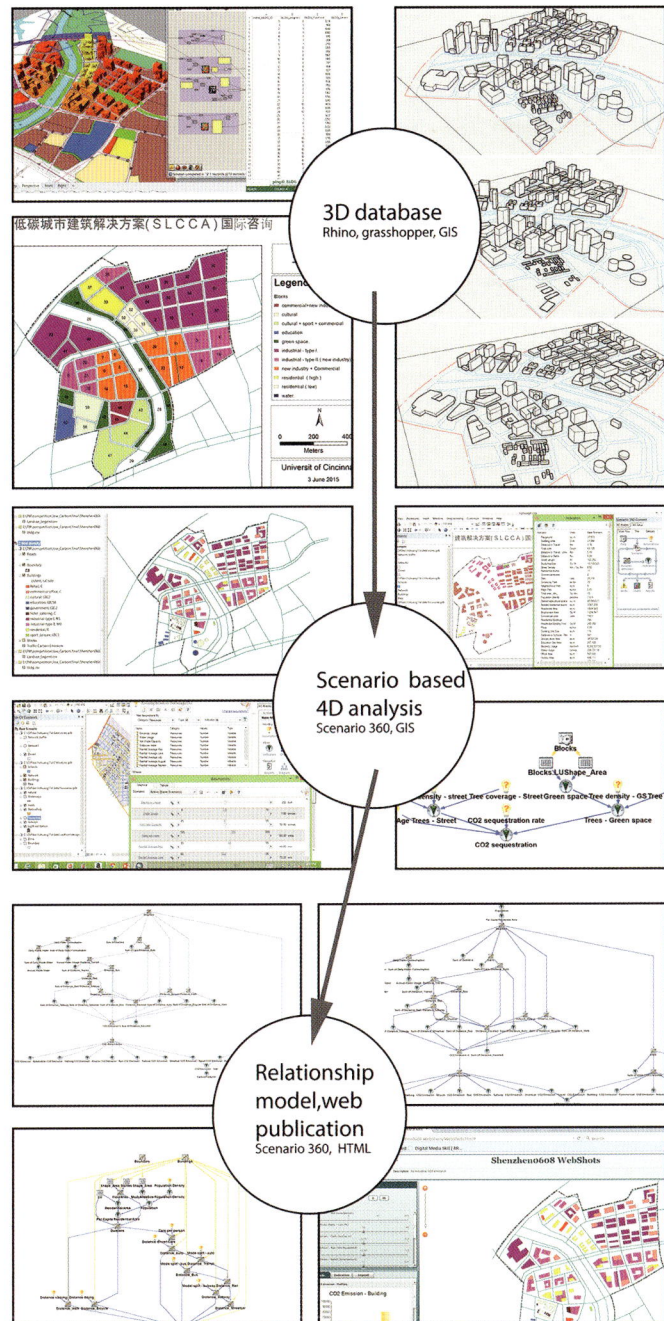

Figure 7.7 Process of scenario-based urban modeling.

Source: Ming Tang, Xinhao Wang. http://ming3d.com/pingdi/

potential to evaluate various scenarios and optimize a solution. The research is extended to the mathematical interaction within the planning parameters and their controlled geospatial outcome. The evaluation was accomplished through the exploration of several modeling techniques, either formula-driven or fixed values from reference. We believe that the results expanded the boundary of conventional GIS planning strategy through relationship modeling and simulation. Adjacent to the topic of scenario-based morphogenetic, the topic of CO_2 sequestration has also influenced designers to think of planning as a part within an eco-system where the impact of each element is multiplied across an urban field. Here, the formal order of individual components, such as FAR, population density, zoning, etc., is decentralized from the predetermined rules and exclusively ordered through its relation with all other elements of the system. So instead of thinking about the planning code as the center, scenario-based analysis has taught architects, planners, and developers to specify the process of planning before defining the multiplicity of elements and local sources that determine the formal elements, building topology such as mass, type, size, or materials. This scenario-based process is inherently new to the architecture and planning profession and can only be applied if there exists an understanding of complex relationships amongst the local conditions. As developers, we need to be methodical about the system of inputs we feed into the parametric utility.

However, to facilitate this new analysis process, the marriage between the human planning decision and computer analysis rules needs to have a seamless integration that allows planners, developers, and decision makers to set the right rules to evaluate the urban development iterations. In our research, a web-based interface was developed to give the entire team access to these variables and exercise various manipulation methods (http://ming3d.com/pingdi/). Through this web-based 4D interface, users can rely on the rules to change the design and observe the evaluation related to carbon emissions, transportation, population, and employment directly. Developers can test different inputs and try to find the answer to questions such as 'How much carbon emission will my site generate if the industry CO_2 emissions are reduced by 20 percent? What if the estimated population is increased from 5,000 to 15,000? What if the tree coverage along the street is increased from 20 percent to 50 percent?' The final results of the analysis can also be reviewed regarding how successful the CO_2 sequestration was in determining the tree density, renewable energy generation, amount of green roof, and many other factors.

We can conclude that the scenario-based analysis process and 4D data representation have created a concept of relationship model, instability, and de-centralization of the static solution. The paradigm in the digital landscape has been conceived as an ideal solution captured as a single design scheme. It was not until parametric urban theorists such as Patrick Schumacher noted the possibilities of parametric relationships between urban systems that we were critical of the design, planning process, and outcome. From the interactive model constructed by 4D-based scenario analysis, we can see a much more interactive process influencing the evolution of urban infrastructure as a dynamic system composed of a vast number of interrelated parameters. Within the process of scenario-based design and web distribution, digital landscape is now understood as a process of conceptualizing various urban components, or modulating the set of variables through an open end process, to the specific planning criteria (such as carbon neutral) it has to meet.

Data simulation

A digital landscape can also be constructed from data simulation and bottom-up methods.

> *An agent-based simulation (ABS) consists of numerous agents, which follow simply localized rules to interact with an environment, thereby formulating a complex system over time. The concept of the agent-based system has been widely used, including swarm intelligence, decentralized social networks simulation, and economic growth modeling.*
>
> *(Tang 2015)*

In terms of spatial modeling, agents can be defined as autonomous 'physical or social' entities or objects that act independently of one another (Batty 2007).[1] Our research defines the agent as the physical entity within the field of urban and landscape simulation. It focuses on the agent's properties and processes used to respond to external changes, specifically how the agents can 'sense' and 'act' to form a bottom-up system.

Our research began with an abstract landscape form by creating a movement network across an open field. The goal was to create optimized paths. This approach uses a few simple behaviors of individual agents to interact with the environment and other agents, which ultimately increases the complexity of the system as a whole. First, a group of agent-based spatial nodes are woven into an initial, rigid network. Once the two respective nodes are set to represent the start point and destination, a straight line is used to connect two nodes to represent the initial trajectory. A network optimization script is developed to generate the minimum paths using Frei Otto's wool simulation method. Instead of a simple 'dumb' static system, each agent along a path becomes an active, moving element. The agent interacts with the neighboring agents and their trails based on rules such as proximity, attraction, alignment, and collision. The external landscape is formed by a series of contextual elements, including existing buildings, land obstacles, and non-destructive topographic boundaries. As reactive agents seek equilibrium between external forces and other agents and their trails, every agent's movement is continually modified by the microenvironment by various operations such as attracting, following, repulsing, or keeping distance. The initial, rigid network thus evolves into a complex, self-organizing pattern.

With the external forces and interaction among agents, the autonomous 'action' of each agent lies in modifying its movement based on the repulsion or attraction to neighboring agents in addition to the environment itself. A complex movement organization is automatically formed over time. Visually, the agents' trails appeared to be deformed and merged into one another based on their contextual relationships. Different behaviors can be assigned to form alternate emerging patterns (Figure 7.8).

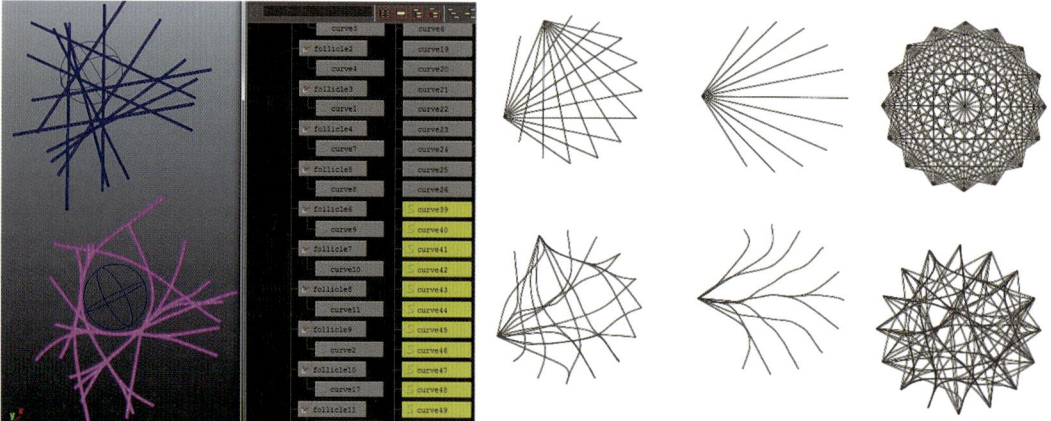

Figure 7.8 A system of agents with unique values and behaviors are calculated and manipulated. The initial grid is optimized similarly to Frei Otto's wet grid network, which is a physics-based analog method.[2] A movement system is optimized by the computer simulation based on the proximity and interaction of agents and their trails. Tools: Autodesk Maya, Rhino, Grasshopper.

Source: Ming Tang.

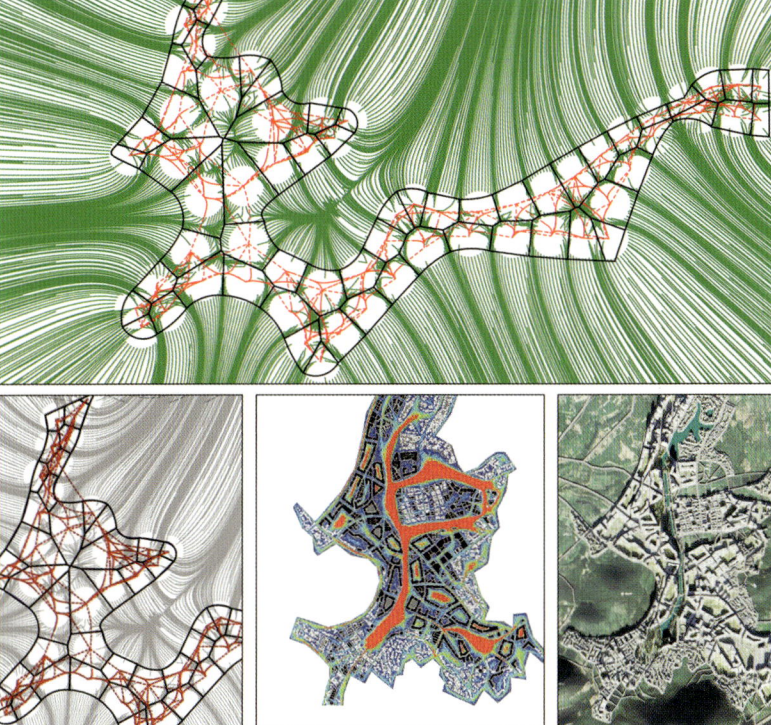

Figure 7.9 Silicon Valley of China. Tools: Space Syntax, ESRI City Engine, ArcMap, Autodesk Maya. Phase I: The self-organizing pattern was accomplished through an ABS bottom-up approach. Then, the movement network was optimized. Phase II: Space Syntax was used to analyze the movement network and generated an 'attraction map.' Two historic villages and the proposed public space are evaluated based on the spatial integration and accessibility values. Phase III: digital landscape based on 'attraction map.' Green corridor, central park, and riverside park system were added to the 2D parcel system. Three-dimensional buildings were automatically loaded from a building library and adapted to each parcel based on the 'attraction map.' The map combined various data such as proximity to the urban infrastructure, proposed zoning, and development intensity. After the automatic modeling process had been completed, the skyline along the river and east–west axis were evaluated and modified by designers.

Source: Ming Tang.

Ming Tang

PROJECT: SILICON VALLEY OF CHINA

This commissioned project is called 'Silicon Valley of China,' a large urban design project in the TJW Valley near Zhuhai. The project goal is to create a 6,000,000 square meter sustainable and ecological valley, which includes residential, commercial, cultural, and institutional spaces. A new water system is required to improve the existing hydraulic network. We applied the data-driven design methods in the conceptual design stage. Space Syntax was used to create an 'attraction map' and combined with other GIS data in the schematic design phase. Then, we used a parametric method to construct a fully detailed 3D landscape model in the end. A self-organizing pattern of movement networks emerged based on the external rules including the proximity to the existing urban infrastructure, the slope of the topography, and the distance to the water body. The 'soft grid' automatically adopted a set of forces that drive movement patterns with various magnitudes. An extremely efficient circulation and transportation system for pedestrian, vehicle, and bike was achieved by agent-based simulation. As a result, neighborhoods, blocks, and parcels were automatically constructed based on the field pattern to promote the most efficient pedestrian flow and vehicular streamline (Figure 7.9).

CONCLUSION

The research presented in this chapter is intended to realize the potential of streaming the abstract geospatial data into a parametric landscape. In these methods, the integration of non-geometrical parameters within the form seeking, animation, scenario-based analysis, simulation, and fabrication process resulted in a series of conceptual make-up models. Manipulating zoning, transportation network, city block, and various building types developed the digital landscape. Ultimately, the data-driven design looks to build upon the strengths predefined in the various representation and simulation methods and capture the benefits of emerging computational technology. It can seamlessly integrate vital geospatial components in the equation and alter the way people explore the possible design solutions to generate the ideal landscape forms, either 2D, 3D or 4D. We believe the geospatial database can provide a rich resource to produce design solutions with respect to ecological performance criteria. The demographic, traffic, and economic data from the dataset contains the trace of activity and event parameters of the urban life process. As Schumacher described in the parametric city, 'parametricist continuation is always possible in myriad, unpredictable, and qualitatively diverse ways, but it is never random' (Schumacher and Hadid, 2010). Different from traditional landscape design process, the data-driven model provides us with a range of the abstracted diagram, rather than a particular design solution. In other words, the outcome of data-driven design is the constantly morphing forms driven by the changing relationship of information, which can be interpolated into physical landscape features. The value of parameterizing landscape related data, either conceptual or diagrammatic, became a valuable design method in the planning, architectural, landscape, and urban design fields through digital computation and fabrication. It created an interesting notion of the data representation and simulation, and further exploited the idea that design solutions can evolve from the massive volume of data available and accessible to us.

ACKNOWLEDGMENTS

Thanks for the contributions and support from Enrique Sanchez, Craig Moyer, Xinhao Wang, Chris Auffrey, Mingming Lu, Ellen Crawford, Kelsey Reichenbach, Connor Borchardt, David Schaengold, Yinan Wu, Kyle Zook, Lydia Yen, Dihua Yang, and Yan Zhou.

NOTES

1. Batty defined the environment as a cell-based landscape and agents as 'objects or events that are located with respect to cells but can move between cells' (Batty 2007). Agents are objects that do not have fixed locations but act and interact with one another as well as the environment in which they exist according to some purpose.
2. Frei Otto's wool-thread machine is a form of analog computer. Analog computers use a continuously changing aspect of a physical phenomenon to model a problem being solved. Otto's wool-thread machines change the degree of freedom that water (a physical phenomenon) can act on the wool threads. By changing the degree water acts on the wool threads, Otto solves the problem of path optimization. The end geometry is a result of material interaction, elasticity, and variability.

REFERENCES

Bally, Michael. 2007. *Cities and Complexity, Understanding Cities with Cellular Automata, Agent-Based Models, and Fractals*. Cambridge MA: MIT Press.

Schumacher, Patrik, and Zaha Hadid. 2010. *Recent Projects*. Tokyo: A.D.A. Edita.

Tang, Ming. 2015. 'Self-Organizing City: Experiments Using Multi-Agent Model and Space Syntax.' Paper presented at the 2015 Symposium on Simulation for Architecture and Urban Design (SimAUD). Washington DC: Society for Modeling and Simulation International (SCS).

Tang, Ming, and Jonathon Anderson . 2011. 'Information Urbanism – Parametric Urbanism Injunction with GIS Data Processing and Fabrication.' Paper presented at 2011 Annual Architectural Research Centers Consortium (ARCC) Spring Research Conference. Detroit, MI.

Part II

Innovative processes

8

Manufacturing resonance

Michael Beaman and Zaneta Hong

Landscapes are open systems, always in a state of perpetual information exchange with surrounding conditions. This exchange activates and sustains the material processes that continually form, inform, and transform landscapes. For landscape architecture, as with any practice of spatial design, the capacity to understand these processes and the ability to intervene in them lies within the representational models that practice employs. As we find the need to generate more responsible, responsive, and effective environmental interventions – a pressing issue for design – manufacturing resonance between these representational models and the complex environments they describe challenges the anthropogenic basis on which these models have been constructed.

Michael Beaman and Zaneta Hong

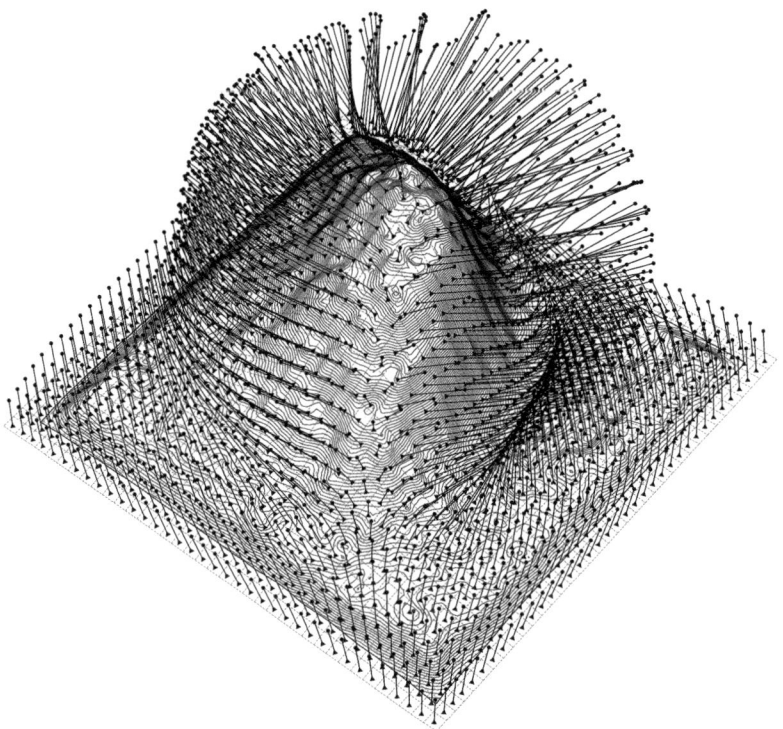

Figure 8.0 A representational model of a speculative landform that simulates a hydrokinetic phenomenon according to two particular data sets – flow velocity and vector.

> *Landscape, in this instance, implies process and change, not form: it cannot be designed and controlled as a totality but instead must be projected into the future and allowed to grow over time.*
>
> (Allen and McQuade 2001, 23)

Landscapes are spaces of flux, shaped and reshaped by flows of information expressed through energy and matter. Their autonomy is ephemeral, if existent at all. Intrinsically, landscapes are spaces continuously in a state of becoming – formed, informed, and transformed by manifold exchanges of information between their material composition and environmental conditions. This is the very definition of an open system (Luhman 1995a, 28).

Material processes define landscapes, in as much as they constitute them. Likewise, material processes don't inhabit spaces; rather they form them. Unlike strictly controlled environments bounded by enclosures that regulate

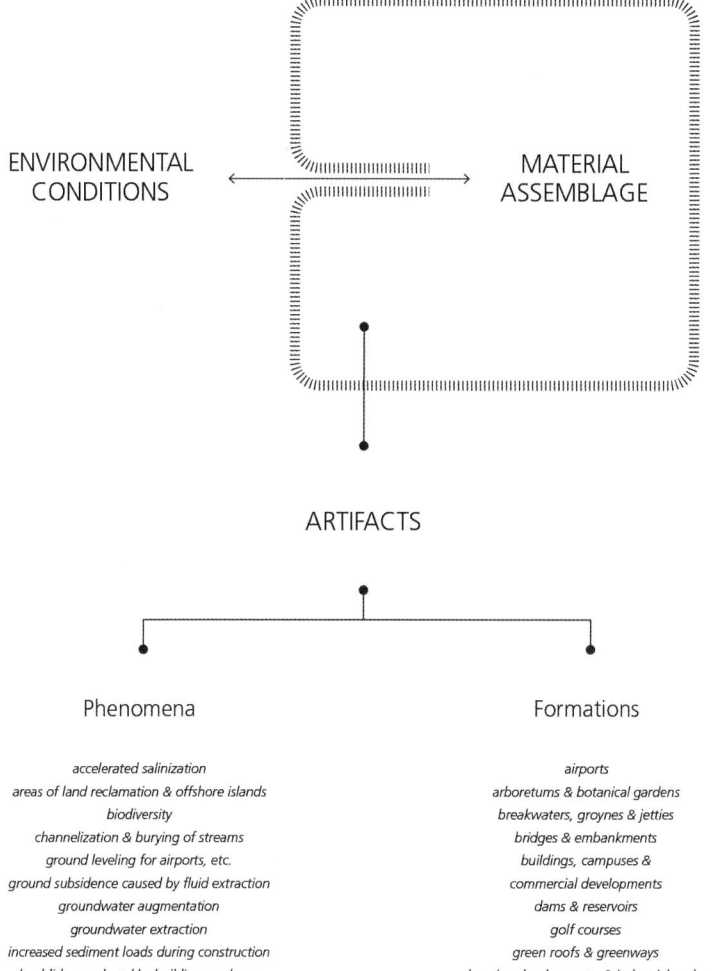

Figure 8.1 Material effects are spatiotemporal manifestations of the exchange of information between a landscape's environment and its material assemblage. The manifestations include phenomena and formations.

or mediate their exchange of information (e.g. submarines, spacesuits, or biological testing labs), landscapes are directly subjected to and are part of changes in their surrounding conditions. They have no spatial perimeter – their finitudes are expressions of behavioral qualities rather than dimensional boundaries. They are in a perpetual indeterminate state.

The pattern of responses that result from the exchange of information between material processes and their surrounding environmental conditions manifest as *material effects* – phenomena and formations. Phenomena are the events that are produced as a result of this exchange; formations are the artifacts of those events. Both phenomena and formations, as physical embodiments of material processes and environmental conditions, exist within a reciprocity, where landscapes affect and are affected by the environments they are a part of (Figure 8.1).

ENVIRONMENTS AND REPRESENTATIONAL MODELS

It is within these processes of information exchange that anthropogenic interventions occur; a collective reshaping of the interdependent processes and effects that constitute landscapes extend affordance and mitigate vulnerabilities (Turkl 2011). The capacity to understand material processes, many of which are beyond our ability to perceive in whole or even in part, underlies an ability to influence future material effects.

The interconnectivity of constituent agents and artifacts in any environmental condition undermines the formation of discrete and isolated interventions. Any attempt at direct intervention takes place in the larger information assemblage they seek to modify, producing residual phenomena and formations, some of which are unwanted and potentially catastrophic, climate change being the most cogent example. As James Corner notes, landscape manifestations include 'human intervention' (Corner 2002, 130–131).

Landscape design is a creative, projective practice that derives agency through an ability to generate descriptions and instructions for producing future environments. This ability creates the possibility of intervention ad infinitum – through processes of iteration, analysis, and proposition. To achieve this projective position, design practice employs frameworks or systems, which create distinction between representational and actual interventions.

This formulation follows sociologist and systems theorist Niklas Luhmann's assertion that a system's function is to reduce the complexity of its environment through operations of information selection. Luhmann writes, 'The system's own complexity already forces it to make selections: the order the system chooses in relating its elements results from the difference in complexity between it and its environment' (Luhmann 1995b, 25–26). For landscape design, the methodology and act of selection determine what environmental information is salient and what is not. As Luhmann writes, this selection is contingent on the system doing the selecting.

> *The system draws its own boundaries by means of its own operations, that it thereby distinguishes itself from its environment, and that only then and in this manner can it be observed as a system. This always happens in a very specific way, not just in any way, but in a way that we can determine more precisely with the concepts of operation and the operational – which is to say, by means of the manner in which the system produces itself through system-specific operations.*
>
> *(Luhmann 1995a, 63–64)*

This distinction between environmental conditions, and a system's ability to recognize and incorporate information from that environment is a product of the operations of the system – what we term the system's *operational domain*. Luhmann further writes, a system gains *access* to its environment 'only as information,' experiences it 'only as a selection,' and apprehends it 'only as changes' (Luhmann 1995b, 174). We term this capacity to "access" an environment the system's *observational domain*. For landscape design, the combination of an observational domain (information accessibility) and operational domain (information integration) creates a model for intervention through reduction by way of representation (Figure 8.2). These models are a product of the histories, practices, technologies, and discourses, which collectively define the discipline – a framework from and for the generation of new knowledge (Badiou 2007, 14).

These models are representational in that they subsume the environments they distinguish themselves from into new information assemblages of reduced complexity. Luhmann notes:

> *Systems lack the 'requisite variety' [Ashby's term] that would enable them to react to every state of the environment, that is to say, to establish an environment exactly suited to the system. There is, in other words, no point-to-point correspondence between system and environment (such conditions would abolish the difference between system and environment).*
>
> *(Luhmann 1995b, 25)*

Michael Beaman and Zaneta Hong

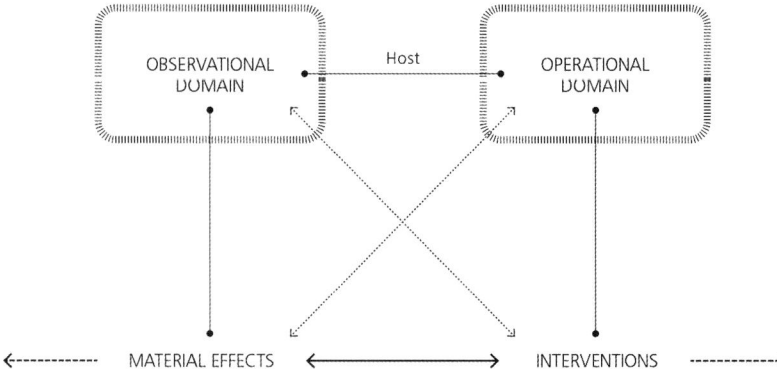

Figure 8.2 For landscape design, the combination of observational domain (information accessibility) and the operational domain (action upon information) creates a model for intervention through reduction by way of representation.

Representational models are able to extend disciplinary agency through their capacity to describe existing processes and material effects within frameworks that facilitate speculative intervention.

Representational models are not neutral, unbiased systems for the displacement, reduction, and translation of information. They do not produce benign artifacts. Rather they form the structure through which designers access, integrate, and manipulate information. Those structures in turn imbue new organizational relationships by establishing hierarchies, boundaries, and preferences; reducing material effects into representational constructs, and increasing accessibility and operability. In other words, representational models re-construct landscapes, converting captured information into new assemblages better suited for speculative interventions.

OBSERVATIONAL DOMAINS

The loss of a sense of the whole in a landscape is not due to the world we inhabit, but rather to the methods we employ.

(Girot 2013, 92)

The capacity to access and register information defines the ability to observe. Information that is both accessible, and can be captured by a representational model defines that system's observable domain. Observability is a relationship between the observer (which does not have to be human or biological in nature) and the observed. Observation within this context emerges through the transfer of information between the object of observation and the observer. A phenomenon, for example, is an observable event, only when that transfer takes place and the observer registers it. This transfer is the overlap of: 1) information the object of observation makes available; and 2) the observer's ability to register that transfer. The qualities a material effect exhibits (scale, occurrence, persistence) impact the availability of information to an observer, whereas the ability to register information is a function of an observer's observational range.

Material effects emerge and exhibit behaviors at various spatiotemporal scales and degrees of complexity. Scale is the extent to which material qualities overlap with the dimensional range of an observer – how large or small and for how long or short a material effect can be observed. Observability of these effects as a function of scale is a measure of both registration and recognition. Figure 8.3 shows spatiotemporal units of measure in powers of 10 ranging from the plank length to the size of the visible universe (and the time it takes light to travel either). Direct observation from humans makes up only a small portion of that range. From the infinitesimal to the cosmological, most of the information that exists eludes human capacity to register and recognize, impacting the anthropocentricity of representational models.

Phenomena and formations generated from material processes are iterative products; they re-occur. Occurrence, whether intermittent or patterned, is the frequency and regularity at which material effects emerge (e.g., streams, cycles) and their adherence to ontological and morphological constraints (e.g., forms, geometries, densities, compositions). Streams are continuous or stable states of occurrence. They produce dynamic phenomena, which once completed may not occur again. Cycles invert this stable relationship by producing material effects as either intermittent or patterned instances of emergence. Both examples are temporally constrained characteristics. Geometries, features, densities, and compositions, on the other hand, characterize the spatial consistency of material effects generated from a process in any given environmental condition. Occurrence in this instance is a measure of semblance between like-generated effects rather than absolute spatial dimensions.

The degree to which a material process is affected by changes in environmental conditions determines the persistence of its material effects. Perturbations, in the flow of information (e.g., rate, type, pattern, volume), vary the manifestations of material processes, altering the phenomena and formations these processes manifest. Material processes with 'the capacity to buffer change' exhibit resilience (Folke et al. 2002, 437–440). The degree to which these changes impact – either access or recognition of material effects by an observer – are a measure of

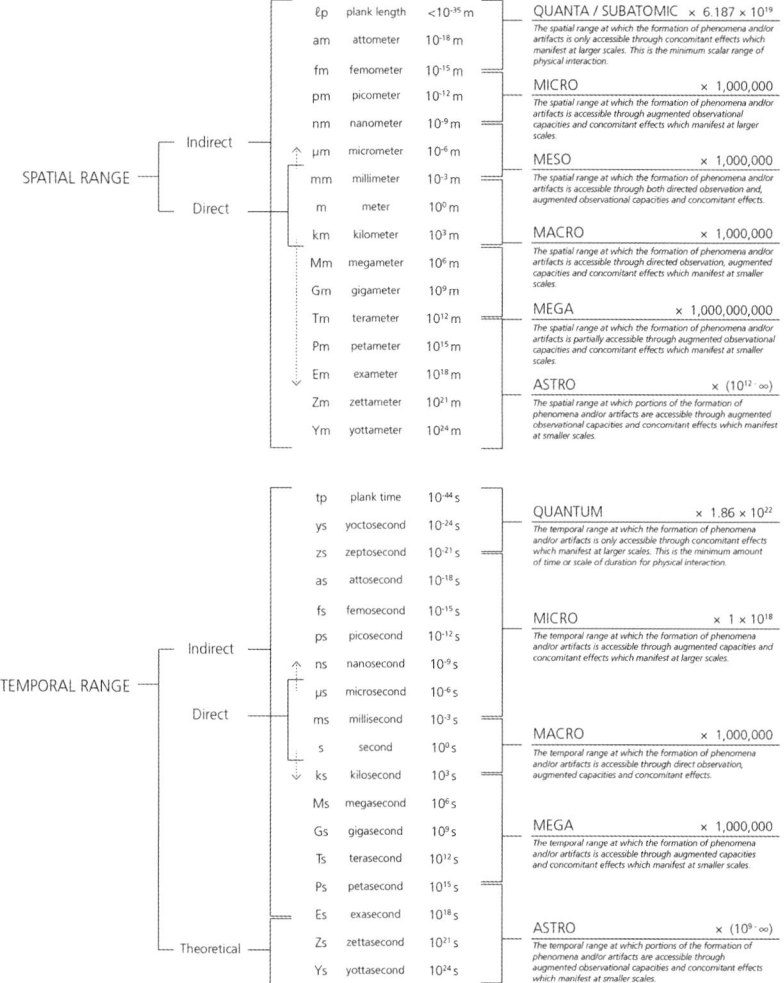

Figure 8.3 Observational range is comprised of indirect, direct, and theoretical units of measure and the capacity of an observer to register information at each scale.

how invariant the process of observation is to the degree of frequency of perturbation, marking a threshold at which material effects are fundamentally and globally changed (Mitov 2012, 2).

We often ascribe the term observer with a tacit anthropocentricity, though that definition is not implicit in the emergence of phenomena. The above criteria do not specify humans as the sole agent of observation. Though we often use the limitations of the human body as the datum by which we gauge access, and observational range, the boundaries of an observational domain are not completely constrained by the capacities of the human body. Technologies extend agency, and it is through the development and utilization of technologies that anthropogenic observational limitations have been surpassed. These have been developed through four distinctive modalities: 1) enhancements; 2) extensions; 3) associated effects; and 4) sensitivities. Each describes the way in which our innate observational range is overcome, providing new possibilities to observe previously inaccessible information. These modifications often incorporate multiple technological developments into a single device, system, or set of standardized techniques (Arthur 2009, 27–43).

- Enhancements modify the observational domain by changing the format of communication. Night vision goggles enhance the amount of light reflected from objects in our visual field so that information is available to us via our existing capacity for sight. Here, inaccessible information is formatted to the limitations of our eyes. Enhancements supply more information into the observational domain.
- Extensions modify the observational domain by changing the scale or frequency of communication. The microscope magnifies the reflection of light from objects so that they are discernible to the eye. Extensions rescale information to fit our capabilities.
- Associated Effects modify the observational domain by changing the vehicle of communication. This may be a change in material, modality, or strategy. As heat is transferred to a thermometer from the surrounding air, the mercury inside expands, registering and visualizing the transfer. Associated Effects correlate one material effect which is observable with one that is not.
- Sensitivity modifies the observational domain by increasing or decreasing the resolution with which information is observed. The hanging spring of a seismograph absorbs the earth's movement at intervals undetectable by the human eye, expanding our ability to detect and register movement at regional, global, and astronomical scales. Sensitivities change the threshold between information that is available and the registration of that information.

In each case, information available to the observer is amplified, revealing more of a material effect's qualities, which allow for a more thorough registration of properties and processes. Observation provides the base set of information from which design intervention takes place; this, in turn, becomes the function of the observational domain. However, the registration and recognition of information is not the same as incorporating information into the design process. This function resides in a representational model's operational domain.

Michael Beaman and Zaneta Hong

OPERATIONAL DOMAINS

> *We throw away 99% of what is specific about each object to represent only 1%*
> *– in the hope of revealing patterns across this 1% of objects' characteristics.*
>
> (Manovich 2010)

If the observational domain is defined by the capacity to capture information within a representational model, then the operational domain is defined by the collection of discourses, techniques, and technologies that assemble (or act upon) that information. As more information is made available and captured by a representational model's observational domain, it becomes increasingly representative of its environment. The operational domain provides methods for the assembly of that information into a set of relationships, which, as a whole or in part, attempts to re-make their environment with reduced complexity. As new information is brought into the representational model, new forms of knowledge are produced, and novel interventions generated.

New media and cultural theorist Lev Manovich identifies two considerations of a representational model's capacity to elicit new forms of knowledge. He emphasizes that rather than asking what information is converted into a representational model, the question instead becomes: What is the capacity of a representational model to convey those sets of information, and how do the model's operations reveal inaccessible information? This is the 1 percent that Manovich refers to in the quote above, and the first consideration for representational models – fidelity.

Information captured through a representational model's observational domain becomes organized within the logic of representation that system establishes. For example, landscapes are typically distinguished one from another or between themselves and their surrounding territory, by a number of delimited methodologies. These delimiting methodologies are derived from the representational model's mode of communication – lines delineated on two-dimensional orthographic projections of terrain for example.

Not all landscapes have clearly delineated or *bonafide* boundary conditions (Smith and Mark 2003, 411–427). Geological and constructed elements offer discreet bounding entities, whereas political borders, administrative sectors, or property lines often serve as *fiat* delimitations, boundaries wholly imposed from the mode of information representation (Smith and Varzi 2000, 401–420). Boundaries, whether constructed or implied, are projections of a representational system's discretization method onto dynamic environmental conditions (Figure 8.4). Differences in geological, ecological, or climatological zones offer more amorphous boundaries, where separations between two spaces are provisional, conditional, and fluctuating. These fuzzy finitudes become codified as landscape boundaries through institutional, legal, or traditional practices of defining space and communicating information.

The recognition of these elusive aspects of landscape (boundaries between processes, occurrences of phenomena, and morphological definitions of formations) challenge the fidelity of representational models to select and represent information from a surrounding environment. The degree of infidelity the representational model exhibits in comparison to actual material effects imparts uncertainty in any delineation not explicitly present in the environment. That uncertainty transfers to design interventions based on these representational models.

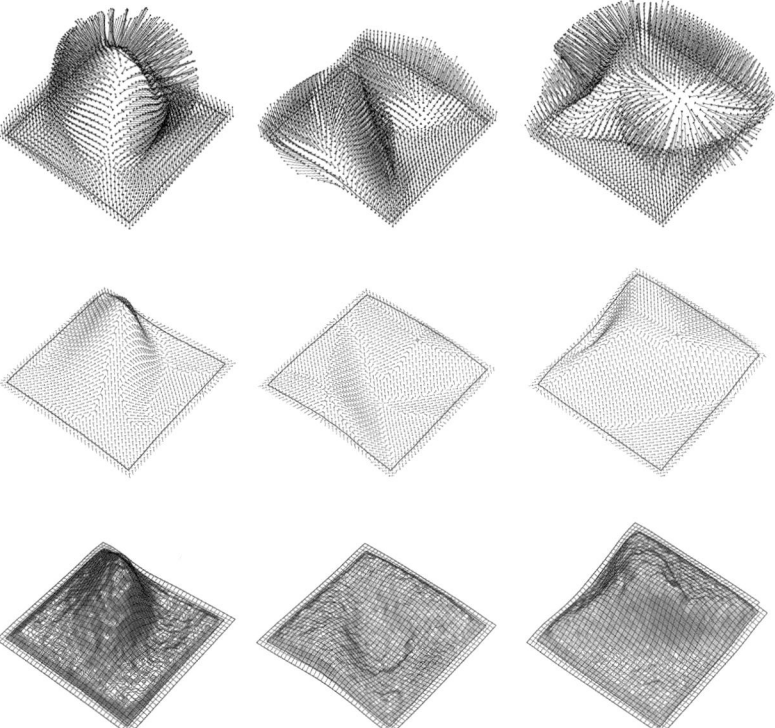

Figure 8.4 Slope intensity and flow rate describe the likelihood of certain hydrokinetic behaviors on a given surface. Speculative landforms above are derived computationally and formed to generate specific phenomena.

The second consideration is how information is hosted. Manovich notes that visualization practices (the use of visual representations as modes of knowledge creation), which emerged in the early eighteenth century for the sciences and plastic arts, utilized 'visual primitives' as a form of information reduction through representation. These predominately visual models operate though the 'privileging of spatial over other visual dimensions' (Manovich 2010). In this scenario, spatial variation (e.g., sizes and positions) serve as the representational model's *hosting logic*.

The protocol or set of relationships and rules imposed on information within a representational model are how that system hosts information. Hosting is built on the logic of representational models, and it carries with it all of the preferences and defaults embedded in its formulation. This becomes especially apparent in drawing conventions. The representation of a landscape through drawing relies on standardized methods of production, communication, and expression. When using drawings to assemble information, designers are importing not only information from the observational domain but also other latent organizational strategies embedded in the process of representation. Though drawing hosts' information through visual means, representational systems are not necessarily visual. Other hosting regimes exist where visualization is only a method of communication, e.g. databases, catalogues (Figure 8.5).

Unlike drawings, databases defy adherence to a singular communicative device, in that its means of hosting and communicating information are not governed by the same protocols. A database is an organized collection of information, which can be integrated into multiple modes of communication. As such, databases offer a democratic approach to expression where the information it contains is accessible and replicable in a multiplicity of forms, states, and conditions. For the database, observations and operations are available in simultaneity (Manovich 1999, 80–99). The metric for information in a database is without graduation or calibration, rendering inherent values explicitly. A database, because of the separation of host and communication method, can be prompted into new assemblies with new structures, affinities, and relationships – communication becomes a malleable and responsive endeavor.

With developments in technologies and techniques that have allowed humanity to move beyond the human observational range, purely anthropocentric approaches limit the epistemological effectiveness for representational models. The dissonance between material effects and their reconstruction through representational models results from the operational constraints developed to reduce complexity. These include the reliance on hierarchies and sequences to

Manufacturing resonance

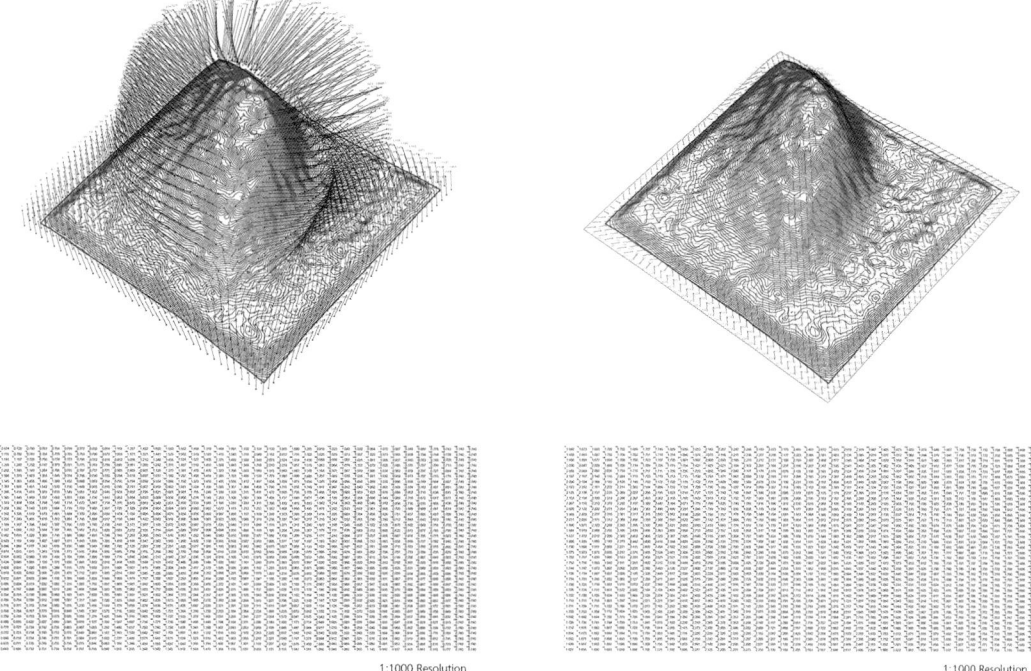

Figure 8.5 In this specimen, hydrokinetic processes defined as functions of representative data sets were used to articulate form and features. Their terrain is determined and recorded by data points related to flow velocity (left) and movement vector (right).

organize and reduce information; the inability to instrumentalize dynamic and temporal formation processes; the exploration and communication of complex physical objects or spaces through conventional forms of deconstruction, which render unsympathetic and incomplete wholes; the binary nature of possible material formations; and the reliance on fixed symbolic meanings. As a consequence, design production that relies on a particular representational model exhibits that model's suppression of environmental processes, material effects, and their agency as non-human actors. In other words, as more information becomes available about our world, the representational models we employ resonate less and less.

Michael Beaman and Zaneta Hong

MANUFACTURING RESONANCE

> *'Whole' is now nothing more than a provisional visualization which can be modified and reversed at will, by moving back to the individual components, and then looking for yet other tools to regroup the same elements into alternative assemblages.*
>
> (Latour 2010, 159)

As has been stated, representational models re-assemble landscapes as collections of selected information brought together through new operational regimes. The capacity to perform this re-assembly resides in the representational model itself, and is a function of how the model creates distinction between itself and its environment. A model's effectiveness is largely a question of assessing how well speculative material effects that are generated within the model resonate with actual material effects produced through constructed interventions. The dominant governing criteria (at least for designers) is that of analogical resonance. To position another way, resonance is achieved through resemblance, typically visual resemblance. This approach has defined spatial design practice and operative models for the last five hundred years (Evans 1997, 152–193). This longevity, and what assures its future usefulness, is that its calculation of resonance is an anthropogenic one.

To enact a greater or even different calculation of resonance, and thereby alter the course of landscape design, we may first need to address the ways in which the discipline draws distinctions between the systems it employs and the environments it hopes to impact. An expansion of the observational domain would make more information available to a representational model. Though there are many technologies of observational augmentation yet to be explored by landscape design, more information does not necessarily denote greater operational capacity, just more data to operate.

Computational models, which simulate material processes within a specific scope and resolution, can produce states that correlate to material effects (Beaman 2014, 148–152). These simulated processes rely on the capacity to perform mathematical calculations at a rate and within tolerances that fall outside of human capacity. Representational models that utilize these operations de-center humans as the sole arbiter of resonance. However, logic systems lack the ability to translate simulated phenomena and formations to full-scale/full-resolution environments, de-centering computation from representational models as well.

Manufacturing resonance

Analogical/logical hybridization expands the agency of representational methodologies, by expanding the ways in which resonance can be achieved. With no central or *a priori* method of achieving it, resonance becomes a manufactured property rather than a conditional one. Such is the challenge for innovative design processes. How might these analogical/logical hybrid representational models construct resonance between themselves and their environment?

When we define landscapes as a collection of material processes intertwined with environmental conditions, we are describing a system of immense scope. Manufacturing resonant representational models becomes a question of how to achieve a significant reduction in complexity, making intervention a possibility, while maintaining a correlation between effects generated within the model to those within the environment being represented. A reduction in the scope of representation in favor of simulating material effects with greater resolution offers one approach to resonance. As Bruno Latour suggests, wholes when constructed as representational models are provisional, suggesting that the operative domain of landscape practice might exchange some simulations for others. This heuristic method of development allows one to incrementally modify the applied representational model.

The distinction of data sets into a descriptive or notational element, such as what we use in orthographic drawings, is useful when representing material effects with *bonafide* boundaries. This is less the case when we are interested in reducing the complexity of processes into a single representational model. Representation here functions to truncate data or impose extrinsic boundaries that represent the behavior of a process. Modeling parts of processes or analogous behaviors starts to chip away at the preferences, default assumptions, or regimes of reduction employed by existing representational models. Those behaviors are then mapped between the original process and the representative one, so that the phenomena and formations that emerge from the target environment and the simulation are correlated in a way that allows designers to predict future states of an environment. At this point, the designer can intervene in the model in some way, changing its configuration, relationships, or composition, and assess the resultant effects.

Conversely, working with lower resolution simulations in which its scope extends to intrinsic boundary conditions provides representational models the capacity to resonate with global effects. Lower resolution simulations may be less sensitive, smaller in scale, and composed of fewer elements and relationships, but which nonetheless are phenomenal and formal wholes that provide a catalog of formations sufficient to represent actual material effects (Ankeny 2007, 46–58,

52–54). Low-resolution wholes resonate with high resolution, large-scope landscapes by dealing directly with the complete data set that defines it, and without the need to operate within a strictly representational regime. As architectural theorist Mario Carpo notes, 'In the new world of algorithmic, or differential, reproducibility, visual sameness is replaced by similarity' (Carpo 2011, 101).

The need to generate more responsible, responsive, and effective environmental interventions has emerged as a pressing issue for landscape designers and all spatial design disciplines that derive agency from the ability to project future worlds (Figure 8.6). The question of how to manufacture resonance between representational models and the material effects stands at the forefront of addressing these issues. Information when conceptualized, integrated, and utilized as a focus of inquiry in and of itself, allows designers to move beyond conventional methodologies of representation. A reformulation of the observational/operational domain relationship and the ways in which information is reconsidered in the design processes for landscape architects, allows future practitioners of both theoretical or actual interventions to more effectively impact our environment.

REFERENCES

Allen, Stan and Marc McQuade. 2001. *Landform Building: Architecture's New Terrain.* Zurich: Lars Muller.

Ankeny, Rachel A. 2007. 'Wormy Logic.' In *Science without Laws, Model Systems, Cases, Exemplary Narratives*, edited by Angela N. H. Creager, Elizabeth Lunbeck, and M. Norton Wise, 46–58. Durham: Duke University Press.

Arthur, W. Brian. 2009. *The Nature of Technology: What It Is and How It Evolves.* New York: Free Press.

Badiou, Alain. 2007. *The Concept of Model: An Introduction to the Materialist Epistemology of Mathematics.* Melbourne: Re.press.

Beaman, Michael Leighton. 2014. 'Other Complexities.' In *ii Journal: International Journal of Interior Architecture and Spatial Design: Corporeal Complexities*, edited by Meg Jackson and Jonathon Anderson. Houston: University of Houston, 148–152.

Carpo, Mario. 2011. *The Alphabet and the Algorithm.* Cambridge, MA: MIT Press.

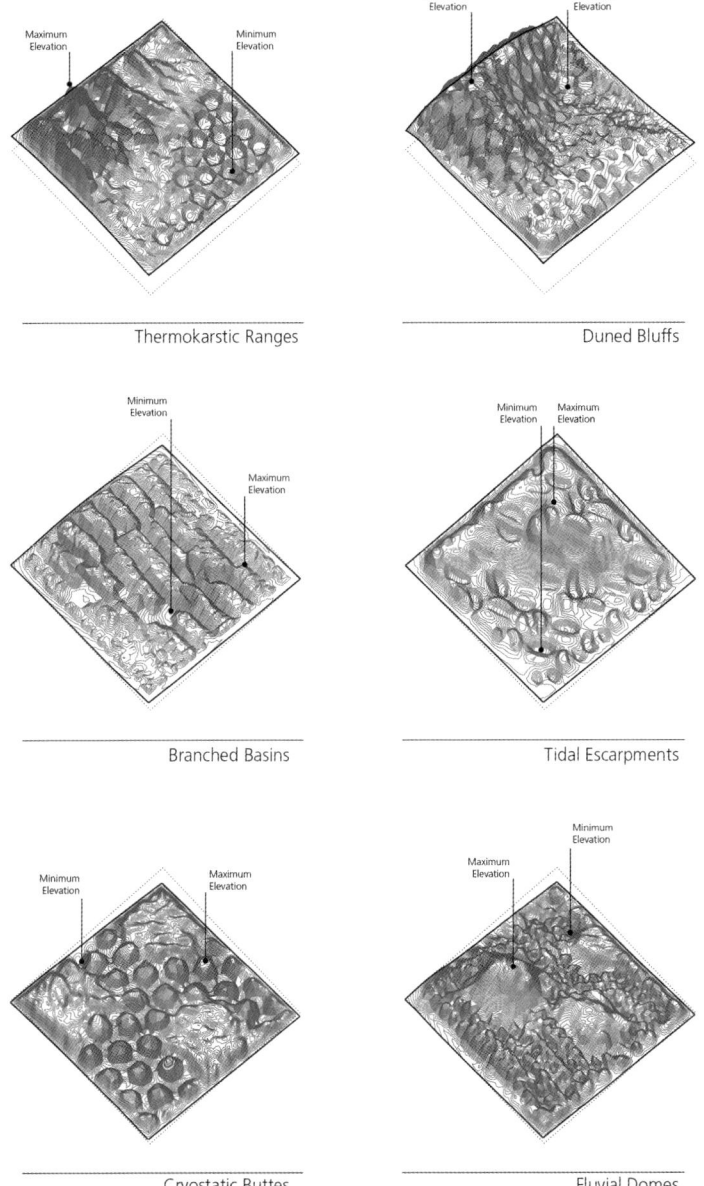

Figure 8.6 Represented are six speculative landforms: thermokarstic ranges, duned bluffs, branched basins, tidal escarpments, cryostatic buttes, and fluvial domes (top to bottom, left to right). Each landform bridges a particular formation process with a unique surface morphology, resulting in patterns of feature-dominant or terrain-dominant conditions.

Corner, James. 2002. 'The Hermeneutic Landscape.' In *Theory in Landscape Architecture: A Reader*, edited by Simon Swaffield, 130–131. Philadelphia: University of Pennsylvania Press.

Evans, Robin. 1997. 'Translations from Building to Drawing.' In *Translations from Building to Drawing and Other Essays*. Cambridge, MA: MIT Press.

Folke, Carl and Steve Carpenter, Thomas Elmqvist, Lance Gunderson, C.S. Holling, and Brian Walker. 2002. 'Resilience and Sustainable Development: Building Adaptive Capacity in a World of Transformations.' *Ambio*. 31(5): 437–440.

Girot, Christophe. 2013. 'The Elegance of Topology.' In *Landscript: Topology 3 – Topical Thoughts on the Contemporary Landscape*, edited by Christophe Girot, Anette Freytag, Albert Kirchengast, and Dunja Richter, 79–116. Zurich: Institute of Landscape Architecture ILA, ETH Zurich.

Latour, Bruno. 2010. 'Tarde's Idea of Quantification.' In *The Social After Gabriel Tarde: Debates and Assessments,* ed. Mattei Candea. London: New York: Routledge.

Luhmann, Niklas. 1995a. *Introduction to Systems Theory.* Stanford: Stanford University Press.

Luhmann, Niklas. 1995b. *Social Systems.* Translated by John Bednarz, Jr. with Dirk Baecker. Stanford: Polity Press.

Manovich, Lev. 1999. 'Database as Symbolic Form.' In *Convergence: The International Journal of Research into New Media Technologies*, 5(80): 80–99. Accessed on February 5, 2009. http://con.sagepub.com/cgi/content/abstract/5/2/80.

Manovich, Lev. 2010. 'What is Visualization?' Accessed on January 6, 2015. http://manovich.net/content/04-projects/062-what-is-visualization /61_article_2010.pdf.

Mitov, Michel. 2012. *Sensitive Matter: Foams, Gels, Liquid Crystals, and Other Miracles.* Cambridge, MA: Harvard University Press.

Smith, Barry and Achille C. Varzi. 2000. 'Fiat and Bona Fide Boundaries.' In *Philosophy and Phenomenological Research*, 60(2): 401–420.

Smith, Barry and David M. Mark. 2003. 'Do Mountains Exist? Towards an Ontology of Landforms.' In *Environment & Planning B (Planning and Design)*, 30(3): 411–427.

Turkl, Sherry. 2011. 'Does This Technology Serve Human Purposes? A Necessary Conservation with Sherry Turkl (Part One).' Accessed November 10, 2014. http://henryjenkins.org/2011/08/an_interview_with_sherry_turkl.html.

9

Expanded 'thick description'

The landscape architect as critical ethnographer

Alison B. Hirsch

While landscape architecture has evolved into an urban profession that deals with consequential questions of climate change, ecological sustainability, and land-use reclamation, it has moved further away from the sociocultural dimension of landscape. This chapter addresses the recognizable ambiguity over the 'cultural agency' of landscape architecture as it is theorized and practiced today. Specifically, it promotes creative methods that use cultural rituals and social practices, as well as contested memories or suppressed cultural histories, as the interpretive starting point for design generation.

The term 'thick description' comes from anthropologist Clifford Geertz (borrowed originally from Gilbert Ryle) and refers, in simplest terms, to an interpretive ethnographic approach (Geertz 1973).[1] Geertz insisted on ethnography as an interpretive practice – a 'thick description' of social and symbolic action – emphasizing the particular over the universal or cross-cultural. While more than forty years have passed since his seminal essay 'Thick Description: Toward an Interpretive Theory of Culture,' Geertz's methodology still poses a model for landscape architecture as the field attempts to retain its position as an alternative to twentieth-century 'utopian' practices of urban planning and design. Equally important, however, is the criticism Geertz's approach has received – specifically, its political neutrality or the focus on locality at the expense of situating meaning into a broader context of political, economic, and social structures. It is for this reason that I title this chapter *'expanded* thick description.' In addition, while adapting the subtitle from Hal Foster's 1996 essay 'The Artist as Ethnographer' (Foster 1996),[2] I have inserted 'critical' to refer to this expanded and politicized form of ethnography – ethnography responsive to its post-colonial and globalized contexts. In her book *Critical Ethnography: Methods, Ethics, Performance* (2011), performance scholar D. Soyini Madison explains,

> *The critical ethnographer … takes us beneath surface appearances, disrupts the status quo, and unsettles both neutrality and taken-for-granted assumptions by bringing to light underlying and obscure operations of power and control. Therefore, the critical ethnographer resists domestication and moves from 'what is' to 'what could be'.*
>
> *(Madison 2011, 5)*

The implication of transformative action rather than passive description is pivotal to this investigation of landscape architectural methodology.[3]

The primary emphasis here on methodology is the sociocultural dimension of today's 'mongrel' cities (Sandercock 2003) and what processes of globalization imply for a culturally interpretive practice of landscape architecture.[4] In the context of the globalization of capital and the 'global cultural flows' that it has catalyzed (Appadurai 1990), culture can no longer be considered static or essentialist. In this new urban condition, it is consistently renegotiated through citizens' search for both personal and collective expressions of identity. This plays out in the space of the city through the negotiation of 'conflictful edges and turfs' (Soja 1998, 444) and the appropriation of space through acts of 'insurgent citizenship' (Holston 1998).[5]

Expanded 'thick description'

The provocations below are intended to encourage an activist on-the-ground practice that responds to these dynamic sociocultural processes as a creative catalyst for design generation. The following will situate this sociocultural emphasis in the theoretical context of the field and neighboring disciplines (I. Theory), then attempt to provide a methodological framework for this renewed form of practice (II. Methodology). The figures are intended to illustrate how some of the methodological values could be applied in action. They were either generated by *foreground design agency,* my research practice (with partner, Aroussiak Gabrielian) or by our students experimenting with the methodological framework I outline here.

THEORY

Expanded thickness

The hope is here to frame landscape architecture as an interpreter of culture; not as a neutral or scientific analysis or a means to sustain the status quo, but an imaginative interpretation that challenges people to think beyond the conventions of familiar expectation – from 'what is' to 'what could be.'

It is thus time we return to the thickness of landscape – its temporal and sectional thickness, as well as the thick complexity of the cultural processes that shape it. The language of Landscape Urbanism (and its legacy) – which continues to contribute to the field's theoretical debates – is still largely dependent on the postmodern language of surface over depth (excusing the binary logic inconsistent with this language). While in the anthology of essays *Recovering Landscape: Essays in Contemporary Landscape Architecture* (1999), landscape architect and theorist James Corner and others insisted on the 'excavation' of site as a critical cultural practice (Corner 1999a), this discussion on depth was soon fully eclipsed by the language of 'staging surfaces' (Corner's own shifting language; Corner 2006, 28) within the 'horizontal field of urbanization' (Waldheim 2006, 15). While the global reach and horizontal spread of urbanization are significant to the present endeavor, the emphasis is not an either/or but an 'and/also' as Edward Soja (after Lefebvre) describes the introduction of a third alternative that diversifies and opens up the limitations of binary thinking (Soja 1996). Again, it is for this reason that I have titled the chapter 'expanded "thick description"' (expanded, from the Latin *expandere*, to spread out) – implying both broad

Alison B. Hirsch

understanding of the global spread of cultural flows and a deep search for cultural meaning in highly localized contexts.

Urbanization and destabilization

Returning to *Recovering Landscape*, a number of the authors address the thickness or depth of a site's past lives and suggest an interpretive practice. They emphasize the traces and relics that mark these past lives and trigger the creative process (see particularly Girot 1999). Physical relics and ruins are inarguably compelling for their imaginative dimension – triggering the mind to piece together stories of their past existence. Ruins have clearly been integral to landscape architecture's development in the western world, as they were an 'essential ingredient' to the eighteenth-century Picturesque (Hunt 1978, 796). Part of landscape's 'recovery' has been especially focused on 'post-industrial' relics and ruins which are undeniably alluring in their heroic dimensions and as reminders of the great manufacturing economy whose loss still haunts our cities. Yet places such as the quintessential and experientially thrilling Landschaftspark Duisburg-Nord, the transformation of part of the massive steelworks in Germany's Ruhr Valley, rarely interpret difficult aspects of the site's social history as integral to the design, thus sacrificing the interpretive agenda for a kind of fetishization of our monuments (objects) of production. David Harvey's provocation about such sites published in a symposium brief titled 'Where is the Outrage?' asks, 'converting an old iron and steelworks into a magnificent park or play space is one thing, but then I thought to myself, have we stopped using iron and steel? Where is the iron and steel now being made?' To this he explains the working conditions of Chinese manufacturing in the Yangtze and Pearl River deltas where much of this industry has moved:

> *Having witnessed 16 year old girls working, usually for the grand total sum of $15 a month ... then you realized our world is being constructed in a certain kind of way and that there is a certain luxury which is allowing certain areas of the advanced capitalist world to somehow or other engage in this act of atonement [i.e. transforming decommissioned industrial sites into 'play space'].*
>
> (Harvey 2005)

As landscape historian John Beardsley additionally notes, the site is sanitized of 'the close connection between the steel industry and the Nazi party during World

Expanded 'thick description'

War II [and] ... the widespread use of prisoner of war and slave labor in German factories in those years' (Beardsley 2007, 209).

An expanded and critical 'thick description' might ask *what are the cultural impacts of processes of industrialization and globalization in terms of identity, history, and meaning?* Clearly, it would be difficult to argue that it should be a designer's ethical obligation to address a site's fullest sociocultural narrative, as it would be extraordinarily stymieing to the imaginative project. However, what I would like to argue is that the interpretation – through design – of the not-so-comfortable past or the stories of those marginalized citizens that occupy a site in the present, would provoke discourse – activating the public realm – and potentially enhance empathy for and understanding of those 'Other' from us.

Landscape architectural theorist Elizabeth Meyer takes on the issue of polluted or contaminated landscapes resulting from industrial processes and the field's too prompt instinct to ameliorate and restore without a critical interpretation of the processes of production *and consumption*, that contributed to the site's 'disturbed' condition (Meyer 2007). She calls this uncritical approach 'landscape camouflage' (after Engler 2004) which, she claims, 'masks the histories and processes of disturbed industrial sites and obliterates a connection that might render these parks more meaningful to the public' (Meyer 2007, 62). While she focuses largely on the interpretive potential of design to catalyze an environmentally responsible form of citizenship, which is not necessarily the primary emphasis here, Meyer's opposition to disguising the 'uncertainty and risk' associated with disturbed sites as 'places of anxiety and discomfort' is most essential to the current argument, particularly as applied to socially contested urban sites. She states,

> *Witnesses who encounter landscapes of disturbance, doubt, uncertainty, and beauty in their everyday experiences of a large park might be bewildered, moved to wonder and recentered ... What might happen if that experience of beauty within risk caused a collectivity of individuals to act differently in their everyday lives? We might truly know what the cultural agency of landscape could be.*
>
> (Meyer 2007, 82)

This same form of 'recentering' or 'destabilizing' the limits of our comfortable expectations – through a practice of expanded 'thick description' – may provoke us into awareness to think more critically about the social, cultural, political, and economic processes that impact the built world around us. This may, in turn, stimulate public discourse and heighten human compassion.

Alison B. Hirsch

Influences: interpretation and cultural landscape frameworks

The 'cultural agency of landscape' is most primary to a discussion on design as 'thick description' in the Geertzian and post-Geertzian sense. When Carl Sauer defined the term 'cultural landscape' in his 1925 essay, 'The Morphology of Landscape,' he stated simplistically yet provocatively, 'Culture is the agent, the natural area is the medium, the cultural landscape the result' (Sauer 1925). Clearly Sauer's description is too linear and ordered to resonate in our twenty-first-century context, and his line of inquiry inspired generations of scholars invested exclusively in rural, pre-industrial, and stable societies. Yet this idea of cultural *agency* is significant to the current study. It is through rituals, performances, and practices that culture is truly an agent of physical change. Significantly, geographer Kenneth Olwig challenges the lacking political dimension in cultural landscape studies by tracing the term's etymological associations with *landschaft,* a type of medieval settlement that retained some local autonomy from feudal administration. Neither Olwig nor I are suggesting that we can use this stable and contained form of pre-modern settlement as a point of comparison for understanding the city of today, but it is certainly useful to remember that landscape is a term whose roots are related to territory identified by 'its customs and culture, not by its physical characteristics' (Olwig 1996, 633; see also Cosgrove 2004, 61).

Cultural geographers and cultural landscape scholars are trained to read and interpret cultural process as it has shaped the environment. Yet their interpretive response remains in descriptive analysis while the objective of design is to not just describe (or map) but make physical moves – in the context of this chapter, moves that emerge from these sociocultural readings. Traditional ethnography is also a descriptive practice, hence the emphasis here on its more recent *critical* and transformative dimensions. Geertz's 'thick description' is an interpretive (representational) practice rather than (an impossible to achieve) neutral or objective description. Geertz states,

> *In short, anthropological writings are themselves interpretations, and second and third order ones to boot. By definition (only a 'native' makes first order ones: it's his* culture.*) They are, thus fictions; fictions, in the sense that they are 'something made,' 'something fashioned' – the original meaning of* fictio *– not that they are false, unfactual, or merely 'as if' thought experiments.*
>
> (Geertz 1973, 15)

Expanded 'thick description'

The creative implication of Geertz's argument – the 'something made' – is what is most significant to us here. Design (an outsider's task) becomes that interpretive process that generates new fictions or stories that ultimately stimulate transformative futures.

The work of architectural and social historian Dolores Hayden is clearly essential to my emphasis on 'thick description' and critical ethnography. Her comprehensive interpretive focus on both the sense of place and the politics of space are what propel the methodological ideologies presented below. Her writings, which aim to 'extend public history in the urban landscape' (Hayden 1995; 1997), prompted my question: *how do we interpret sites as socially contested territories in order to 'destabilize' and 'recenter' the public into new forms of awareness and engagement?*

Landscape architect Walter Hood's observational and interpretive practice partially responds to such questions. His method of registering – without judgment – the human patterns and practices that exist in a particular place to develop proposals for an enhanced public realm parallels the primary aim here. Amidst the discourse within the last fifteen to twenty years on landscape as infrastructure, Hood uniquely asks how 'public landscapes can be transformed to "perform better" as social infrastructure.' He continues,

> *As social infrastructure, public landscapes should build upon the common and the mundane practices that take place within them. The idiosyncratic arises from this process and forces us to learn more about one another. Meaning comes out of use, event, spectacle and the continuous practice of the everyday.*
>
> (Hood 2005, 145, 164)

Hood's method, proposed in *Urban Diaries* (Hood 1997) and implemented in meaningful places such as Poplar Street in Macon, Georgia and Lafayette Square in West Oakland, California, represents a highly localized practice (Hood and Erickson 2001). We might question how to apply these ideas to critically interpret the everyday in the context of larger social, economic and cultural flows that shape the city.

In 1991, James Corner called for the alternative of hermeneutics to counter the 'crisis of meaning' that he traces to the eighteenth-century 'break with tradition.' His framing of hermeneutics is another point of reference, as a transformative interpretation and translation of the circumstances of life into something new and fresh, both prompting us into awareness of our given situation and provoking us to think outside the confines of what is known. While Corner theorizes a poetically hermeneutical stance, he does not suggest how it can be deployed in the dynamic sociocultural context of the city. It is not until he abandons hermeneutics (meaning) for agency (use) that Corner begins to recognize the processes and politics of urbanization as perhaps integral to the landscape architectural project (Corner 1991; 1999a).

Within the field of landscape architecture, contemporary theory and practice that is focused on forces and processes of urbanization around the globe are predominantly invested in large-scale logistics or mitigating and interpreting sites of contamination ('disturbed sites'). But these same processes have clearly affected the social fabric of cities where 'difference, otherness, fragmentation, splintering, multiplicity, heterogeneity, diversity, plurality prevail' (Sandercock 2003, 1). It is through a thick description of these large-scale processes and the 'localization of [such] global forces' (Holston and Appadarai 1998, 3) that we can begin to shape an interpretive and transformative practice of landscape architecture.

METHODOLOGY

The methodology I am proposing might be best outlined by three phases: *observation* (in the form of on-the-ground fieldwork – as well as methods of historical ethnography); *interpretation* (of the fieldwork through representational practices of drawing, modeling, i.e. making); and *translation* (of interpretive drawings and readings into physical proposals for an expanded and enhanced public realm).

Observation: fieldwork

The intention is to frame the landscape architect as an ethnographer who conducts rigorous first-hand observational research in the field (Figure 9.1). This investigative process is pre-empted by anthropologist James Holston in his essay on 'Spaces of Insurgent Citizenship,'

> *In terms of methods, I mean to emphasize those of an urban ethnographer – or of a detective, which are similar: methods of tracing, observing, decoding, and tagging, at one moment of the investigation, and those of reconstructing identifying, presenting and rearticulating, at another. Both the trace and the*

Expanded 'thick description'

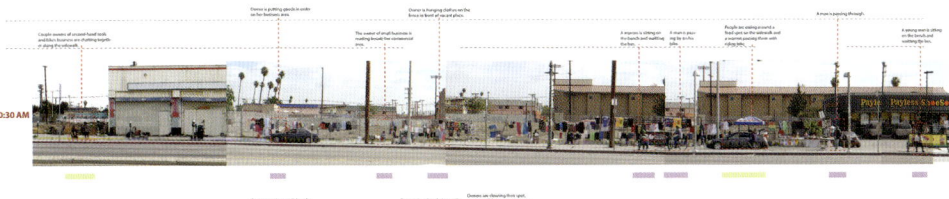
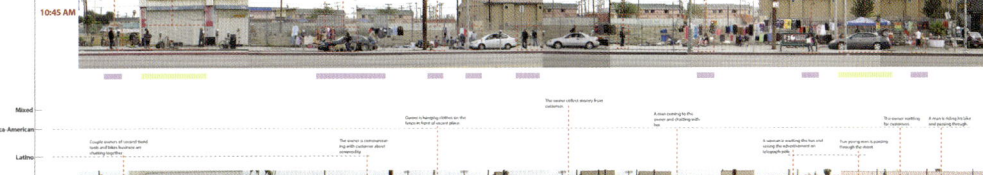

Figure 9.1 For my USC landscape architecture design studio course called *The Geography of Civil Unrest: Designing the Public Realm in the Insurgent Spaces of the City*, student Nan Cheng conducts fieldwork recording cultural appropriations along two major vacancies (still vacant since they were destroyed during the 1992 Uprisings) in South Central Los Angeles. She notates cross-cultural interaction and shifting rhythms throughout the day.

reconstruction compose this engagement with the ethnographic present. In this proposal, I am not suggesting that planners and architects become anthropologists, for anthropology is not reducible to ethnography. Rather, I suggest that they learn the methods of ethnographic detection and also learn to work with anthropologists … To reengage the social after the debacle of modernism's utopian attempts, however, requires expanding the idea of planning and architecture beyond this

> *preoccupation with execution and design. It requires looking into, caring for, and teaching about lived experience as lived. To plan the possible is, in this sense, to begin from an ethnographic conception of the social and its spaces of insurgence.*
>
> (Holston 1998, 172–173)

While the musings here do not directly address collaborations with social scientists, this is clearly worthwhile.[6] However, the social sciences rely on data – whether quantitative or qualitative – while the practice of landscape architecture is a creative endeavor, not a data-driven science. Too often designers have attempted to take a data-oriented approach to 'designing for user needs' (Francis 2003) and end up measuring and expressing the norms of the culturally dominant majority through the generation of design principles. William H. Whyte inevitably comes to mind here, as does Jan Gehl, both of whom have contributed significantly to the humanization of the urban environment, but have bordered on the formulaic. Rather than rely on the social sciences for data-driven design methods, the emphasis on the writings of anthropologists such as Geertz is to set the framework for a practice of landscape architecture that creatively interprets how people use, appropriate, and actively spatialize the city (Figure 9.2).

The fieldwork method is a tactical on-the-ground approach to design that clearly resists the modernist inheritance of 'master planning,' or an impositional practice of utopian dimensions. It is another means of setting up a '[landscape] architecture of resistance' put forth by Kenneth Frampton in 1983 (Frampton 1983). The theoretical foundations and methodological values of 'Everyday Urbanism' are useful here, including the reliance on Michel de Certeau and the tactical practices of everyday life (Certeau 1984), as well as Henri Lefebvre's rhythmanalytical project (Lefebvre 2004). However, while the ethnographic approach parallels attitudes of EU, it suggests that such means of studying the everyday can have more transformative results than the 'micro-utopias' proposed in the book (Crawford 2008, 10; Figure 9.3).

While Lefebvre's intellectual emphasis is the *spatial* – challenging the Marxist over-emphasis on the temporal or historical dimension – his writings on rhythmanalysis represent an effort to understand the relationship of time and space made manifest by the social and economic processes of everyday life. The spatio-temporal dimension is most primary to landscape, as a medium that is perpetually in the state of transformation. Thus, Lefebvre's studies of the rhythms of space–time are particularly applicable.

Expanded 'thick description'

Pushpanjali is an offering of flowers to Indian Gods. In Sanskrit, pushpam means "flower" and anjali means "offering with folded hands". So Pushpanjali means offering of flowers with folded hands.

Aarti is a part of puja, in which light from wicks soaked in ghee (purified butter) or camphor is offered to one or more deities. Aartis also refer to the songs sung in praise of the deity, when lamps are being offered.

Naivedhya - a Sanskrit word meaning supplication, is food offered to a Hindu deity as part of a worship ritual.

Anulepana or **gandha**. Perfumes and ointments are offered to an image or deity.

Vastra ("clothing"). A cloth is offered to symbolically adorn the godess ganga

Dhupa is, in dharmic religions (such as Hinduism, Buddhism, Jainism, etc.), the ritual offering of incense during puja to an image of a deity, or other object of veneration. It is also the Sanskrit word for incense or perfume itself.

Ganesha is one of the deities best-known and most widely worshipped in the Hindu pantheon regardless of religious affiliations. Devotion to Ganesha is widely diffused and extends to Jains, Buddhists, and beyond India. Although he is known by many other attributes, Ganesha's elephant head makes him particularly easy to identify. Ganesha is widely revered as the Remover of Obstacles and more generally as Lord of Beginnings and Lord of Obstacles patron of arts and sciences, and the deva of intellect and wisdom.

PUJA

(Sanskrit: reverence, honour, adoration, or worship) is a religious ritual performed by Hindus as an offering to various dieties, distinguished persons, or special guests. It is done on a variety of occasions and settings, from daily Puja in the home, to temple ceremonies and large fesivals, or to begin a new venture. Puja is modeled on the idea of giving a gift or offering to a diety or important person and recieving their blessing, (*Ashirvad*). There are many variations in scale, offering and ceremony. Puja is also performed on special occasions such as Durge Puja and Lakshmi Puja. The Puja ritual is performed by Hindus worldwide.

Figure 9.2 For our design studio called *Grounding Diaspora: Negotiating between Home and Host*, taught with Aroussiak Gabrielian at the University of Toronto, student Matthew Blunderfield traces the 'ritual deposition' along the shore of Jamaica Bay in Queens, NY. As a substitute for the Ganges River, the South Asian and Guyanese Hindus in the neighborhoods north deposit such offerings in Jamaica Bay during the Puja ritual, while Gateway National Park (Jamaica Bay) rangers continue to argue that the practice causes harm to the bay's fragile ecosystem. This point of contestation became the seed for the studio, which asked that the students design a public space infrastructure that accommodates the complex diasporic and transnational communities that make up this area. Here Blunderfield conducts fieldwork, recording the ritual deposits and their mythical sources and associated symbolism.

Lefebvre writes,

No rhythm without repetition in time and space, without reprises, without returns, in short without measure. But there is no identical absolute repetition … When it concerns the everyday rites, ceremonies, fêtes, rules and laws, there is always something new and unforeseen that introduces itself into the repetitive: difference.
(Lefebvre 2004, 6)

Lefebvre's 'theory of moments' – challenging Henri Bergson's *durée* or temporal continuum – emphasizes such instants when 'existing orthodoxies are open to challenge, when things have the potential to be overturned or radically altered'

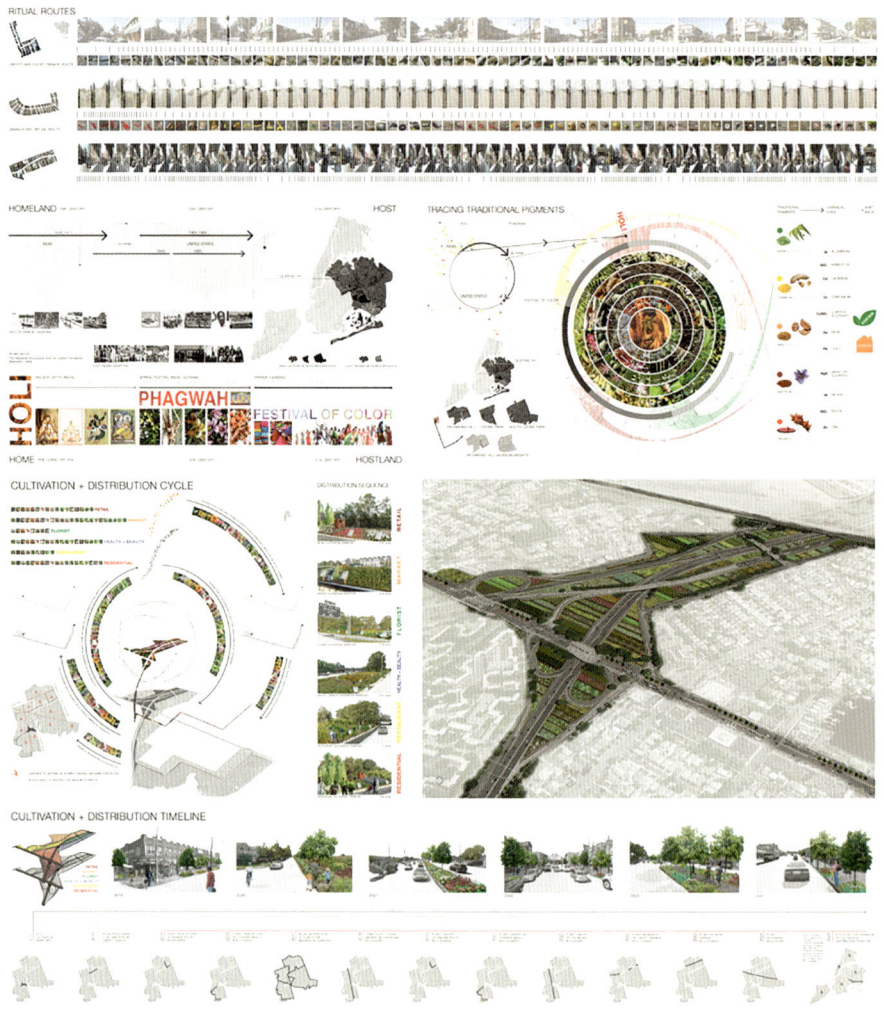

Figure 9.3 For our studio, *Grounding Diaspora*, student Robin O'Connell traced the transported cultural rituals (ritual processions) occurring in this area – the Hindu Puja ritual of depositing offerings at the water's edge, the Holi parade (or Phagwah, harvest festival), as well as the processions of daily life particular to this area. Her study continued with emphasis on Phagwah during which colored dyes and powders are strewn about to chase away the winter grays. Because synthetic dyes are now used rather than importing the natural source, the festival has been confined to a very small area. She meanwhile catalogued the Puja offerings found on the beach, including flowers, fruit, food, powder, and leaves (some which can also create natural powders for Holi) and then generated a list of alternative plants that are either native or naturalized in NY with specific attention to the original plants' traditional symbolism, its form and structure, and its range of uses. From this research she designed a cultivation infrastructure for those natural alternatives that would both generate offerings and other ritual products for sale in local shops along the processional routes. The entirety of this project is shown to demonstrate how this fieldwork/interpretation/translation process can catalyze large-scale transformative interventions (vs. the 'micro-utopias' of Everyday Urbanism).

(Elden 2004, x). The designer here must act as rhythmanalyst – measuring not just the production of space but the rhythms (and ruptures) that shape lived experience. While we register and notate the rhythms of the city through fieldwork, we *interpret* them through the intervening medium of drawing (modeling, etc.) and ultimately *translate* these drawings into physical design interventions – providing infrastructures that sustain and heighten both joyful interactions and those moments of 'difference' that 'destabilize' or 'recenter' us, allowing us to see beyond our existing circumstances and into new ways of occupying and negotiating the city.

Interpretation: representation

As stated, after fieldwork comes interpretation of the thickness of observations gathered, which for the landscape architect initially transpires through the act of drawing. As a creative *process* rather than an object of composition and communication, landscape architectural drawing negotiates between a given reality and an idea and between an idea and its physical embodiment. In other words, it both follows (through interpretation of a given circumstance) and precedes the world it represents. The analytical aspect of rhythmanalysis or fieldwork is not simply observing the dynamics of the city, but – in our case – visually interpreting these rhythms to see new patterns and relationships emerge (Figure 9.4).

In this framework, representation is critical action – an ideational process and speculative inquiry, rather than merely a vehicle for communication and delivery. Here I largely rely on James Corner's essays 'Representation and Landscape' (1992) and 'The Agency of Mapping' (1999b), which consider how visualization of the dynamic phenomena and temporal qualities of landscape serve as creative vehicles for design. Borrowing and elaborating on such ideas, the ethnographic method encourages the use of time-based representational techniques (sequential views, movement notations, filmic processes, etc.) to record and interpret the rhythms and rituals of the city and translate these interpretive frameworks into physical proposals (Figure 9.5).

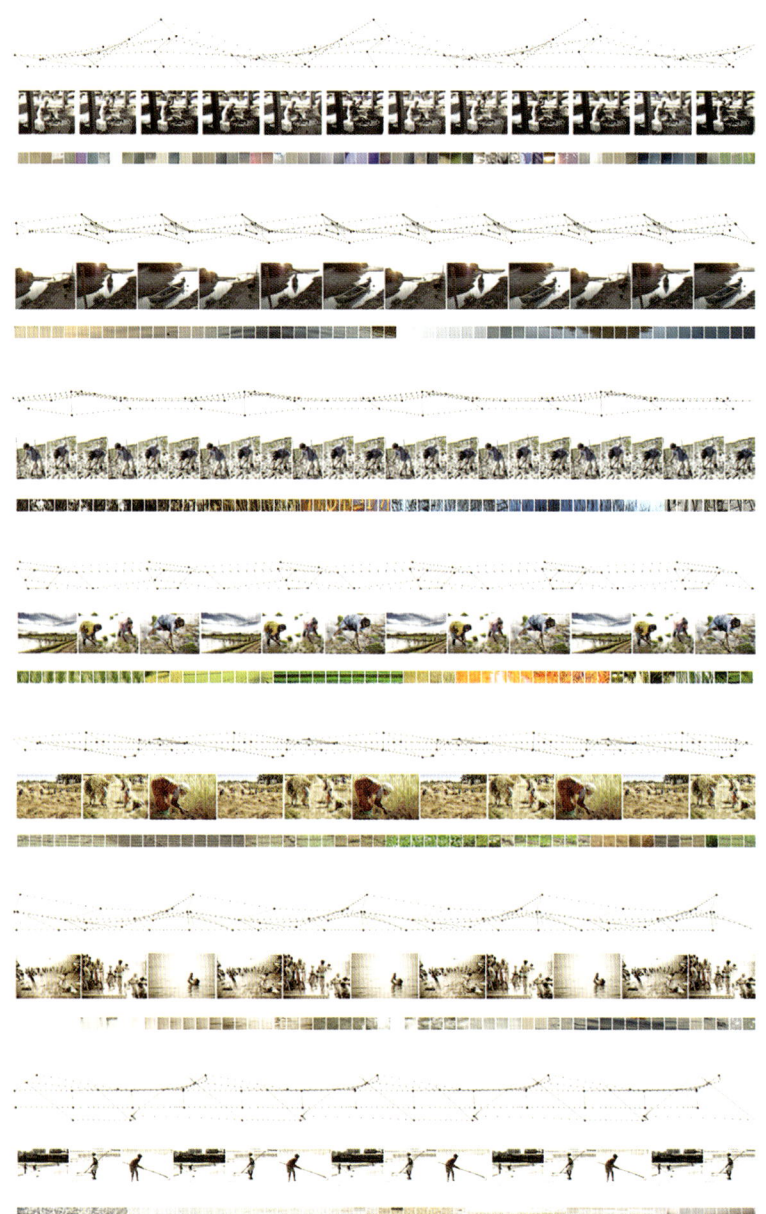

Figure 9.4 For this study, *foreground* (Gabrielian) generated a movement notation of the various acts of everyday labor that have profound impact on the shaping of the landscape of Mumbai and its region. This drawing contributed to the development of an infrastructural system that integrated and juxtaposed these cultural acts.

Figure 9.5 Detail from *foreground*'s competition proposal for the access points to the defunct elevated railway in Queens, New York (showing one of six designed sites of access). As one of the most ethnically diverse urban areas in the world, this proposal emerged from a rhythmic analysis of the musical traditions represented along the cultural transect of the railway. Intensive study of the characters and qualities unique to each musical genre – the meter, transitions, tonal range, level of improvisation, as well as the 'fusion of other cultural traditions – was translated into physical parameters that endow each of the sites with their own rhythmic experience and prompt variant forms of movement. As rites of passage or movement from the everyday city streets to this new elevated public realm, the rhythmic infrastructures are intended to heighten the transformative character of this thickened threshold.

Translation: physical propositions

The methodological and theoretical values proposed here support processes of insurgent citizenship, and the interpretation of the narratives, histories, and practices of the marginalized, the displaced, and the diasporic. The hope is – through methods of 'thick description' – we might transform urban places into discursive arenas for public debate, the negotiation of identities and new forms of collectivity. This aligns the pursuit with Richard Sennett's long insistence on living together not simply in tolerant indifference, but in active and meaningful intercultural engagement (Sennett 1994, 1970; Sandercock 2003, 358). Similarly, geographer Ash Amin identifies tangible sites of 'banal transgression,' or places of habitual engagement where such forms of negotiation and exchange are currently possible – such as the workplace, schools, sports clubs, and community and youth centers, etc. (Sandercock 2003, 94; Amin 2002). Amin continues:

> *Cultural change in these circumstances is likely to be encouraged if people can step out of their daily environments into other spaces acting as sites of 'banal transgression'. Here too, interaction is of a prosaic nature, but these sites work as spaces of cultural displacement and destabilisation. Their effectiveness lies in placing people from different backgrounds in new settings where engagement with strangers in a common activity disrupts easy labelling of the stranger as enemy and initiates new attachments. They are moments of cultural destabilisation, offering individuals the chance to break out of fixed relations and fixed notions, and through this, to learn to become different through new patterns of social interaction.*
>
> (Amin 2002)

I include this quote to provoke designers to take on the challenge of providing physical frameworks for places of cultural destabilization and initiation and new patterns of social interaction. It is through culturally interpretive practices that that such 'banal' or everyday places can be appropriately situated and designed for new forms of encounter. Amin justifiably declares that sanctioned public spaces are too often 'territorialized by particular groups' and are places of surveillance, ensuring that people are operating within particular standards of behavior. The need for sites of *discursive negotiation* is more pressing today than ever as we exist in a period of heightened fear and suspicion of 'the Other' (Figure 9.6). Through adopted methods and practices of expanded thick description and critical ethnography, the landscape architect can transform the specific and circumstantial realities of 'what is' into such meaningful proposals for 'what could be.'

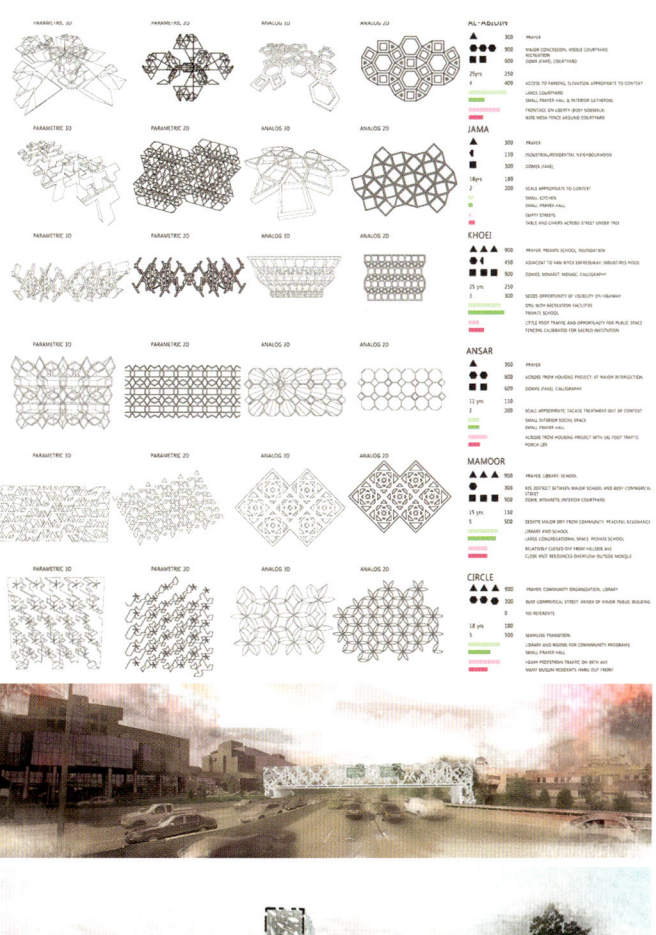

Figure 9.6 For our studio, *Grounding Diaspora*, student Javid Alibhai addressed diaspora and security and access by focusing on the Islamic presence within the site. The six mosques that occupy it were then surrounded by security fencing and surveillance. The student transformed that particular marking of territory from one of defense and restriction to one that heightened access, urban experience, and creative exchange. Since the arabesque plays an essential role in the identification and marking of Islamic space, the student generated his own arabesque patterning through analog and digital scripting by assigning certain characteristics or parameters embodied by the mosques to specific geometries. Using the patterns generated for each mosque, he proposed interventions for each. The three pictured (top to bottom) include: (1) a bridge crossing over the highway to the mosque that provides enhanced access and processional experience, extending the sacred space into the public realm; (2) a minaret or 'public observatory' – that marks a new community center underground; (3) the transformation of an underutilized portion of the mosque's parking lot into a basketball court that dually serves as a prayer space with qibla wall.

Alison B. Hirsch

NOTES

1. On a few occasions, landscape architect James Corner has adopted Geertz's notion of 'thick description' (see Corner 1999a; 2013). Yet what Corner's writings seem to leave for future scholarship is how such ethnographic investigation into sociocultural dynamics of a particular place might also serve as an 'agent of creativity,' a phrase he uses often.

2. Hal Foster's essay is highly critical of the 'artist as ethnographer,' in which he claims 'the turn to the ethnographic' is actually a pseudoethnographic practice that is still 'commissioned, indeed franchised,' thus framed by the institution, which often means little actual contact with communities and sites and thus it is not the artist that is 'decentered' but 'the other' that is 'fashioned in artistic guise.' While a useful critique for our purposes, the intention here is to frame a tactical practice that attempts to subvert institutional order. Foster does admit that such practices have been successful at such things as 'recovering suppressed histories' (Foster 1996).

3. I am using the term 'methodology' deliberately here as opposed to 'method' since 'methodology' refers to the study of the principles from which particular methods have developed (while methods refers to the specificities of techniques).

4. Rather than 'multicultural,' planning theorist Leonie Sandercock's term 'mongrel' is more apt for the condition of the contemporary city because of the sterilization of the former term (Sandercock 2003; see also Hall 2000).

5. Holston's term 'insurgent citizenship' refers to the opposition to the modernist political (and spatial) project which declares that the state is 'the only legitimate source of citizenship rights, meanings, and practices.' In the essay he focuses on the spaces that subvert the order, regulation and homogeneity of modernist city space.

6. Setha Low, for instance, has long been contributing to cultural landscape management and designs for the public realm and her ethnographic method informs the 'thick description' framework here.

REFERENCES

Amin, Ash. 2002. 'Ethnicity and the Multicultural City.' In *Report for the Department of Transport, Local Government and the Regions and the ESRC Cities Initiative*. Durham, UK: University of Durham.

Appadurai, Arjun. 1990. 'Disjuncture and Difference in the Global Cultural Economy.' *Theory, Culture & Society* 7(2): 295–310.

Beardsley, John. 2007. 'Conflict and Erosion: The Contemporary Public Life of Large Parks.' In *Large Parks*, edited by Julia Czerniak and George Hargreaves, 199–213. New York: Princeton Architectural Press.

Certeau, Michel de. 1984. *The Practice of Everyday Life*. Berkeley: University of California.

Corner, James. 1991. 'A Discourse on Theory II: Three Tyrannies of Contemporary Theory and the Alternative of Hermeneutics.' *Landscape Journal* 10(20): 115–133.

Corner, James. 1992. 'Representation and Landscape: Drawing and Making in the Landscape Medium.' *Word & Image* 8(3): 243–275.

Corner, James. 1999a. 'Introduction: Recovering Landscape as a Critical Cultural Practice.' In *Recovering Landscape: Essays in Contemporary Landscape Architecture*, edited by James Corner, 1–26. New York: Princeton Architectural Press.

Corner, James. 1999b. 'The Agency of Mapping.' In *Mappings*, edited by Denis Cosgrove, 213–252. London: Reaktion.

Corner, James. 2006. 'Terra Fluxus.' In *The Landscape Urbanism Reader,* edited by Charles Waldheim, 21–33. New York: Princeton Architectural Press.

Corner, James. 2013. 'The Thick and the Thin of It.' Paper presented at the *Thinking Contemporary Landscape* conference, Hanover, Germany, June 20–22.

Cosgrove, Denis. 2004. 'Landscape and *Landschaft*.' *GHI Bulletin* 35: 57–71.

Crawford, Margaret. 2008. 'Introduction.' In *Everyday Urbanism: Expanded,* edited by John Chase, Margaret Crawford, and Kaliski John, 6–11. New York: The Monacelli Press.

Elden, Stuart. 2004. 'Rhythmanalysis: An Introduction.' In *Rhythmanalysis: Space, Time and Everyday Life,* by Henri Lefebvre, vii–xv. London/New York: Continuum.

Engler, Mira. 2004. *Designing America's Waste Landscapes*. Baltimore: Johns Hopkins University Press.

Foster, Hal. 1996. 'The Artist as Ethnographer.' In *The Return of the Real*, by Hal Foster, 171–204. Cambridge, MA: MIT Press.

Frampton, Kenneth. 1983. 'Critical Regionalism: Six Points for an Architecture of Resistance.' In *The Anti-Aesthetic: Essays on Postmodern Culture,* edited by Hal Foster, 16–30. Seattle: Bay Press.

Francis, Mark. 2003. *Urban Open Space: Designing for User Needs.* Washington: Island Press.

Geertz, Clifford. 1973. 'Thick Description: Toward an Interpretive Theory of Culture.' In *The Interpretation of Cultures: Selected Essays*, by Clifford Geertz, 3–30. New York: Basic Books.

Girot, Christopher. 1999. 'Four Trace Concepts in Landscape Architecture.' In *Recovering Landscape: Essays in Contemporary Landscape Architecture*, edited by James Corner, 59–67. New York: Princeton Architectural Press.

Hall, Stuart. 2000. 'Conclusion: The Multicultural Question.' In *Un/settled Multiculturalisms: Diasporas, Entanglements, Transruptions,* edited by Barnor Hesse, 209–241. London/New York: Zed Books.

Harvey, David. 2005. 'Where is the Outrage?' *The Newsletter of the Architectural League of New York*: 4–7.

Hayden, Dolores. 1995. *The Power of Place*. Cambridge, MA: MIT Press.

Hayden, Dolores. 1997. 'Urban Landscape History: The Sense of Place and the Politics of Space.' In *Understanding Ordinary Landscapes,* edited by Paul Groth and Todd Bressi, 111–133. New Haven: Yale University.

Holston, James. 1998. 'Spaces of Insurgent Citizenship.' In *Cities and Citizenship*, edited by James Holston, 155–174. Durham, NC: Duke University.

Holston, James and Arjun Appadurai. 1998. 'Introduction: Cities and Citizenship.' In *Cities and Citizenship*, edited by James Holston, 1–18. Durham, NC: Duke University.

Hood, Walter. 1997. *Walter Hood: Urban Diaries*. Washington, DC: Spacemaker Press.

Hood, Walter. 2005. 'Landscape as Social Infrastructure.' In *The Mesh Book: Landscape/Infrastructure*, edited by Jessica Blood and Julian Raxworthy, 148–168. Melbourne: RMIT.

Hood, Walter and Melissa Erickson. 2001. 'Storing Memories in the Yard.' In *Sites of Memory: Perspectives on Architecture and Race*, edited by Craig Evan Barton, 171–189. New York: Princeton Architectural Press.

Hunt, John Dixon. 1978. 'Ut pictura poesis, the Picturesque, and John Ruskin.' *MLN* 93(5): 794–818.

Lefebvre, Henri. 2004. *Rhythmanalysis: Space, Time and Everyday Life*. London/New York: Continuum.

Madison, D. Soyini. 2011. *Critical Ethnography: Methods, Ethics, Performance*. New York, Sage.

Meyer, Elizabeth. 2007. 'Uncertain Parks: Disturbed Sites, Citizens, and Risk Society.' In *Large Parks*, edited by Julia Czerniak and George Hargreaves, 58–85. New York: Princeton Architectural Press.

Olwig, Kenneth R. 1996. 'Recovering the Substantive Nature of Landscape.' *Annals of the Association of American Geographers* 86(4): 630–653.

Sandercock, Leonie. 2003. *Cosmopolis II: Mongrel Cities of the 21st Century*. London/New York: Bloomsbury Academic.

Sauer, Carl. 1925. 'The Morphology of Landscape.' *University of California Publications in Geography* 2(2): 19–53.

Sennett, Richard. 1970. *Uses of Disorder*. New York: Vintage Books.

Sennett, Richard. 1994. *Flesh and Stone*. New York: W.W. Norton.

Soja, Edward. 1996. *Thirdspace: Journeys to Los Angeles and other Real-and-Imagined Places*. New York: Wiley/Blackwell.

Soja, Edward. 1998. 'Los Angeles: 1965–1992.' In *The City: Los Angeles and Urban Theory at the End of the Twentieth Century*, edited by Allen J. Scott and Edward W. Soja, 426–462. Berkeley: University of California.

Waldheim, Charles. 2006. 'Introduction: A Reference Manifesto.' In *The Landscape Urbanism Reader*, edited by Charles Waldheim, 13–19. New York: Princeton Architectural Press.

10

Urban morphology phenomena

Post-industrial urban landscapes

Laura Lovell-Anderson

Deindustrialization phenomena imperils urban form and infrastructure caused by the acute alteration of topographies that are vulnerable to ecological, economic, and social decline. Interwoven within the built urban periphery, these sites are often misunderstood as 'waste landscapes', and frequently perceived as deteriorated, hazardous, and unusable. It is a growing cross-cultural problem that continues to grow exponentially in both size and complexity as the global economy shifts from a system reliant on the tangible (via products and manufacturing) towards a market dominated by the intangible (via services and data). The consequence is a complex emerging urban phenomena consisting of post-industrially scarred sites and topographies within the dense urban landscape.

Urban morphology phenomena

Defunct economic and production systems founded on principles of globalization, outsourcing, and decentralization have forced previously thriving industrialized sites to discontinue activity, leaving behind a collection of urbanized post-industrial landscapes (Berger 2006). The remains of these large industrial built environments are static and marked by fragility, as the planning and development strategies relied on at their inception frequently omitted comprehensive consideration for the end of use and landscape reprogramming for future uses. Marked by fragmented environments and structures along an altered topography interwoven within the urban periphery, these sites are often understood to be 'waste landscapes' in that they are characteristically understood as deteriorated and unusable (Berger 2008; Loures 2006). This emerging urban phenomenon spurs an altered type of decline among the cultural, social, ecological, and economic fabric of communities prone to the onset of waste landscapes.

While deindustrialization and waste landscape phenomena have been extensively researched and documented, absent from the discussion are: the larger system(s) in which this condition or phenomena is an instance of; a set of forms or a vocabulary to define the boundaries of such, and the reciprocal design/morphology and policy/structure premise for the occurrence of these phenomena (Steadman 1979; Pawlyn 2011). Further it is unclear as to how these conditions impact the productive reintegration of dormant and static urban landscapes (Mehrotra 2011). This chapter will explore the innovative processes associated with public policy and land reclamation while adding to the current discourse of sustainable landscapes. Finally, the chapter is organized to identify and describe the formation, defining characteristics, permeation/occurrence attributes, and phenomena of obsolete post-industrial urban landscapes; current policy narratives shaping 'waste landscape' revitalization through a design for sustainability discourse; and prospective surrounding the concept of kinetic urban morphology in the phenomena's context.

FORMATION CONDITIONS

The sprawling implementation of mechanized manufacturing processes was the primary impetus for economic expansion that occurred during the first 'industrial' revolution of 1760. In a global transition from hand production to machined production processes, Industrial manufacturing sites were methodically planned and situated to effectively make use of a region's natural climate and landscape. In concert to the growth of the industrial infrastructure was the formulation of dense urban areas that emerged around hubs of activity, especially in the northeastern United States. These industrial cities were situated in close proximity to a variety of natural resources such as quarries, coastlines, and forests, as well as access to transportation via canals, roads, and railways. The revolution perpetuated the rise of modern capitalism when new, efficient machinery introduced unprecedented possibilities for expanding material development. Innumerable benefits were instantly recognized, yet there were both short- and long-term consequences that gradually yet persistently began to reshape the world.

In a mode of expansion, the second industrial 'technological' revolution began in 1860, where the electrification of factories amplified mechanized production methods, thus increasing the capacity for mass production via the production line (Bluestone and Harrison 1982). Concurrent to the technological advancements was the unprecedented rise of transportation infrastructure in the form of roads, railways, and canals (Cowie and Heathcott 2003). This expansion was possible due to the progression in steam, oil, and electricity as primary energy sources, in conjunction with the introduction of electrical communication.

In progression, the third industrial 'digital' revolution of the 1950s initiated a transition from the analog mechanical processes and electric technologies towards a digital industry. In such a culture, a cooperative and decentralized technological network has created momentum in developing a complex, dynamic global information and communication network revolving around the interrelationship of technological and human interactions. The deviation to a network-reliant society is a result of a monumental shift from the isolation of computers and technology for data storage and processing to integration, reliance, and sharing of information and power in global electronic networks. The global economic transition from mass production and mass consumption of the tangible products and manufacturing towards a market dominated by the intangibility of services and data have resulted in the evolution of post-industrial systems for design, recognized as post-industrial urbanism.

The unwavering knowledge-oriented economy marked by digital industry comes with the consequence of urban deindustrialization phenomena. Decades of economic globalization, overseas outsourcing, and decentralization have forced these industrialized sites to discontinue activity, leaving behind a collection of scarred physical landscapes.

Urban morphology phenomena

PERMEATION AND OCCURRENCE ATTRIBUTES

Clusters of urban blight and decay amass post-industrial areas and their surrounding communities throughout the United States, where more than 40,000 US manufacturing sites have closed between 2001 and 2008 (McCormack 2009). This results in immediate economic decline, and long-term stagnation. Acres of unkempt, vacant lots have a decreased property value and overall appeal to investors and new businesses, obstructing local development plans and threatening opportunities within the residential, economic, and social sectors. These physical locations are now sagging under the weight of the planning and development strategies relied on at their inception which omitted comprehensive consideration of some potential long-term consequences regarding the impact of the interrelationship between natural resources and responsible human consumption of such, along with reuse and elimination (Kirkwood 2001). The resulting negative outcomes on cultural, social, ecological, and economic systems cannot be isolated from one another and independently viewed.

While post-industrial landscapes should be recognized as dynamic or in flux, and in constant transformation, six forms of waste landscapes operate in the contemporary urban context including wastescapes of dwellings, transition, infrastructure, obsolescence, exchange, or contamination (Berger 2006). Of these sites, wastescapes of contamination which Berger (2006, 220) describes as including 'public and federal installations such as airports, military bases, ammunition depots and training grounds, and sites used for mining and petroleum and chemical operations' are resistant to site remediation and waste containment, proving to be extremely difficult or impossible to be reintroduced as urban environments. This is largely attributed to the fact that these landscapes are abandoned or underutilized, having been permanently altered due to actual or perceived contamination by hazardous or toxic substances introduced in their prior use. Further, the sites are prone to urban decay, a condition of waste landscapes marked by ecological peril, economic dysfunction, infrastructure decay, racial polarization, social turmoil, and cultural disorientation (US Environmental Protection Agency 2015). Many waste landscapes are an amalgam of the six classifications in conjunction to elements of urban decay, further complicating the unique nature of these sites. Further complicating the phenomena is the correlational gap between design-based post-industrial urbanism phenomena and current policy narratives for design for sustainability.

Laura Lovell-Anderson

THE LEGAL LANDSCAPE

With regard to urban morphology and the post-industrial landscape, public policy guides designers, architects, and urban planners in the productive reintegration of dormant and static urban waste landscape through a design for sustainability discourse. Policy and law provides the contextual framework, courses of action, regulatory measures, and funding strategies that may be used to reduce the impact of damages of complex, interwoven issues including ecological, economic, and social problems frequently associated with post-industrial urban landscape phenomena. The process of reprogramming a post-industrial waste landscape dramatically alters the social, ecological, and economic fabric of communities. Environmental risks are related to natural resource consumption required for remediation; disposal processes of toxic waste and soil excavation; air pollution resulting from aeration of soils at a contaminated site; vegetation changes should bioremediation be implemented; unintended groundwater contamination; disruption of water flow, and containment of soil contaminants. Additionally, there are social risks related to public health and increased focus on the possibility of public health impacts from exposure to hazardous substances during reclamation. As such, a series of federal, state, and municipal regulatory laws and programs function to protect the environment, reduce blight, and lessen development pressures of green spaces and working lands, however, in the context of post-industrial urban landscape phenomena, policy is disconnected from the design practices and sustainability measures of reprogramming and reintegration efforts.

Pertinent national policy and legislation such as the current Pollution Prevention Act, the Clean Air Act, the Safe Drinking Water Act, as well as the Comprehensive Environmental Response, Compensation, and Liability Act (CERCLA or 'Superfund') provide provisions designed to prevent the occurrence of or reduce the risk of water, air, and land contamination surrounding active and inactive sites at the urban periphery. They typically include short-term provisions, where governmental agencies are authorized to take action to address releases or threatened releases requiring prompt response, as well as long-term responses designed to permanently and significantly reduce the hazards associated with releases or threats of releases of toxic substances (US Environmental Protection Agency 2015). However, omitted from such policy and legislation is the inclusion of provisions to blend the complex and multidisciplinary aspects of the biological and physical sciences, law, and economic aspects of productive reintegration and reprogramming often orchestrated by non-governmental agencies (Berger 2008).

Further, the skewed balance between economic, environmental, and social benefits exist, where the economic benefits are the primary driver of these acts, and the social and ecological characteristics considered secondary. This is largely due to the fact that the prevention of environmental disasters avoids the need for expensive federally- and privately-funded investments in waste management or cleanup initiatives.

PROSPECTIVE

The larger system(s) in which this condition or phenomena is an instance of has yet to be distinguished, as this contemporary phenomenon is unique and without precedent, and reflects a symptomatic consequence with no root cause born from another existing problem (Rittel and Webber 1972). Additionally, the complex dynamics with which it intersects are idiosyncratic. The boundaries between such phenomena and context are not clearly evident (Yin 2003), therefore, its body of knowledge and conceptual home must be shaped through identification and study of spatial and behavioral patterns from the phenomena relationships. In the phenomenon, a simultaneous process of deindustrialization and urbanism (Berger 2008), it is essential to identify and develop a set of forms and vocabulary to define the boundaries, characteristics, and patterns of the phenomena. As new and increasingly complex issues surrounding these sites emerge, it will be necessary to develop a framework for understanding and analyzing the many forces directed at dormant and static post-industrial urban landscapes. Current research omits the development of such framework, further complicating the balance between design/morphology and policy/structure issues related to programing and reuse. Therefore, these post-industrial situations require the careful consideration and analysis of its previous architecture, landscape elements, and programming.

REFERENCES

Berger, Alan. 2006. *Drosscape: Wasting Land in Urban America*. New York: Princeton Architectural Press.

Berger, Alan. 2008. *Designing the Reclaimed Landscape*. London: Taylor & Francis.

Bluestone, Barry and Bennett Harrison. 1982. *The Deindustrialization of America: Plant Closings, Community Abandonment, and the Dismantling of Basic Industry*. New York: Basic Books.

Cowie, Jefferson and Joseph Heathcott. 2003. *Beyond the Ruins: The Meanings of Deindustrialization*. Ithaca: ILR Press.

Kirkwood, Niall. 2001. *Manufactured Sites: Rethinking the Post-Industrial Landscape*. London: Spon Press.

Loures, L. 2006. *(Re)-developing Post-industrial Landscapes: Applying Inverted Translational Research Coupled with the Case Study Research Method*. IPP – Politecnic Institute of Portalegre – ES AE; CIEO – Centre of Spatial Research and Organizations – UALG.

McCormack, R.A. 2009. *Manufacturing a Better Future for America*. Washington, DC: Alliance for American Manufacturing.

Mehrotra, Rahul. 2011. 'The Static and the Kinetic.' In Richard Burdett and Deyan Sudjic, *Living in the Endless City: The Urban Age Project by the London School of Economics and Deutsche Bank's Alfred Herrhausen Society*. London: Phaidon Press Ltd.

Pawlyn, Michael. 2011. *Biomimicry in Architecture*. London: Riba Publishing.

Rittel, Horst W.J. and Melvin M. Webber. 1972. *Dilemmas in a General Theory of Planning*. Berkeley: Institute of Urban and Regional Development, University of California.

Steadman, Philip. 1979. *The Evolution of Designs: Biological Analogy in Architecture and the Applied Arts*. Cambridge: Cambridge University Press.

US Environmental Protection Agency (2015) *Superfund: Law, Policy, and Guidance*. www.epa.gov/superfund/superfund-policy-guidance-and-laws (accessed July 3, 2015).

Yin, Robert K. 2003. *Case Study Research: Design and Methods*. Thousand Oaks, California: Sage Publications.

11

Ecological urbanism
The synthesis of ethics, aesthetics, and cybernetics

Iman Ansari

In the past decade, ecological urbanism has emerged as an interdisciplinary design process that responds to unprecedented environmental challenges such as rapid urbanization, the exponential growth in population, a growing scarcity of natural resources, and the looming consequences of climate change. This chapter traces the genesis of ecological urbanism in the synthesis of three modes of cultural consciousness: ethics, aesthetics, and cybernetics. By describing moments, or episodes, where nature and technology converge, the chapter also explores the uncharted territories opened up by this holistic approach to design and their potential for redefining our understanding of the environment.

Figure 11.1 The *Blue Marble* in its original orientation taken by Apollo 17 commander Eugene Cernan from the Command Module *America*, December 23, 1972.

Source: courtesy of NASA.

Ecological urbanism

EPISODE 1: THE BLUE MARBLE

On December 7, 1972, during NASA's last manned lunar mission, the Apollo 17 crew captured an image of Earth (NASA 2012). The translunar photograph, AS17-148-22727, a.k.a. the *Blue Marble,* was taken at about five hours and six minutes into the flight from a distance of some 28,000 miles from Earth (Figure 11.1). In this extraterrestrial image, Earth's fully illuminated hemisphere expands from the Mediterranean Sea to Antarctica and from the Indian Ocean to the Atlantic. As white clouds swirl over deep blue oceans, Africa appears at the center of the globe – what a beautiful irony! Thousands of years of evolutionary history, from our first migration out of Africa to our last voyage into space, is collapsed into a single image: as we leave home and embark on a new journey, pondering our fate in the outer space, we look back at the continent – and now the planet – we leave behind. The closed circle of our warm, colorful planet is framed by an infinite, cold, and dark void of uncertainties that surrounds us.

The *Blue Marble* was more than a snapshot of our space odyssey. It revealed the fragility of our planet: a borderless, interconnected, and isolated mass suspended in a vast expanse of space. As soon as the photograph surfaced on magazine covers, newspapers, posters, and television programs, it became ingrained in our subconscious. The photograph became a Lacanian mirror in the developmental stage of our global psyche. For most of us on Earth, the *mirror* revealed an image of humanity, our collectivity, and our fragile environment. For the astronauts aboard Apollo 17, the *mirror* depicted an image of a closed system, a space capsule floating in the celestial void – what Buckminster Fuller called 'Spaceship Earth' (Fuller 1969). Caught at the intersection of the *symbolic* imagery and the *imaginary* world of Gaia and the Galilean cosmos, the photograph revealed the *real* at a moment when one spaceship looks at another.

But if the image in the *mirror* was familiar to us, it was also alien: Antarctica on top and the North Pole at the bottom, the East to the left and the West to the right. Had we gotten it wrong the whole time? Or did the weightless astronaut holding the camera not know up from down? The image is also without a foreground – or any ground for that matter – to situate or locate the viewer: it has no perspective. It is a perfectly objective representation – a large circle inscribed in a black square. The perspectival vanishing point, the very point on which our cone of vision converges, and the one that orients and locates us in the image, has expanded to an enormous floating sphere that nearly fills the entire picture plane: a translunar selfie without a real self. By offering the viewer an all-encompassing image of Earth and, at the same time, removing the subject from the image, NASA's photographs of the globe, as Denis Cosgrove has described, are "simultaneously 'true' representations and virtual spaces" (Cosgrove 2001, 257).

How are we to read this image or orient ourselves vis-à-vis this new representation of the world? As it turns out, NASA rotated the photograph 180 degrees before releasing it, so the image corresponded to the way Earth had conventionally been represented – after all, the image in a mirror is always reversed. Earth is represented as an astronomical mass, captured, cropped, rotated, and publicized, recalling Martin Heidegger's fear of 'the world conceived and grasped as a picture' (Heidegger 1977, 129). The *Blue Marble* not only collapsed time, but space itself; it is an image becoming a map.

Despite this, the *Blue Marble* reoriented us in more ways than we did the image. Released in the wake of the political upheavals of 1968, during the rise of environmental activism in the 1970s, and just before the 1973 oil crisis and the recession that followed it, the *Blue Marble* almost instantly became a countercultural icon, representing – even catalyzing – a new global consciousness, a call for planetary unity and environmental conscience (Kurgan 2013, 9). The image was embraced across a variety of spectrums: from NGOs advocating human rights in the developing world to social activists fighting for civil rights and environmentalists seeking to protect endangered species and wild habitats around the world. It put a face to the inextricably interrelated challenges of our times: the frailty of our atmosphere, the depletion of our natural resources, the rapid urbanization of our planet, even socio-economic inequalities and political instabilities across the globe. It reminded us that our planet is a closed system, that Earth is as fragile as the spaceships we send to outer space, that we cannot escape the consequences of our actions. And this was perhaps the most significant achievement of our explorations of space. More than a New Frontier leading us towards outer space, as Bruno Latour has observed, the Apollo missions led us to inner space (Latour 2010). The most meaningful discovery of those missions turned out to be nothing but the very planet we left behind: on our way to the Moon, we discovered Earth.

This ecological awakening, materialized by NASA's captivating images of Earth, was a gradual process that began over a century earlier with the work of many naturalists, botanists, scientists, and environmentalists. The result of their work was the development of the concept, and later the science, of *ecology*, which redefined the relations of organisms to one another and to their milieu. But more than a new scientific approach, the underlying premise of this recently emerged mode of understanding was a philosophical one, namely, ethics. With nature no longer considered man's property, a new understanding, or respect, for the nonhuman members of the biosphere emerged. The burgeoning field of ecology implied a moral dilemma: How are we to relate to our fellow organisms in the post-Darwinian world where man's relation to the natural environment has been entirely re-scripted? That is to say, what determines and regulates the relations of organisms to one another and to their environment in the absence of any supernatural or spiritual supremacy?

Aldo Leopold, American scientist and environmentalist, was the first to recognize the philosophical underpinning of this paradigmatic shift. In his 1949 landmark essay, 'The Land Ethic,' he argued for the extension of moral principles to nonhuman members of the 'biotic community' – including 'soil, waters, plants, and animals, or collectively, the *land*' (Leopold 1949, 204). Leopold's concept of *land* embodied, literally and metaphorically, the ground for a new ecological conscience. For him, thinking about the environment ethically was not only an evolutionary possibility but an ecological necessity. Two decades later, Scottish landscape architect Ian McHarg expanded Leopold's ideas to design and planning. McHarg viewed *ecology* as 'the only bridge between the natural sciences and the planning and design professions,' and he devised an 'Ecological Method' – described in a 1967 essay of the same title – that understood nature as a process and, therefore, design as an adaptation to that ecological process (McHarg 1967, 105–107). Through the work of Leopold and McHarg, among others, the concept of *ecology* came to replace traditional notions of *landscape*, signaling a paradigmatic shift that demanded a new theoretical and practical approach to both conservation and planning. By 1972, when the *Blue Marble* appeared, this new approach was understood not only as an environmental necessity or a design strategy, but also as a moral imperative.

EPISODE 2: THE LONDON ZOO

On the morning of July 27, 1844, in Sleepy Hollow, Massachusetts, American novelist Nathaniel Hawthorne narrates a 'little event' in his journal. As he sits in his green retreat, enjoying the harmony and tranquility of nature, he is startled by the shriek of a locomotive whistle: 'But, hark! there is the whistle of the locomotive – the long shriek, harsh, above all other harshness, for the space of a mile cannot mollify it into harmony' (Hawthorne 1932, 102–105). Hawthorne's 'little event' presents us with an astonishing picture of the forces of industrialization in the mid-nineteenth century. The locomotive – powered by the steam engine and associated with fire, iron, speed, and noise – is the emblem of the new industrial power that is shattering the peaceful harmony of the countryside. Hawthorne's portrayal of the machine as a crude, masculine, and aggressive intruder is contrasted with his idyllic, feminine, and submissive view of nature – with man in a very uncomfortable position in between. This vivid contrast, as Leo Marx argues in his book, *The Machine in the Garden*, expresses 'the symbolic power' of the 'little event' in Sleepy Hollow and is emblematic of the great confrontation that took place between the *garden* (nature) and the *machine* (technology) in the nineteenth century. This was no 'little' event. In many ways, as Marx has noted, Hawthorne's 'little event' is 'a miniature of a great – in many ways the greatest – event in our history' (Marx 1964, 27).

The long-held dichotomy between nature and technology existed in Western culture long before the Industrial Revolution. From Homer's accounts of the *Garden of Alcinous* to Virgil's *Eclogues* and the figure-ground cartography of Giambattista Nolli's *Pianta Grande di Roma*, the *machine* and the *garden* have occupied different grounds: the city here, the country there. And this opposition produced two irreconcilable aesthetic approaches to the built environment. Nowhere is the clash of these ideologies more visible than in nineteenth-century industrial cities. While gardens and parks, though man-made, continued to emulate the picturesque aesthetics of nature, cities became increasingly ordered, Euclidean, and *machinic*. With the exception of the *Jardin à la Française*, this aesthetic opposition increased with urbanization, leading to a formal demarcation between 'architecture' and 'landscape'. But Hawthorne's 'little event' implied a radical change in the conventional pattern; an unprecedented situation, where the *machine* is invading the *garden*, transforming the way it looks and sounds, and imposing a new dominion over it. Astutely, Marx embraces 'the machine in the garden' and sees this shift as an abandonment of traditionally sentimental views of nature in favor of a new, complex 'pastoralism of the mind' (Marx 1964, 32). The most distinctive attribute of this new order is technological power, which is no longer confined to its traditional boundaries and threatens to break down, once and for all, the conventional polarity between the *garden* and the *machine*, between the country and the city, between *ecology* and *urbanism*.

How did this transformation come about? During the Industrial Revolution, the steam engine was instrumental in determining relations of force around processes of displacement. Informed by the second law of thermodynamics – which state that the overall level of entropy, or disorder, tends to increase in any closed system – energetics provided the framework by which moving bodies in space could be understood as fields of force, what historian Anson Rabinbach has

Ecological urbanism

called a 'physiognomy of labor power' (Rabinbach 1990, 117). These developments paralleled the evolution of *biology* as a fully codified science, which, in turn, did away with earlier distinctions between *mechanism* and *vitalism* in favor of a new hybrid concept of *organism*. The living being was no longer conceived as a simple association of organs, each working autonomously, but rather as a whole whose parts are interdependent, each performing a particular function for the common good (Jacob 1973, 83). During this process, the concept of *organization* – the pattern of relationships binding and integrating separate parts into a coordinated whole – redefined the conventional understanding of organisms, to the extent that it designated the possibility for life itself. The vitality of an organism came to be seen not only as analogous but synonymous to mechanical processes in machines powered by water, steam, or electricity – in Mary Shelley's novel, *Frankenstein; or, The Modern Prometheus,* for instance, Victor Frankenstein gives life to his creature (made up of an assemblage of human body parts) by using electricity (Shelley [1818] 1982). This increased awareness of the integration of structure and function within an organism was eventually extended to the relation of an organism to its *milieu*. The result was an idea of a tripartite assemblage, consisting of structure, function, and environment, that defined the regulatory mechanisms of *organized*, and thereby *organic*, bodies

Figure 11.2 Berthold Lubetkin, Penguin Pool at the London Zoo, 1934.
Source: courtesy of Morley von Sternberg/RIBA Collections.

(Martin 2005, 17). Therefore, not only were the relations between organic parts, or organs, and the organism radically transformed at the beginning of the nineteenth century, relations extending beyond the body, uniting all organisms into a collective network of organization, were also reorganized (Jacob 1973, 111). And through this process, the *machine* came to be seen as an external artificial organ, a prosthetic extension, that connects the *organism* to its social, cultural, and technological *milieu*.

If the *organism* and the *machine* are now part of the same organizational network, then which aesthetic approach is the most appropriate for the environment that the two now share? And how are we to adapt *organic* bodies to their increasingly *machinic* surrounding? In the late 1930s, the London Zoo became a testing ground, a scientific laboratory, for exploring the relationship between organisms, in this case animals, and their environment – with implicit implications for the human built environment. In 1933, the Round House for gorillas, designed by Berthold Lubetkin, became one of the first Modernist buildings in Britain (Allan 1992). A year later, the Zoo unveiled a Penguin Pool, designed by the same architect. Having carefully studied the lifestyle and habits of penguins, Lubetkin recreated the penguins' natural habitat within an artificial setting – albeit inspired by modern architecture. A white concrete structure with a futuristic pool, dual spiral ramps, and ribbon windows with multiple vistas, the Penguin Pool resembled a Corbusian villa more than a conventional shelter for animals (Figure 11.2). Lubetkin's pool house also challenged him to explore innovative construction techniques, such as the use of "shotcrete" or "gunite" – a reinforced concrete spray – for the construction of the double-spiral ramp.

These design experiments re-emerged in the 1960s. The Elephant and Rhino House, for instance, completed in 1965, was designed by Sir Hugh Casson and Neville Conder in the Brutalist style. Made of brick and encased in pick-hammered concrete with concealed top-lighting, coarse textures, curved walls and asymmetrical timber-roof frames clad in weathered copper, the building received the Royal Institute of British Architects award in 1965 for the best building in London. But the most notable example in this lineage is the Snowdon Aviary. Designed by renowned British architect Cedric Price with Tony Armstrong-Jones and Frank Newby, and completed in 1964, the Aviary was Price's first and one of his very few built projects (Figure 11.3). It employed some of the most advanced technologies of its time – including the use of aluminum castings, stainless steel forgings, welded aluminum mesh and tension cables – to create a lightweight enclosure that maximized flying space for the birds. The Snowdon Aviary was also the first walk-through aviary, a massive birdcage where humans and animals

Ecological urbanism

Figure 11.3 Cedric Price, Tony Armstrong-Jones and Frank Newby, Snowdon Aviary at the London Zoo, 1964.
Source: courtesy of Architectural Press Archive/RIBA Collections.

occupy a shared environment. The project is a net-worked structure: an aluminum web wrapped around a matrix of diagonal structural poles. And in its rational yet unconventional approach to the design of a natural habitat, the Snowdon Aviary challenges the conventional aesthetics of the built environment. It is a hybrid apparatus that no longer resembles a *machine* or a *garden*, but occupies a space in between; a spatial network of organization that brings – at least for the duration of a visit – all of the participating *organisms* (plants, animals, humans, and machines) together in the same space (Figure 11.4).

Leaving the debate over confining animals to the side, the London Zoo projects succeeded in challenging our preconceptions about the *natural* and the *artificial*, incorporated a more holistic and ecological approach to design, and explored the use of different building materials and construction technologies. But perhaps the most significant accomplishment of these architectonic experiments was the way

Figure 11.4 Cedric Price, Tony Armstrong-Jones and Frank Newby, Snowdon Aviary at the London Zoo, 1964.

Source: photograph by Eric de Maré, 1965. Courtesy of Eric de Maré/RIBA Collections.

they dissolved the ideological opposition – and with that, the formal, or aesthetic, dichotomy – between the *garden* and the *machine*. By exploring new aesthetics, each project, in its own way, blurred the distinction between the *natural* and the *artificial*, challenging the disciplinary boundaries between *architecture* and *landscape* and signaling the possibility of a new typology that resists disciplinary distinction. The projects made us realize that we were asking the wrong question all along. The dilemma is not about how to adapt the *garden* to the *machine*, or whether the *machine* is killing the *garden,* but rather, whether the *garden* itself is a *machine*.

EPISODE 3: THE WORLD GAME

The December 18, 1950, issue of *Life* magazine featured an article, provokingly titled 'How US Cities Can Prepare for Atomic War' (Wiener et al. 1950, 76–84). Supported by a series of maps and diagrams, the article outlined a detailed proposal that called for the decentralization of urban infrastructures to mitigate the aftermath of a nuclear strike. Arguing that the panic and chaos caused by the breakdown of transportation and communication networks would be far more devastating than the immediate consequences of the explosion, the plan called for the creation of a series of exurban 'life belts' – infrastructural networks arranged in radial patterns around major cities – that would regulate the city's equilibrium in the event of a nuclear strike by sustaining the flow of transportation and information.

The article was co-authored by Norbert Wiener, an American mathematician whose influential book, *Cybernetics: or Control and Communication in the Animal and the Machine,* had launched an interdisciplinary research program of the same name two years earlier. Cybernetics considers systems in a closed self-regulating signaling loop, where information is adjusted through a feedback mechanism. But implicit in the subtitle of Wiener's book is the notion of *control* – regulating the behavior of organisms (*the animal*) and the new information processing devices (*the machine*) – by means of *communication*. As he wrote, 'if the seventeenth and early eighteenth centuries are the age of clocks, and the later eighteenth and nineteenth centuries constitute the age of steam engines, the present time is the age of communication and control' (Wiener 1948, 38).

Wiener's reference to the 'age of clocks' and, especially, the 'age of steam engines' is noteworthy. During the nineteenth century, as discussed earlier, both the relations established between the parts of an organism and those uniting all organisms were radically transformed. Until then, what was distributed and transmitted between these biological (or mechanical) organs and the organisms they inhabited were natural substances required for their vitality or function: force or energy in the form of water, steam, fire, or electricity. Information, or data, was only processed by the human subject and was transmitted to machines by virtue of inputs, commands, or operations. By the turn of the twentieth century, however, a dramatic increase in the volume of production, the speed of transportation, and the quantities of goods being circulated and consumed resulted in new problems of organization and management – what James Beniger called the 'crisis of control' (Beniger 1986). From factory floors to offices, the question of how to resolve this new crisis led to the production and accumulation of more data, time charts, inventories, customer files, etc. (Picon 2010, 18). Information began to be seen as a formidable force that demanded a new level of organization and management. This in turn, led to the emergence of an information-based society, or what has often been referred to as the 'Second Industrial Revolution' (Landes 1969). If in the beginning of the nineteenth century 'physiognomy of labor power' or the relations between bodies in space was completely reconfigured, at the turn of the twentieth century those very relations were translated into objective, quantifiable, and electronically transmittable data. Therefore, if the Industrial Revolution prosthetically extended the human body and its mechanical functions, the Second Industrial Revolution extended the human nervous system by enabling communication between man and machine.

Wiener's book, dedicated to his collaborator, neurophysiologist Arturo Rosenblueth, is the first exposition of research conducted by the two on the links between communications networks and the human nervous system. Applying ideas from nineteenth century thermodynamics to systems of information measurement and management, Wiener defined information in relation to entropy. He proposed – referring to the second law of thermodynamics – that, like energy, the amount of information or 'negentropy' within a system is subject to a process of breaking down and leveling off (Wiener 1950). As a result, cybernetics considers systems in a self-regulating signaling loop, where organization is achieved through a continuous cycling of information (feedback), obtained by artificial 'sense organs' and transmitted back into the system (communication) in order to correct its course or modify its output (control).

Wiener's 1950 article was an early instance of the application of cybernetic principles to spatial organization and the planning of cities. The article also signaled an attempt to popularize a debate about urbanism between scientists and planners and to reorient urban development and planning towards the use of new computational tools (Picon 2010, 40). For Wiener, the city was defined as 'a net of communications and of traffic,' and he viewed the danger of blocked communications in a city subject to emergency conditions as 'analogous to the danger of blocked communications in the human body' (Wiener et al., n.d.). Emblematic of the bipolar climate of the Cold War, filled with mistrust and deceit, and the looming threat of a nuclear strike, Wiener's article, with its sociopolitical overtones, suggested a cybernetic approach to a complex crisis of global scale and magnitude far beyond the purely scientific limits he laid out two years earlier. Earth, circled by satellite and telecommunication networks, was now a closed cybernetic system that could drive itself to entropy, chaos, or even self-destruction should the system fail to regulate itself – a Prisoner's Dilemma that could result in the worst outcome for all, should any player choose to *defect* rather than *cooperate*.

One of the most significant contributions of cybernetics and system theory was its influence on the reformulation of *ecology*, as a branch of biology that deals with the relations of organisms to one another and to their physical surroundings. For many, like Leopold, highly influenced by this systems-based approach, cybernetics provided a new theoretical framework for the study of socio-ecological networks. Earth – like a brain, a thermostat, an aircraft controller, or a spaceship – was viewed as a cybernetic machine that carefully monitors any change in its environment and responds to it. Buckminster Fuller was one of the leading figures who adopted this holistic approach to the world's problems. Like Wiener, Fuller was convinced that the world required a more global form of management. His 'Great Logistics Game' or 'World Peace Game' – later shortened to simply the 'World Game' – developed in 1961, was an attempt to devise a systems approach to tackle socio-ecological problems, such as overpopulation and the uneven distribution of global resources. For Fuller, it was no longer the city, state, or nation, but the entire world that was a relevant unit of analysis. Using the Dymaxion Map to plot world resources, trends, and scenarios, the game required a group of players to cooperate to collectively solve a set of metaphorical scenarios, thus challenging the dominant nation-state perspective in favor of a more holistic view (Figure 11.5). The rules were simple: 'Make the world work, for 100 percent of humanity, in the shortest possible time, through spontaneous cooperation, without ecological offense or the disadvantage of anyone.'

The logic of the World Game reflected Fuller's approach to governance and social problem solving – his goal was to make the tool accessible to everyone. He viewed the game as a democratic process whereby individuals use their values, imagination, and problem-solving skills to tackle global crises – a bottom-up mobilization rather than a top-down planning. In its attempt to create an infrastructural network of communication and governance, the World Game

Figure 11.5 Buckminster Fuller standing in front of Dymaxion map during the World Game seminars held in the summer of 1969 at the New York Studio School in Greenwich Village, New York. During the workshop, twenty-six people from various disciplines met for eight weeks where they documented Fuller's concepts and ideas through research and simulated plays. The World Game Report, published in the following year, is an overview of the process and products of that workshop.

Source: courtesy of the Estate of R. Buckminster Fuller.

materialized many of the key theoretical components that Wiener deemed necessary for the full realization of cybernetics' organizational potential. Similar to Wiener's control mechanism, a 'defense-by-communications,' the World Game used information management, control, and feedback to defend against and regulate entropy and disorder. But as a communication system, the game also realized Wiener's vision of communicative transparency, not only against hypothetical scenarios, but also against the incommunicative opaque environment that had created them.

To work, the World Game required a comprehensive database to provide the players with an inventory of the world's vital statistics, from quantities and qualities of minerals and manufactured goods and services to human resources and skills from around the world. It also needed an information source to monitor the current state of the world, bringing live news into the 'Game Room.' None of these data-processing and communication services existed when Fuller conceived the World Game. But his vision resonates today in more ways than one, and the socio-ecological challenges he set forth in the World Game are more dire and urgent than they were in the 1960s. At the same time, digital technology has already provided us with essential tools for the World Game that were not available, or even conceivable, back then. With an enormous network of information, multiple means of communication, and highly advanced computational tools, all at our fingertips, we already have Fuller's game board in our pockets. But do we have an incentive to play?

EPILOGUE

As we look back at the *Blue Marble* forty years later, Earth does not look the same. Our planet is increasingly populated, polluted, and urbanized (United Nations 2014). The image we have of our current environment is one of melting glaciers and rising currents, hurricanes and tropical storms, floods and droughts, growing landfills and toxic waste. We are living in an ecology of fear and threats. Nature is no longer the idyllic, feminine, and submissive existence we deified as the 'Garden of Eden' or idealized in our picturesque paintings; nature is now a crude, masculine, and aggressive intruder that is forcing itself upon us, shattering the order and tranquility of our cities. What a tragic irony! Our biggest fear is the damage our actions are inflicting on the planet we inhabit, and our biggest challenge is the maintenance of this Spaceship we call Earth. But perhaps this time, as we look at the *Blue Marble* once again, we will not look 'back' at Spaceship Earth, but we look forward, to the side of the picture. We will look at the four-thousand pound machine made of nickel steel, aluminum and plastic: Apollo. Or we will look at the extraordinary spacesuit (Figure 11.6) that compresses the vital functions of our entire biosphere into twenty-one interconnected layers of fabric (de Monchaux 2011): a miniature version of an ideal habitat, a wearable ecosystem, a prosthetic environment.

The challenge we face today is that we still cannot see Earth as a cybernetic system, as Fuller's Spaceship, nor can we see Apollo, or the spacesuit, as a microenvironment. In many ways, our perception of the environment, and of nature, is still obscured by the traditional binary between the *garden* and the *machine*. Disciplinary distinctions are a consequence of this and, in many ways, reinforce it – a rationalization based on technical, material, or scalar dimensions, further complicated by professional and disciplinary power struggles. But as we have already learned, these categories are increasingly irrelevant in resolving the

Figure 11.6 Apollo 11 lunar module pilot Edwin Aldrin as he looks down at the systematized list of mission procedures sewn onto the surface of his left sleeve. The photograph was taken during the two-and-a-half hour moonwalk by Apollo 11 commander Neil Armstrong who can be seen along with the lunar module in the reflection on Aldrin's visor, July 21, 1969.
Source: courtesy of NASA.

larger socio-ecological problems of our time. Working across fields, with complex problems of global scale and magnitude, demands a holistic, systems-based approach, one that, similar to cybernetics, can organize dynamic relationships through a kind of 'communicative transparency.' Ecological urbanism, as the "new ethics and aesthetics of the urban," may not yet have sufficient mechanisms in place to tackle all these issues, but it suggests a more promising, a more creative form of practice than those suggested by separate disciplines (See: Mostafavi and Doherty 2010). It has already succeeded in putting our trust back in the metropolis and providing a new formal and conceptual framework to rethink the future of our cities. Above all, as a new paradigm for a 'machinic landscape' (Mostafavi and Najle 2003), ecological urbanism rids us of our traditionally sentimental views of nature and, in my view, has made us realize that the garden and the machine, ecology and urbanism, are not opposites but are essentially the same. This may be the greatest legacy of ecological urbanism.

REFERENCES

Allan, John. 1992. *Lubetkin: Architecture and the Tradition of Progress.* London: RIBA Publications.

Beniger, James. 1986. *The Control Revolution: Technological and Economic Origins of the Information Society.* Cambridge: Harvard University Press.

Cosgrove, Denis. 2001. *Apollo's Eye: A Cartographic Genealogy of the Earth in the Western Imagination.* Baltimore: John Hopkins University Press.

de Monchaux, Nicholas. 2011. *Spacesuit: Fashioning Apollo.* Cambridge: MIT Press.

Fuller, Buckminster. 1969. *Operating Manual for Spaceship Earth.* New York: Simon and Schuster.

Gabel, Medard. 2002. 'Buckminster Fuller and the Game of the World.' In *Buckminster Fuller: Anthology for the New Millennium,* ed. Thomas T.K. Tung. New York: First St. Martin's Griffin Edition.

Hawthorne, Nathaniel. 1932. *The American Notebooks by Nathaniel Hawthorne, based upon the original manuscripts in the Pierpont Morgan library, and edited by Randall Stewart.* Philip Hamilton McMillan Memorial Publication Fund.

Heidegger, Martin. 1977. *The Question Concerning Technology and Other Essays.* Trans. William Lovitt. New York: Harper & Row.

Jacob, François. 1973. *The Logic of Life: A History of Heredity.* Trans. Betty E. Spillmann. New York: Pantheon.

Kurgan, Laura. 2013. *Close Up at a Distance: Mapping, Technology, and Politics.* New York: Zone Books.

Landes, David S. 1969. *The Unbound Prometheus: Technological Change and Industrial Development in Western Europe from 1750 to the Present.* Cambridge, New York: Press Syndicate of the University of Cambridge.

Latour, Bruno. 2010. 'Forty Years Later – Back to a Sub-lunar Earth.' In *Ecological Urbanism,* ed. Mohsen Mostafavi and Gareth Doherty, 124–127. Baden: Lars Müller Publishers.

Leopold, Aldo. 1949. *The Land Ethic*. In *A Sand County Almana, and Sketches Here and There.* New York: Oxford University Press.

Martin, Reinhold. 2005. *The Organizational Complex: Architecture, Media, and Corporate Space.* Cambridge: MIT Press.

Marx, Leo. 1964. *The Machine in the Garden: Technology and the Pastoral Ideal in America*. New York: Oxford University Press.

McHarg, Ian. 1967. 'An Ecological Method for Landscape Architecture.' *Landscape Architecture 57,* 105–107.

Mostafavi, Mohsen, and Ciro Najle. 2003. *Landscape Urbanism: A Manual for the Machinic Landscape.* London: AA Publications.

Mostafavi, Mohsen, and Gareth Doherty (eds). 2010. *Ecological Urbanism.* Baden: Lars Müller Publishers.

National Aeronautics and Space Administration (NASA). 2012. 'Apollo Imagery.' http://spaceflight.nasa.gov/gallery/images/apollo/apollo17/html/as17-148-22727.html (accessed May 2014).

Picon, Antoine. 2010. *Digital Culture in Architecture: An Introduction for the Design Professions.* Basel: Birkhauser GmbH.

Rabinbach, Anson. 1990. *The Human Motor: Energy, Fatigue, and the Origins of Modernity.* Berkeley: University of California Press.

Shelley, Mary Wollstonecraft. [1818] 1982. *Frankenstein; or, The Modern Prometheus.* Chicago: University of Chicago Press.

United Nations. 2014. *World Urbanization Prospects: The 2014 Revision, Highlights.* ST/ESA/SER.A/352.

Wiener, Norbert. 1948. *Cybernetics: or, Control and Communication in the Animal and the Machine.* Cambridge: MIT Press.

Wiener, Norbert. 1950. *The Human Use of Human Beings: Cybernetics and Society.* Boston: Houghton Mifflin.

Wiener, Norbert, Carl Deutsch, and Giorgio de Santillana. n.d. 'Cities that Survive the Bomb.' Undated draft, box 12, folder 638, Norbert Wiener papers, MIT. Quoted in *The Organizational Complex: Architecture, Media, and Corporate Space,* Reinhold Martin. (Cambridge: MIT Press, 2005)

Wiener, Norbert, Carl Deutsch, and Giorgio de Santillana. 1950. 'How US Cities Can Prepare for Atomic War: MIT Professors Suggest a Bold Plan to Prevent Panic and Limit Destruction.' *Life,* 76–84.

12

Engineering nature

Patrick Franke and Nick Christopher

The current trend in architecture and architectural design is one that places greater emphasis on landscape as an integral element to the building. Earth's landscape has always held influence over the design of buildings; after all, the land itself predates any concept of construction by several millennia. The way in which landscape influences our built environment is something that continues to change. Beginning with the earliest moments of human ancestry and ending with the highly involved megaprojects of today, the built environment represents a physical manifestation of humankind's relationship to the planet and its landscape. This relationship between humanity and the planet is one that takes place in both the real world (the physical, tangible world) and also in the fictional stories we create (the world as we perceive it). Many of today's constructions appear, to our senses and minds, to be green, natural, and healthy. When these same structures are considered within the reality of their construction, the resources they require, and the energy they consume, we see that they are more akin to massive engineering efforts than to the *greenscapes* and *living buildings* as which they are perceived. The task of designing to meet the needs of both worlds – the real and the perceived – remains the foremost challenge of architects and designers today.

A focus on skyscrapers tends to dominate conversations about architecture in the United States. This is understandable, given their high visibility and iconic presence, however there are many equally impactful projects that happen at ground level – or even below ground, for that matter. The Central Artery/Tunnel project in Boston, Massachusetts, known as 'the Big Dig,' is one such undertaking. Begun in 1982 and not completed until 2007, this massive project sought to re-route Boston's downtown highway traffic through a tunnel buried below the city, costing an estimated $22 billion when completed (Johnson 2006). The purpose of the Big Dig was to hide a portion of our noisy, man-made infrastructure and banish it from sight, and over its scar create a greenway to be enjoyed by the city's pedestrians. In this case, an incredible amount of effort was put forth with the goal of *obscuring* architecture and creating the appearance of a natural, lightly-touched landscape.

We see this phenomenon happening everywhere, not just on megaprojects like the Big Dig. Visit any construction site today and one is likely to see giant mounds of earth; the soil on which a building will sit is excavated, pushed around, carted away, and reshaped until the ground bears little resemblance to its former self. This same reality exists on construction budget spreadsheets, where large sums of money are marked for 'site work,' and the larger the site, the greater the figure. Parallel to this evolution in construction is the increased involvement of civil engineers and landscape architects, whose impact far exceeds the simple planting of trees and grading of the site. The construction of a building is more than the erection of a superstructure; there is an immense amount of investment put into augmentation of land below it and around it. The result: our impact on earth's landscape is universal. There is little of earth's surface that is not in some way 'designed,' yet it is increasingly engineered in such a way as to appear natural, organic, and untouched (Figure 12.1).

The following text seeks to examine this phenomenon: why do we go to such great lengths to create the appearance of nature? What are the consequences of this act of benign deception? First we will review the evolution of this trend, beginning with earth itself and highlighting key past events that demonstrate the relationship between landscape and architecture, as well as the notable aesthetic similarities or differences between the two. Next we will consider the current zeitgeist and how it is shaping our world architecturally, and finally we will look to the future of landscape and architecture and consider the question: are these two distinct pursuits, or have they become the same? This chapter does not seek to support this notion of architecture-disguised-as-landscape, nor does it seek to admonish it; rather, we hope to draw attention to a deserving topic and encourage debate, both within the design community and the greater public.

Engineering nature

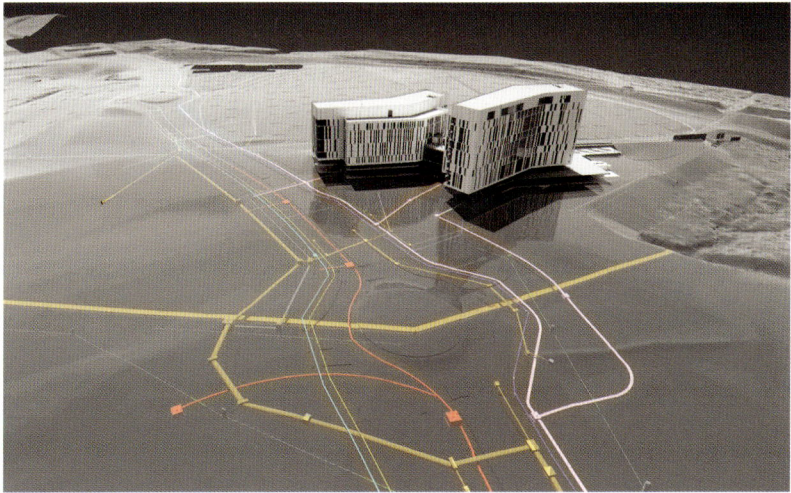

Figure 12.1 North American Office Development: Mass Grading and Site Utilities. Prior to constructing the portions of the project that are above ground and visible to the average observer there is a massive amount of earth moving and site utility work required to connect the project with the local infrastructure and greater city planning. In this way architecture almost always reinvents the landscapes it is built within in one capacity or another.

Source: Cerner.

To clarify: when referring to *landscape* we are speaking about the ground plane. *Natural landscape* is then the land as it exists without the involvement of man and *artificial landscape* is land that has been augmented by man in some way. *Architecture*, for our purposes, is simply a building enclosure created by man and for the purpose of occupancy. We have chosen these simple yet specific definitions for the terms as a means of providing clarity; after all, the words 'landscape' and 'architecture' are both broadly used with many different connotations to describe a plurality of conditions.

PREHISTORY

In 1968, Charles and Ray Eames directed and released the first version of the film *Powers of Ten*. The film highlighted both the infinite qualities of the universe and the finite essence of earth (*Powers of Ten* Video 1977). In the final version of the film, the scene opens with a view from the vantage point of one meter from Earth's surface, a familiar scale and typical setting. The camera frames a couple picnicking in the park. From one meter, the camera zooms out toward outer space and into the cosmos. As the camera recedes from Earth at an exponentially increasing rate, it captures the shear vastness of the universe. The viewer is confronted with the reality that Earth is a speck in comparison with the boundless extent of the universe. Returning home and back toward Earth the camera zooms back to where it started to a distance of one meter from Earth's surface. The camera then begins to zoom in and magnify the couple picnicking in the park and captures life at a cellular level. From this perspective we can appreciate the elemental scale of the building blocks, which coalesce to make our world. At the atomic level, we can sympathize with the fact that everything is from the same cloth, birthed from years of biological and environmental evolution in which circumstances and time have formulated the context in which we find ourselves.

Time is relative, and relatively speaking Earth is quite old and architecture is quite young. An accepted prediction puts Earth at around 4.54 billion years old (Lide 2005). In comparison, what we consider modern humans have only been on the planet for around 200,000 years (O'Neil 2015). In other words, for every year humans have been on Earth, Earth has been in orbit for 22,700 years. This is to say that the planet has existed without architecture and without human intervention for nearly 4,539,800 billion years. Architecture is just a newborn – in truth, it is closer to a mere pin-prick in time when compared to the history of the planet. When we ask ourselves how landscapes have influenced the way we build and the way we think about architecture, we must first understand that architecture is a very new concept (Figure 12.2).

Like the concept of time, the scale or perceived size of Earth is a relative notion. Technically speaking, Earth has a radius of around 3,959 miles making for around 196.9 million square miles of surface area (Pianka 2015). However, not all of that surface area is land nor habitable. Land area accounts for around 57.2 million square miles, and of that, only about 43 percent is considered habitable, making for about 24.6 million square miles of habitable land (Pianka 2015). Taking into consideration the habitable land and Earth's current population of 7 billion people we can calculate that each person could have approximately .0035 square miles of land to themselves or just above two acres per person. Conceivably there was a time in human history where Earth was perceived to be fairly infinite. In contrast, looking back to the beginnings of the first modern humans and the earliest societies of foragers (about 200,000 years ago) we find a planet and a series of landscapes untouched by human hand. The concept of a built environment did not exist. Architecture had yet to be invented – the closest thing was shelter, and the first shelter was the mere makings of the land (Figure 12.3).

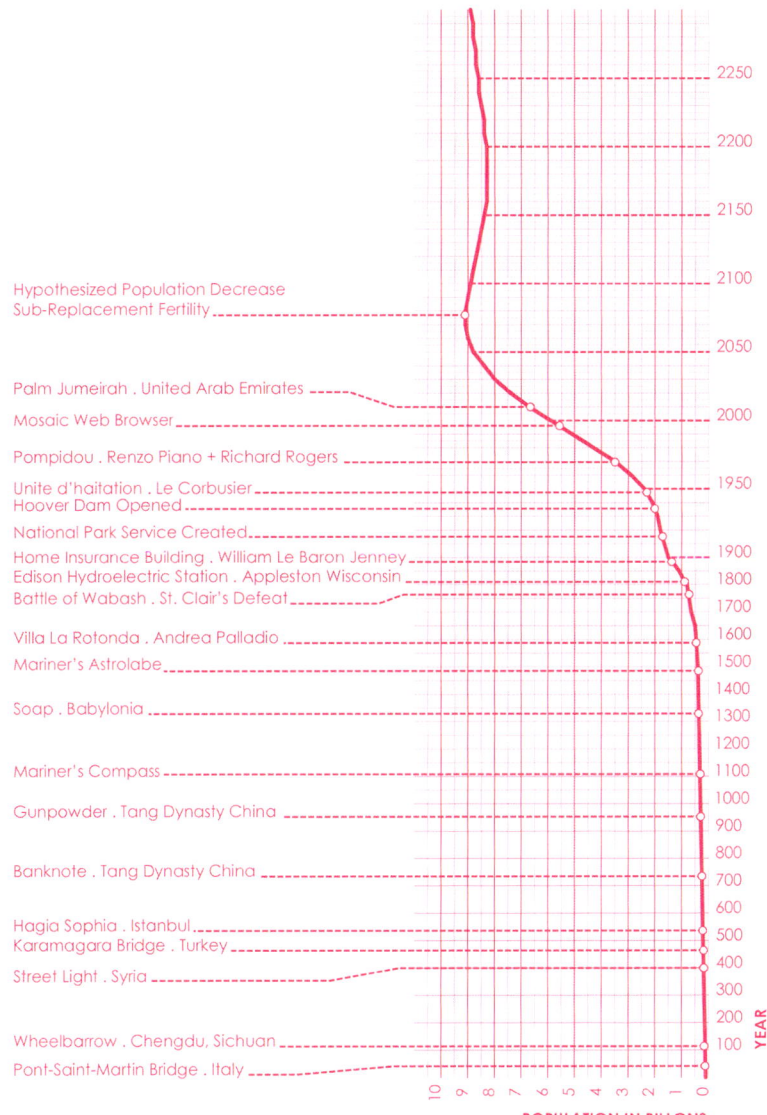

Figure 12.2 Timeline: Human Events and Population. Over the course of human history our population has exponentially increased. In step with our population are a series of human milestones and events that have altered the course of humanity, architecture, and the way we develop within the framework of the planet we occupy. Foreshadowing an unprecedented human condition, some future population calculations predict a plateauing of human population followed by a decline which would have unprecedented implications for how our economies function and the way we live and develop land.

Source: United Nations (2004). Drawn by Patrick Franke and Nick Christopher.

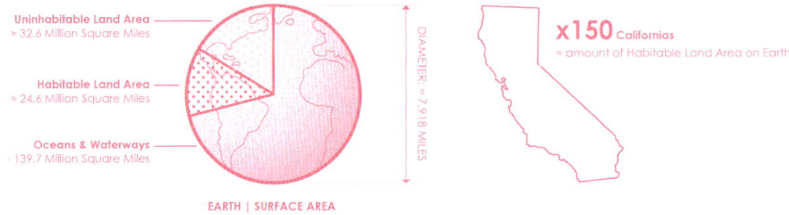

Figure 12.3 Our Planet – Surface Area and Habitable Land. While the way in which we build and live on the planet has greatly changed over the last 200,000 years and will continue to evolve going forward, the amount of area on which we are able to build and utilize for development resources is a fixed and somewhat finite parameter. Will we expand what is considered habitable area for humans by expanding into the terra incognita?

Source: Williams (2015). Drawn by Patrick Franke and Nick Christopher.

Shelter was a well-situated cliff, cave, or embankment. The earliest shelter was a naturally occurring place within the landscape that was just a bit more comfortable when compared to another part of the land. Out of shelter emerged architecture. In her book titled The *Old Way,* author Elizabeth Marshall Thomas writes of her experiences and observations from her time living with one of the last remaining hunter-gatherer societies – the Ju/wasi (Thomas 2006). Interestingly, the concept and consideration of shelter within this society was relatively unremarkable. Despite the danger of being preyed upon by wild animals, their shelter was a fragile aggregation of reeds found on the land nearby. Their shelter was purposefully minimal. It was more important to the Ju/wasi that their shelter be nomadic than be protective. In this way, the landscapes that supported their way of life were more important than the shelters that they utilized. Architecture, which is often perceived to be static, concrete, and long lasting, has no place in a society that is constantly on the move (Figure 12.4 and 12.5).

Tracing our lineage a long way back we find that we all came from some tribe of foragers and hunters. The desire for a connection with the land is a genetic disposition in all of us, dating back to these early times when the land was fundamental to our survival. The time before architecture was a time when it was a greater risk to lose touch with the landscape than it was to be taken as prey.

Figure 12.4 and 12.5 Campus Housing: Congo Basin Institute – partnership between UCLA and IITA (International Institute for Tropical Agriculture: Working closely with UCLA, Gensler developed a concept for an environmentally positive research hub in Cameroon, Africa, which would be both a resource and a catalyst for the people of the region. A portion of the design included housing for visiting educators and researchers traveling from other countries. While the historic vernacular of Cameroon, once embedded the dwelling directly in the land, the proposed housing concept is lifted from the land allowing for more ample air movement. By lifting the residents off the ground-plane a literal and perceived security is given to the architecture and the residents. Source: Gensler.

Patrick Franke and Nick Christopher

TAMING OF LANDSCAPE

With the agricultural revolution came a change in the relationship between human shelter and the landscape. Permanent, sturdy dwellings replaced the ephemeral shelters of mankind's ancestors, and with this permanence a new contrast was created between the *civilized* or *cultivated* world and that which was *uncivilized, untamed,* wilderness. Implied by this distinction is the association of safety with dwelling.

The philosopher Martin Heidegger refers to this concept in his discussion of threshold and the significance of that line between 'home' and 'the outside.' He makes this point through an analysis of Georg Trakl's poem, *A Winter Evening*. As Christian Norberg-Schulz points out, 'the poem distinguishes between an *outside* and an *inside*,' with the outside consisting of '*natural*' elements and therefore being representative of that which is inhospitable. In contrast to this is a home that 'offers man shelter and security by being enclosed and "well-provided"' (Norberg-Schulz 1979, 8). While Heidegger's analysis may be making a larger point about the importance of place, this remains a powerful illustration of the relationship between architecture and security.

In the most literal sense, architecture creates security by providing shelter. However, it is also the presence of man's influence that contributes to this feeling; a building or landscape that is *man-made* is a representation of humans conquering nature and all of the dangers associated with it. In order to extend the boundary of safety, civilization extends beyond the building's footprint in a similar, visible fashion. Landscapes are physically altered in the interest of production and profit, namely the parceling and tending of land for agriculture as well as the damming of rivers. At an even more impressive scale, coastlines are expanded as ambitious groups of people take on the task of creating (or perhaps more appropriately, *rearranging*) the land itself. Boston is a prime example of this physical growth; entire neighborhoods sit on artificially-created land that was added incrementally. The city's very geography is shaped by the economic forces that simply demanded more real estate. In today's world, Abu Dhabi and Dubai are also expanding in the interest of economy.

We see this human inclination to instill order at an incremental scale through the arrangement of landscape elements. While regimented columns of orchard trees or grapevines are undoubtedly a product of efficiency, there is also precedent for its use as an aesthetic representation of perfection and control. By taking a closer look at three examples – the gardens of Versailles in France, Oak Alley

Engineering nature

Plantation in Vacherie, Louisiana, and Central Park in New York City – we can understand how a tradition of ordered landscape flourished in Europe, was carried over to the Americas, and was subsequently replaced by a natural, organic-appearing style of landscape architecture.

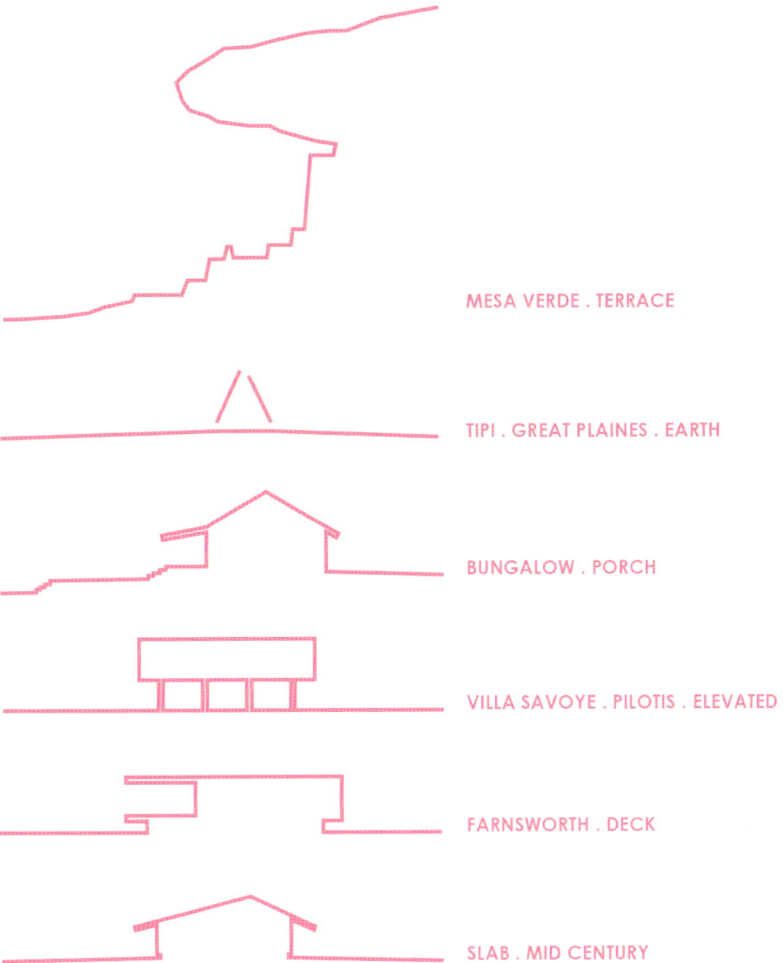

Figure 12.6 A brief history of housing's relationship with the land. Throughout time architecture has both been the manifestation of man's desired relationship with the land as well as the provocateur for nuanced ways in which we are connected with the landscapes we occupy and alter.

Patrick Franke and Nick Christopher

The Baroque era of architecture called for abundance and order, and nowhere is this more apparent than in the immaculately planned gardens of Versailles. Plantings and pathways are carefully plotted to create a manicured environment that is heavy with the presence of human involvement. To wander through Versailles is to experience a version of nature that has truly been bent to the will of its designers. Its scale suggests a massive empire, while the precision of its execution seems to imply submission and domination. For these reasons the Palace at Versailles and its gardens were a fitting symbol of the French monarchy; both showed little tolerance for variation or individuality within the ranks, and both required a level of maintenance and resources that were outrageously difficult to support or justify. Landscape, in this sense, is acting as a symbol of power and authority.

The design and layout of plantation properties in the Americas used a similar strategy of employing the landscape as a symbolic display of supremacy. The Antebellum structures were often built in the Greek Revival or Classical styles as an indication of wealth and upper-class status (Whiffen and Koeper 1983). The landscape surrounding them was similarly ordered, as seen in the layout of Oak Alley plantation in Vacherie, Louisiana. Large live oak trees line the entry road to create an impressive canopy that today feels more like a living green tunnel. The landscape, in this case, is being used to delineate a threshold. In many ways it mirrors the hubristic attitude with which the plantation system operated for decades; not only is nature made to support the plantation owner's operation, so too are the enslaved people who tend to the land and the buildings.

Following the Industrial Revolution, the fashion of regimented order decreases as city dwellers lament the loss of the natural landscape. We now see the pendulum swing in the opposite direction, and efforts are made to re-introduce wilderness, or the appearance of wilderness, into everyday life. The zeitgeist of

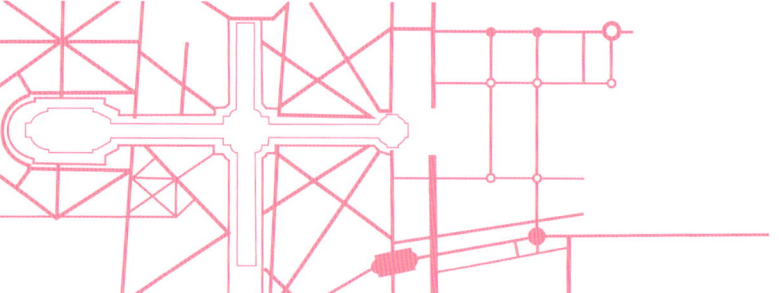

Figure 12.7 Site plan – gardens of Versailles, circa 1746. The precise geometry and meticulous planning of the gardens of Versailles are a demonstration of man's desire to apply order and regiment to nature.

Engineering nature

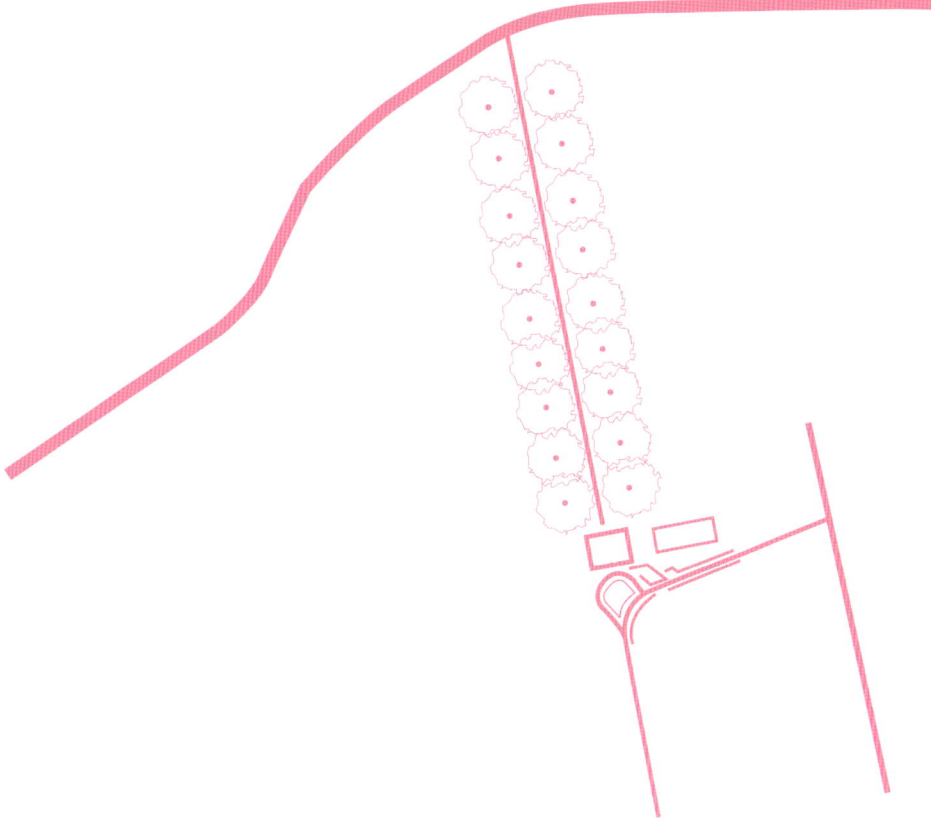

Figure 12.8 Site plan – Oak Alley Plantation, Vacherie, Louisiana, circa 1840. The use of oak trees along the plantation's entry has the effect of establishing a threshold.

early nineteenth-century American landscape design culminates in Frederick Law Olmstead's design for Central Park in New York City.

The beautiful and bucolic park is often referred to as *preserved green space,* implying that its current state is an untouched piece of the virgin landscape as it always was, simply roped off while the skyscrapers of Manhattan rose around it.

This of course is far from accurate; the experience of nature which Olmstead created is more akin to a stage set than to the land's original appearance. Rem Koolhaas explains in his retroactive manifesto, *Delirious New York*: 'a series of manipulations and transformations performed on the nature "saved" by its designers. Its lakes are artificial, its trees (trans)planted, its accidents engineered, its incidents supported by an invisible infrastructure that controls their assembly.' He goes on to call the great park 'a synthetic Arcadian Carpet' (Koolhaas 1997, 21–23).

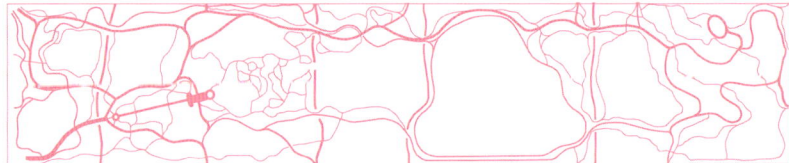

Figure 12.9 Site plan – Central Park, New York City, circa 1875. The park's network of paths is split into visitor passages and service roads; while they may appear to be organic, the landscape architect, Frederick Law Olmstead, carefully planned for their separation.

Aesthetically, Central Park presents a sharp contrast to the gardens of Versailles; a comparison of Figures 12.7 and 12.9 highlights the radical difference between the two. It is interesting to note that while Central Park appears to be much less 'designed,' it is in fact engineered to an even greater degree than is Versailles. The question of whether an act of benign deception such as this is desirable is a good one; it seems dishonest, in a way. But there is no arguing with the success of Central Park and the immeasurable joy and health it has generated for New Yorkers since its inception. As Henry David Thoreau said: 'It's not what you look at that matters, it's what you see' (Thoreau 2015).

MODERNISM'S RESPONSE

The appearance of Modernism is not often associated with the natural landscape. Its alternate name, the 'International Style,' suggests a uniformity of design that would seem to ignore the natural setting altogether. It is not difficult to find examples from Modernism's repertoire to illustrate this point. Le Corbusier's Une Cite Industrielle, with its massive, repetitive ivory towers makes a convenient example. This avant-garde city plan relentlessly uproots and covers the urban landscape of Paris with complete disregard for 'pre-existing conditions.' His famous *Five Points for Architecture* are no exception, which is visible enough in his characteristically site-less diagrams. The first point – pilotis, or 'the replacement of supporting walls by a grid of reinforced concrete columns' – lifts the building off of the ground plane and in so doing liberates it from the landscape (Le Corbusier 1985).

Le Corbusier's reasoning for elevating buildings like the Villa Savoye is straightforward: to make room for the automobile. This is easy to accept as fact, given the machine-driven functionality on which Modern architecture stakes its reputation. It is possible, however, that there is a much more natural, visceral human sentiment that motivated this design decision. Researcher and Le Corbusier historian Adolf Max Vogt proposes that it was Le Corbusier's childhood fascination with the Swiss lake house vernacular that *actually* inspired his raised architecture. He goes a step further, claiming that this subconscious tendency is a human one – that we all have an embedded desire for this relationship to the ground (Vogt, 2000).

Mies van der Rohe, the other titan of the Modern movement, echoed this sentiment in a more direct way. In his 1928 essay titled 'The Preconditions of Architectural Work,' he says: 'the building art is man's spatial dialogue with his environment and demonstrates how he asserts himself therein and how he masters it' (Mertins 2001, 604). This seems to imply that architecture is a physical expression of how we as a society feel about our environment, as well as how we position ourselves within it. Whether Modern architects chose to set buildings above the ground plane looking down (as in Le Corbusier's Villa Savoye) or to allow the architecture to dissolve into the landscape itself (as at Mies' Farnsworth house), the decisions were in both cases heavily influenced by the natural context into which the projects were to be inserted. While mid-century Modernism in many instances appeared to clash with the natural environment, it was actually influenced by the land, consciously or subconsciously.

FICTIONAL REALITY OF TODAY

Increasingly, the world we live in is a world that is not naturally occurring. Rather, the landscapes we occupy are those of human creation. Some of this, by way of scientific understanding and metaphor, mimics the natural world, but the good majority of our built environment is completely foreign. In this way, much of the built world (and our understanding of it) is now self-referential; buildings are informing buildings as opposed to the environment itself informing new construction.

> *Seventy thousand years ago, homo sapiens was still an insignificant animal minding its own business in a corner of Africa. In the following millennia it transformed itself into the master of the entire planet and the terror of the ecosystem. Today it stands on the verge of becoming a god, posed to acquire not only eternal youth, but also the divine abilities of creation and destruction. Unfortunately, the Sapiens regime on earth has so far produced little that we can be proud of. We have mastered our surroundings, increased food production,*

Patrick Franke and Nick Christopher

> *built cities, established empires and created far-flung trade networks. But did we decrease the amount of suffering in the world? Time and again, massive increases in human power did not necessarily improve the wellbeing of individual Sapiens, and usually caused immense misery to other animals.*
>
> (Hariri 2015, 415)

In his book *Sapiens*, Yuval Noah Harari brings to our attention the fact that the success and proliferation of the human race owes a great deal to our imagination and to our ability to garner consensus and acceptance around ideas that are not part of the literal–physical world but rather are fictional ideas. Harari discusses how powerful concepts such as religion, governance, and currency are now essential to our behavior and our humanity (Harari 2015). Similarly, architecture serves to reinforce these very human constructs. Architecture is categorized into a myriad of typologies, with each supporting a specific aspect of our life. Buildings are categorical: we have offices for working, schools for learning, houses for living, civic centers for governance, and churches for worship. In this sense, architecture is influenced by our sociological and cultural ideas. The high level of specialization within our building types is evidence of how different our lives have become from those of hunter-gatherers. The simplicity of early man's dwellings is indicative of his relationship to the landscape, and the relative complexity with which we build today is reflective of this same relationship. In short, the world in which we build is a much different one. It is physically different, but the social constructions through which we view it are also vastly different and more complex.

NATURE ENGINEERED

> *We like to look at water because we know deep down that it supports and brims with life; we like to look at flowers because we know that the next step is seed or fruit or food.*
>
> (Benyus 2004)

Many of these up-and-coming projects and neighborhoods appear to be, well, *green*. However, the landscapes and plantings with which we supplement nature are oftentimes highly manicured, engineered, and frequently require an endless amount of resources and maintenance to be kept alive and thriving. Furthermore, a good deal of this imported matter requires replacement within a few years, due to the unmet conditions that are needed to sustain growth. Our world is continuing to become an engineered, man-made version of itself.

The big question we must ask ourselves is: does mimicking nature or its idealized form actually present a problem? After the dust finally settled in Boston, there appeared a beautiful park in the place of a highway. Whether or not this 'Arcadian carpet' is a phony and has been rolled out to cover up our unattractive infrastructure hardly seems to matter when one considers the enormous benefits it provides to the lives and welfare of Bostonians. And the same argument could be made in support of maintaining a lush green golf course in the desert: it is what the golfers prefer, so how could it be a bad thing?

What this psychologically driven approach ignores is the fact that desert golf courses are a gruesome burden on their environments. Massive green projects at the infrastructural scale are likewise resource-hungry and expensive in terms of energy use and maintenance. At some point the question ceases to be *can the taxpayers afford it?* And instead becomes *can our planet afford it?* Increasingly, the answer to the latter seems to be a resounding *no*.

To be sure, not all heavily landscaped projects are problematic; xeriscapes, native plantings, and other nature-conscious mitigation techniques are becoming a popular alternative to the *manicured green*. To suggest that plants themselves are the *root* of the problem would be horribly inaccurate. Rather, it is the material-heavy gymnastics to which architecture turns in order to accommodate some of these designs, and the energy required to create the *green wall* or *green roof* or *green plaza* ultimately outdoes the benefits that the green design is supposedly providing. The solution, it seems, will fall somewhere in between what is *pleasing* and connects us with our ancestral beginnings and what is *efficient* as required by an ever-increasing skyline and man-made world.

REFERENCES

Benyus, Janine. 2004. 'Janine Benyus Ikeda Interview.' Masao Yokota Interview with Janine Benyus. http://www.ikedacenter.org/thinkers-themes/thinkers/interviews/janine-benyus. Accessed July 30, 2015.

Harari, Yuval Noah. 2015. *Sapiens: A Brief History of Humankind.* New York: HarperCollins Publishers, 415.

Johnson, Glen. 2006. 'Governor seeks to take control of Big Dig Inspections.' *Boston Globe*, July 13.

Koolhaas, Rem. 1997. *Delirious New York: A Retroactive Manifesto for Manhattan*. New York: Monacelli Press, 21–23.

Le Corbusier. 1985. *Towards a New Architecture*. New York: Dover Publications.

Lide, David R. ed. 2005. *CRC Handbook of Chemistry and Physics*. Internet version, www.hbcpnetbase.com. Boca Raton, FL: CRC Press. Accessed July 30, 2015.

Mertins, Deltef. 2001. 'Living in a Jungle: Mies, Organic Architecture, and the Art of City Building.' In *Mies in America*, ed. Phyllis Lambert. New York: Harry N. Abrams, 591–641.

Norberg-Schulz, Christian. 1979. *Genus Loci: Towards a Phenomenology of Architecture*. New York: Rizzoli, 5–12.

O'Neil, Dennis. 2015. 'Age of Homo Sapiens.' http://anthro.palomar.edu/homo2/mod_homo_4.htm. Accessed July 28, 2015.

Pianka, Eric R. 2015. 'Habitable Land Area of Earth.' www.zo.utexas.edu/courses/Thoc/land.html. Accessed July 15, 2015.

Powers of Ten Video. 2015. Charles and Ray Eames for IBM. www.youtube.com/watch?v=0fKBhvDjuy0. Accessed June 17, 2015.

Thomas, Elizabeth Marshall. 2006. *The Old Way: A Story of the First People*. New York: Sarah Crichton Books, Farrar, Straus and Giroux.

Thoreau, Henry David. 2015 BrainyQuote.com, Xplore Inc. www.brainyquote.com/quotes/quotes/h/henrydavid106041.html. Accessed July 31, 2015.

United Nations. 2004. *World Population*. www.un.org/esa/population/publications/longrange2/WorldPop2300final.pdf, 179–180. Accessed December 20, 2015.

Vogt, Adolf Max. 2000. *Le Corbusier, The Noble Savage: Toward an Archaeology of Modernism*. Trans. Eadka Donnell. Cambridge: MIT Press.

Whiffen, Marcus and Frederick Koeper. 1983. *American Architecture, Vol. 1: 1607–1860*. Cambridge, MA: MIT Press.

Williams, David R. 2015. 'Planetary Fact Sheet.' http://nssdc.gsfc.nasa.gov/planetary/factsheet/planet_table_british.html. Accessed July 28, 2015.

13

Emergent convergent
Technology and the informal urban communities initiative

Ben Spencer and Susan Bolton

Emergent Convergent: Technology and the Informal Urban Communities Initiative discusses the University of Washington, Department of Landscape Architecture's Informal Urban Communities Initiative (IUCI), an interdisciplinary design activism, service learning and research program based in the slums of Lima, Peru and its recent consideration of technological and industrial development. The chapter discusses how the IUCI is exploring the potential convergence of technologies readily accessible to the urban poor and emergent technological evolution, introducing students to hands-on making and digital fabrication, and challenging them to deploy these skills towards the design of income generating, productive landscapes in urban slums.

Ben Spencer and Susan Bolton

Over the past 300 years, cities, technology, and society have evolved in tandem. The processes of production have shaped urban landscapes and institutions that structure the relationships of urban citizens. Industry has overtaken agriculture as a primary economic driver, and the automated production of goods has overtaken artisanal craft. Local economies have been subsumed by global corporations and, as financial and political capital have concentrated in urban centers, cities have grown into mega-cities regional in scale. As cities have grown so too have urban inequities, especially in the developing countries of the global south. In places as far ranging as Africa, Southeast Asia, and Latin America, more than 200,000 rural migrants move to cities on a daily basis in hopes of finding jobs and escaping the hardships of rural life (Neuwirth 2005, xiii). The urban poor now number close to 1 billion, almost 20 percent of the world's population (United Nations 2013, 42).

The following chapter discusses the University of Washington (UW), Department of Landscape Architecture's Informal Urban Communities Initiative (IUCI), an interdisciplinary design activism, service learning, and research program based in the slums of Lima, Peru and its recent consideration of technological and industrial development. The chapter outlines the evolution of industry that gave rise to modern cities and the expansion of slums and discusses the origins and ongoing influence of the concepts of appropriate and liberatory technology. It goes on to discuss how the UW Department of Landscape Architecture and the IUCI are exploring the potential convergence of technologies readily accessible to the urban poor and emergent technological evolution, introducing students to hands-on making and digital fabrication, and challenging them to deploy these skills towards the design of income generating, productive landscapes in urban slums.

INDUSTRY, CAPITALISM, AND CITIES

During the eighteenth and nineteenth centuries, the advent of technological advances in agriculture, mining, transportation, power production, and manufacture had a transformative impact on the social, economic, and cultural dynamics of Europe and the United States. Economies previously characterized by agricultural production became increasingly driven by factory-based manufacture. The rise of industry was accompanied by the rise of capitalism and cities. Private enterprise operating in the pursuit of profit and the accumulation of financial capital within the context of competitive markets and wage-based worker compensation replaced previously feudal economic systems. Agricultural lands once held in common by tenant farmers were consolidated under private ownership and farmed by fewer laborers. As residents of rural areas migrated to cities, urban populations underwent unprecedented growth (Griffin 2010, 144–161).

The Industrial Revolution benefitted many people. However, scholars such as Charles Feinstein and Simon Szreter have argued that, throughout much of the Industrial Revolution, the living standards of many people did not improve significantly (Feinstein 1998, 649–652; Szreter and Mooney 1998, 109–110). Employed in dangerous work environments and living in overcrowded tenements without ventilation, sanitation, clean water, or other basic amenities, working class citizens often endured a difficult existence. The intimate relationship between livelihood and artisanal processes of making broke down as workers became mired in automated, repetitive tasks.

By the beginning of the twentieth century, the Industrial Revolution was taking root in places as far flung as Japan and South Africa (Domosh et al. 2010, 299). As the century progressed, increasing exploitation of fossil fuels and innovations in industrial organization such as the assembly line and the mass production of consumer goods drove the expansion of a global capitalist system dominated by corporations. The ongoing growth of industry and the concentration of wealth in urban areas fueled the ongoing growth of cities and, in turn, the growth of informal urban settlements (McNeil 2008, 1–11; Cheru and Bradford 2005, 186).

As capitalism, industrialization, and urban expansion reached new heights, critical voices emerged. In his book, *Small is Beautiful: Economics as if People Mattered*, E.F. Schumacher critiqued capitalism and associated processes of industrialization as inhumane. He argued that centralized, capital intensive industrial technologies were inaccessible to the majority of the world's poor and excluded them from the benefits of development. He proposed 'production by the masses' as an alternative to mass production and an 'intermediate' technology with 'a human face,' 'that recognize(d) the economic boundaries and limitations of poverty' and allowed the poor to exercise control over, and benefit from, the processes of production (Schumacher 1973, 138–193). Intermediate, or appropriate technology as it later came to be known, is generally characterized as low cost, small scale and decentralized, hands-on and labor rather than capital intensive, environmentally intelligent, and locally available and accessible. It is intended to contribute to development on a district scale and, historically, focused on providing employment opportunities to residents of rural communities.

Murray Bookchin also condemned corporate capitalism's myopic focus on financial profit and reliance on unrestricted growth as a source of social exploitation. In his works *The Ecology of Freedom* and 'What is Social Ecology?', he asserted that both social and environmental degradation stem directly from the class-based hierarchical organization of capitalist society – that 'the domination of nature by man stems from the very real domination of human by human,' and that 'the root causes of environmental problems [include] trade for profit, industrial expansion, and the identification of progress with corporate self-interest' (Bookchin 1982, 1; 1995, 245). He called for the reconfiguration of society along more egalitarian lines. Distribution of power, participatory democratic processes, and industrial economies that operate primarily at the scale of the locality were central aspects of his vision.

Like Schumacher, Bookchin called for the development of more humane technology. However, he took a more optimistic stance relative to technological progress. In his essay 'Towards a Liberatory Technology,' Bookchin argued that the equitable distribution of wealth at a low level of technology would do little to free people from toil and the struggle to escape scarcity. Eventually, he believed, such distribution would create conditions well-suited to the reproduction of class-based social and environmental oppression. As an alternative, he placed faith in the potential of open-ended technological innovation within the context of a distributed democracy as a means of eliminating menial labor, increasing access to the processes of production, and paving the way for the pursuit of creative and fulfilling livelihoods (Bookchin 1971, 83–139).

In the generation succeeding the publication of *Small is Beautiful* and 'Towards a Liberatory Technology,' both Schumacher's and Bookchin's ideas have exerted considerable influence on the discourse of development. The tenets of appropriate technology have been coopted as core principles of sustainable design and organizations ranging from Practical Action to the US Peace Corps have ascribed to and promoted their application. Participatory methodologies have become increasingly sophisticated and community-driven projects have, in many cases, proven to be more enduring and effective than those conceived of and executed by official or professional 'experts' (Kumar 2002, 23–52). Market-based, social entrepreneurial approaches to community development are transforming business as usual into business that defines profit in terms of its combined social, environmental, and economic benefits (Martin and Osberg 2007, 26–39). Landscape architects and other designers are pioneering systems-based approaches to city making, re-conceptualizing landscape as an infrastructural medium and exploring the possibilities of productive urban spaces (Mostafavi and Doherty 2010, 12–55). Design activism is gaining traction as increasing numbers of students and professionals seek out new ways to apply their design skills to the challenges facing disenfranchised populations (Bell and Wakefield 2008, 8–25).

Meanwhile, many of Bookchin's predictions concerning open-ended technological innovation are coming to fruition. Leapfrog technologies such as solar panels and cell phones are rendering previous large-scale industrial technologies obsolete. Computers that once occupied warehouses now fit in the palm of our hand and cost less than a thousand dollars. The internet and communication software are making previously cloistered information more readily accessible to a broad public and facilitating collaboration between previously segregated populations. Digital fabrication, a more recent entrant into the cast of relatively accessible digital technologies, is also expanding rapidly. Laser cutters, 3D printers, and CNC milling machines have come down significantly in cost and, in some cases, now fit alongside personal computers on desktops. A new breed of inventors or 'makers' are translating digital data into physical form and sharing their design ideas and products over the internet. Fab Labs in cities as far flung as Yogyakarta, Takoradi, and Lima are beginning to democratize access to means of production across the globe. A new industrial revolution is under way (Gershenfeld 2005, 3–17; Anderson 2012, 17–32; Fab Foundation 2015).

Despite these developments, corporate capitalism remains the dominant economic paradigm and the urbanization and large-scale industrialization of countries in the global south continues. The social inequities and slum growth that characterized the cities of both the early Industrial Revolution and its expansion during the twentieth century remain commonplace. Many slum dwellers remain unemployed or underemployed and trapped in a self-perpetuating cycle of poverty. Despite the growing democratization of digital technology, a digital divide stemming from limited access to facilities, insufficient purchasing power, a lack of computer literacy, and other factors continues to exclude the poorest segments of society from the benefits of technological evolution (Kim and Kim 2001, 78–91).

THE INFORMAL URBAN COMMUNITIES INITIATIVE

In response to these ongoing challenges, an interdisciplinary team of faculty and students from the University of Washington Department of Landscape Architecture, School of Environmental and Forest Sciences and Department of Global Health and professionals from Architects Without Borders – Seattle, established the Informal Urban Communities Initiative in Lomas de Zapallal, an informal urban settlement in Lima, Peru. The IUCI is a design activism, service learning, and research program that addresses the challenges of slum development at a local level. Building upon and celebrating the bottom-up processes of urban slum growth, working closely with community members, and responding to their priorities, the IUCI espouses an 'emergent/convergent' approach to design. Small scale, community-driven 'emergent' interventions accumulate over time and 'converge' with adaptive planning at the scale of the neighborhood. The initiative undertakes serial projects in the same community over the course of many years and monitors and evaluates their impacts. The overarching goal is to effect gradual social, economic, and environmental change, substantiate the value of community-based design, and expand the capacity of designers and other professionals to pursue successful projects in poor urban contexts (Spencer et al. 2015, 206–223; 2014, 92–107).

During its first five years, the IUCI has conducted five Seattle-based Design Activism Studios and undertaken five on-site/built projects. On-site projects include two parks and a classroom at LdZ's Pitagoras School and fog collection and household garden pilot projects in LdZ's Eliseo Collazos neighborhood (Figure 13.1). Much of the IUCI's work to date, both in studios and on-site, has been founded on critical assessment of centralized infrastructure and the top-down institutions and processes that support it. The IUCI contends that efforts to improve the living conditions of slums that rely on centralized infrastructure fail to keep pace with slum growth, disempower community members in the process of city making, and contribute to the externalization of environmental burdens – precipitating downstream effects such as climate change which ultimately expose vulnerable urban communities to further hardship.

Recently, the IUCI has begun to focus its critique on the persistence of large-scale industry as the dominant means of production in cities and, acknowledging the aspirations of many slum dwellers to participate in the benefits of technological evolution, to explore the potential of distributed, community-based industry in informal urban settlements. Expanding upon its emergent/convergent approach to community development, the IUCI is exploring the convergence of appropriate technologies that are readily accessible to the urban poor with emergent liberatory technologies. More specifically, the IUCI is asking how we might synthesize hands-on making, digital fabrication, and participatory landscape architectural design as a means of democratizing industry, stimulating local economic development, and generating new forms of productive urban landscape in informal urban communities.

Emergent convergent

Figure 13.1 The Eliseo Collazos neighborhood, Lomas de Zapallal, Lima, Peru.
Credit: IUCI Team.

THE UW DEPARTMENT OF LANDSCAPE ARCHITECTURE AND IUCI CURRICULUM

The tenets of appropriate technology and liberatory technology are embedded within the UW Landscape Architecture Department curriculum, and students are exposed to hands-on making and digital fabrication both prior to and as part of their participation in IUCI studios and projects. As a means of illustration, the chapter first presents key classes in the department's construction and digital media sequences; LARC 332 Materials, Making Landscape Architecture and LARC 441 Digital Media II. It then describes the 2015 LARC 502 IUCI Design Activism Studio and discusses how students are exploring the synthesis of appropriate technology, liberatory technology, and landscape architectural design. Finally, it reflects the 2015 IUCI Design Activism Studio's potential influence on the trajectory of future IUCI on-site projects.

Ben Spencer and Susan Bolton

Construction

LARC 332 Materials Making, Landscape Architecture is a graduate/undergraduate materials and construction class. The class introduces students to material assembly as a means of engaging design at a tactile, human scale, and challenges them to think about the material composition of the built environment in concrete rather than abstract terms, from the bottom-up rather than as an afterthought in a design process that progresses from large to small. It approaches construction as a hands-on, conscientious, and creative pursuit and synthesizes questions of technical performance, ethics, and artistic expression. The class is structured around three modes of learning: 1) lectures focusing on material properties, the detailing of material assemblies, and social and environmental issues related to material selection and use; 2) field trips during which students explore material palettes, weathering, and the sensual qualities of materials in context; and 3) hands-on experimentation with materials including wood, metal, concrete, and the connections between them using both hand and power tools in the UW College of Built Environments Fabrication Labs (Figure 13.2). In addition to

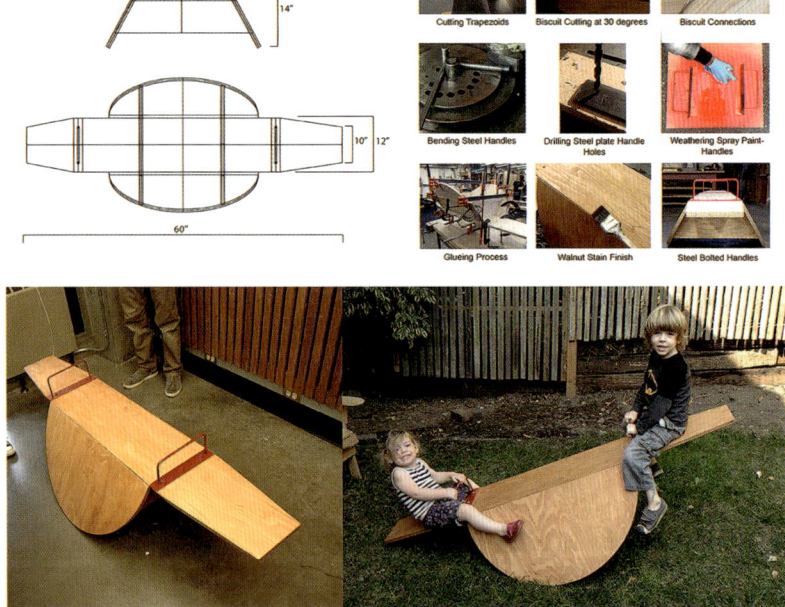

Figure 13.2 LARC 332 Materials and Making, Urban Play See Saw.
Credit: Connor McGarry and Aimee Rozier.

introducing students to materials and construction techniques typically used in the United States, the class also introduces them to materials and construction techniques with applications in developing countries. It imparts both an intellectual and a visceral knowledge of material properties and assemblies that not only deepen student understandings of the material and detailing decisions they make in traditional landscape architectural practice but are also critical to practice in developing communities where design and hands-on construction are intimately related.

Digital media

LARC 441 Digital Media II is a class for graduate and undergraduate UW Landscape Architecture students that promotes digital media as an important tool in the iterative design process and a means of engaging clients and communities through virtual representation and digitally fabricated artifacts. In-class instruction includes theory-based lectures, software demonstrations, and competitive exercises during which students work in teams to complete digital tasks, learning from one another in the process. Two of the assignments in the class involve the synthesis of parametric modeling and digital fabrication. Students first write a parametric definition that controls the relief of a surface inspired by Maya Lin's Wave Field. Once the definition is complete, they translate three virtual wave field models into physical form using digital fabrication processes including laser cutting, CNC milling, and 3D printing (Figure 13.3). The assignments introduce students to flexible approaches to the modeling of topographic form and landscape elements and their extraction from screen-bound virtual environments into three-dimensional, tactile space. They provide foundational skills in digital product development relevant to the incremental and elemental processes of informal urban growth and begin to cultivate the patience necessary to work in developing communities by challenging students to work through software bugs, crashing computers, and the reconfiguration of CNC machines.

IUCI Design Activism Studio

The LARC 502 IUCI Design Activism Studio, a second-year graduate studio, builds upon these classes and emphasizes integrated systems thinking, iterative design, serial prototyping, and participatory processes. Based in Seattle but

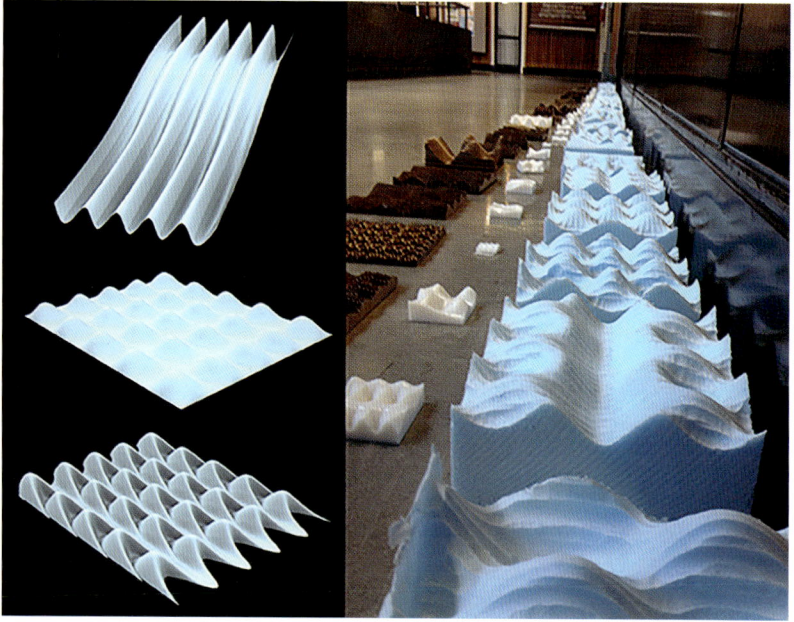

Figure 13.3 LARC 441 Digital Media II, Wave Field parametric and digitally fabricated models.
Credit: James Day and LARC 441 students.

focusing on conceptual design interventions in LdZ, it introduces students to urbanization in developing countries and design in developing urban contexts.

Once known as the garden city and confined to an area close to the Rimac River, Lima's metropolitan area now occupies an expansive stretch of coastal desert that receives less than 1 cm of rain per year. Three million of the city's 9 million residents live in informal settlements. At less than 2m² per capita, green space is scarcer in Lima than in any other major South American city. The majority of this green space is concentrated in the city's affluent districts (Murphy 2013). As the city's population grows and its water supplies are threatened by climate change and melting Andean glaciers, green space is likely to become increasingly scarce, especially in low-income neighborhoods. Gainful employment in Lima's informal urban areas is also scarce. The majority of Lima's formal economy is concentrated in central Lima. In the Eliseo Collazos neighborhood of LdZ, many residents commute 4 hours a day, 6 days a week in search of work. Many earn less than $150 a month (Spencer et al. 2013).

Students participating in the 2015 IUCI Design Activism Studio confronted these challenges. After completing a series of introductory assignments and meeting with Eliseo Collazos community members via Skype to learn more about their neighborhood and priorities, they undertook a six-week assignment consisting of three interdependent parts. They designed: 1) a 'Kit of Parks' product line; 2) 'Fabricated Landscapes' that made use of 'Kit of Parks' products; and 3) 'Landscapes of Fabrication' dedicated to the fabrication of 'Kit of Parks' products.

'Kit of Parks' products diverted recycled PET soda bottles from Lima's waste stream and were loosely organized around the themes of Soil, Structure, Water, and Plants. They included 1) a geo-cell product called 'GeoPop'; 2) a multipurpose textile called 'GeoGrid'; 3) a PET fog collection material; and 4) a modular box that could be arranged and stacked to accommodate a wide variety of uses. The products operated independently or as part of an integrated system.

During product development, students made use of digital fabrication facilities at the UW and attempted to bridge the gap between appropriate and liberatory technology by articulating a process of production that combined digital fabrication and hands-on making. After defining product typologies and interactions in general terms, students experimented with product form and function by constructing a series of virtual and physical 3D models. Students working on the 'GeoPop' geocell product, for example, designed and constructed tools to extract sheet materials from soda bottles and 3D printed a series of plastic clip prototypes to hold these sheet materials together (Figure 13.4). Students working on modular box designs created a parametric definition that provided dynamic control of box size and configuration and experimented with a variety of approaches to melting and shaping waste plastics. For each of the products, students compiled easy to understand, digitally generated graphic instructions detailing the tools and steps involved in product fabrication.

At the same time they were developing 'Kit of Parks' products, students also developed 'Fabricated Landscape' designs. Drawing upon participatory design exercises previously conducted in Eliseo Collazos, the designs were situated on a lot with varied terrain chosen by community members as the site of a future park. Each design demonstrated the use of 'Kit of Parks' products in different ways. For example, one 'Fabricated Landscape' made use of the 'GeoGrid' product as fencing to protect plants from chickens, dogs, and children, as a shade fabric to provide shelter from the sun, and as a soil wrap. Another used 'GeoPop' geocells as part of a layered slope stabilization system that prevented erosion of the community's sandy soils. A third deployed the modular boxes as retaining walls, seating, and play structures (Figure 13.5).

Once 'Kit of Parks' products and 'Fabricated Landscape' designs were well under way, students undertook the additional task of designing 'Landscapes of

Figure 13.4 LARC 502 Design Activism Studio, GeoPop geocells.
Credit: Roxanne Lee, James Wohlers, Ivan Heitmann, Stevie Koepp.

Fabrication.' Whereas 'Fabricated Landscapes' focused on construction *with* 'Kit of Parks' products, 'Landscape of Fabrication' designs focused on construction *with and of* 'Kit of Parks' products. As such they were reflexive, not unlike a reproductive organism, or a self-replicating machine.

Several interesting approaches arose. One design proposed the manufacture of 'Kit of Parks' products as a means of activating Eliseo Collazos' main street. Another design transformed the community center and its surrounding landscape into a site of production on weekdays when the facility was otherwise not in use (Figure 13.6). In all cases, the designs brought together park design, fabrication, and the productive reuse of wastes. In doing so, they sought to engage residents in communal production, strengthen social capital, generate income, and contribute to environmental regeneration.

Students considered the evolution of 'Landscapes of Fabrication' over time and its relationship to community capacity and business development. Rather than starting out big, their interventions started out small and grew incrementally over time in correspondence with the growth of the community's expertise and

Emergent convergent

Figure 13.5 LARC 502 Design Activism Studio, Fabricated Landscape.
Credit: Zhehao Huang, Jiaxi Guo, Ivan Heitmann.

financial means. Products were initially designed by outside collaborators (as in the 2015 Design Activism Studio). Community members then fabricated products on-site and sold them for a profit to other communities and agencies undertaking green space interventions. At the same time, community members participated in capacity building programs in computer literacy, digital fabrication, and design. Over time, 'Landscapes of Fabrication' grew and the community acquired the financial means to purchase increasingly affordable computers and digital fabrication equipment. Responsibility for product design passed from outside collaborators to the community members, placing them in full control of product development, manufacture, and sale. No longer dependent on inconsistent employment in Lima's central districts or burdened by long commutes, they earned their income close to home and were able to spend more time with their families and friends.

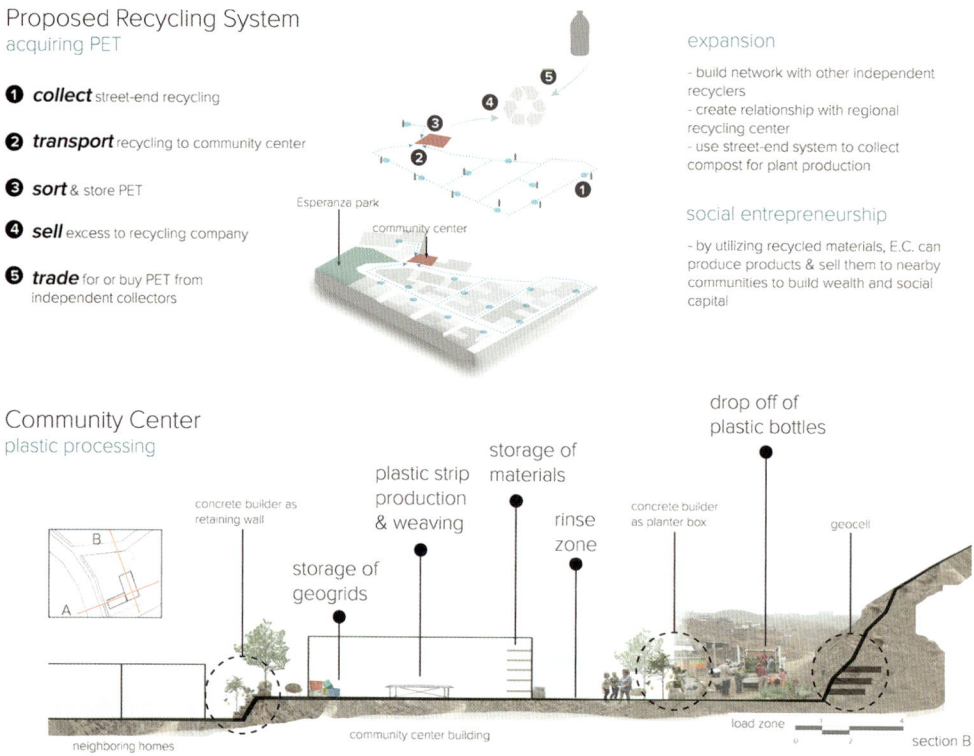

Figure 13.6 LARC 502 Design Activism Studio, Landscape of Fabrication.
Credit: Kenna Patrick, Will Shrader, Xingyu Wang.

On-site projects

Each summer, students travel to LdZ to participate in on-site service learning projects over a period of 4–10 weeks. They work with faculty, professionals, and community members to conduct participatory design workshops, execute design interventions, evaluate the impacts of previous IUCI interventions, and critically reflect upon them. Building upon the knowledge they gain during digital media, construction, and design courses, they learn how to work effectively in developing urban communities through practical engagement.

Although there is not a one-to-one relationship between the work that students complete during IUCI Design Activism Studios and the work they complete during IUCI on-site projects, the two inform one another. Moreover, the work that students undertake one year, whether in studio or on-site, informs the work they

Emergent convergent

undertake during subsequent years. For example, in response to community concerns about water scarcity, students first began experimenting with fog collection technology during the 2011 Design Activism Studio. This experimentation led to an assessment of the fog collection potential of sites near Eliseo Collazos. The positive results of this assessment provided a foundation for the 2013 IUCI Design Activism Studio's focus on fog collection systems. The development of new fog collection materials and initial experimentation with 3D printing during the 2013 studio led to further on-site testing of fog collection materials and informed the 2015 Design Activism Studio's further exploration of digital fabrication and locally manufactured fog collection materials.

It remains to be seen when and how the ideas that students explored during the 2015 Design Activism Studio will manifest during future IUCI on-site projects. The evolution of community priorities, the availability of funding, and other factors will come into play. However, if the history of IUCI serves as an indicator of things to come, these ideas will likely resurface. For example, the project the IUCI is undertaking on-site in 2015 builds upon previous Design Activism Studios focusing on fog collection and involves the design and construction of a large-scale fog collection system (Figure 13.7).

Figure 13.7 IUCI fog collection project.
Credit: IUCI Team.

In the future, students, faculty, and community members will likely have the opportunity to apply their skills in hands-on making and digital fabrication – to undertake projects that strengthen social and intellectual capital, transform urban slum landscapes into vehicles for income generation, and take small but meaningful steps towards bridging the digital divide. As they proceed, it will be important to remember that the creation of new hardware must be accompanied by the cultivation of software – people, places, and processes – that direct its application towards socially and environmentally just ends. By working incrementally, reflecting upon successes and failures and sharing lessons learned, they will have the opportunity to leverage the convergence of appropriate and laboratory technology as an instrument of social change – to put technology to work for those who stand to benefit from it the most.

REFERENCES

Anderson, Christopher. 2012. *Makers: The New Industrial Revolution.* New York: Crown Publishing Group.

Bell, Bryan and Katie Wakefield. 2008. *Expanding Architecture: Design as Activism.* New York: Metropolis Books.

Bookchin, Murray. 1971. *Post-Scarcity Anarchism.* Berkeley: Ramparts Press.

Bookchin, Murray. 1982. *The Ecology of Freedom: The Emergence and Dissolution of Hierarchy*. Palo Alto: Cheshire Books.

Bookchin, Murray. 1995. 'What is Social Ecology?' In *Earth Ethics: Environmental Ethics, Animal Rights and Practical Applications* edited by J.P. Sterba, 245–259. Englewood Cliffs, N.J.: Prentice Hall.

Cheru, Fantu and Collin Bradford. 2005. *The Millennium Development Goals: Raising the Resources to Tackle World Poverty*. London: Zed Books.

Domosh, Mona, Terry G. Jordan-Bychkov, Roderick P. Neumann, and Patricia L. Price. 2010. *The Human Mosaic.* Twelfth Edition. New York: W.H. Freeman and Company.

FabFoundation. 2015. 'Map of Fab Lab Locations.' Accessed February 5, 2015. www.fabfoundation.org/.

Feinstein, Charles H. 1998. 'Pessimism Perpetuated: Real Wages and the Standard of Living in Britain during and after the Industrial Revolution.' *The Journal of Economic History*, 58(3): 625–658.

Gershenfeld, Neil. 2005. *Fab, The Coming Revolution on Your Desktop: From Personal Computers to Personal Fabrication.* New York: Basic Books.

Griffin, Emma. 2010. *A Short History of the British Industrial Revolution*. New York: Palgrave Macmillan.

Kim, Mun-cho and Jong-Kil Kim. 2001. 'Digital Divide: Conceptual Discussions and Prospect.' In *The Human Society and the Internet: Internet Related Socio-economic Issues, First International Conference, Seoul, Korea: Proceedings*, edited by Won Kim, Tak Wang Ling, Yoon Joon Lee, and Seung-Soo Park. New York: Springer.

Kumar, S. 2002. *Methods for Community Participation: A Complete Guide for Practitioners*. London: Practical Action Publishing.

Martin, Roger L. and Sally Osberg. 2007. 'Social Entrepreneurship: The Case for Definition.' *Stanford Social Innovation Review*. Spring. Palo Alto: Leland Stanford Jr. University.

McNeill, John R. 2008. 'Global Environmental History in the Age of Fossil Fuels (1800–2007).' In *The Environmental Histories of Europe and Japan*, edited by K. Mizoguchi. Kobe: Nagoya University Press.

Mostafavi, Mohsen and Gareth Doherty. 2010. 'Why Ecological Urbanism? Why Now?' In *Ecological Urbanism*. Harvard University GSD: Lars Muller Publishers.

Murphy, Annie. 2013. 'What's a Walk in the Park Worth in Peru?' *The Christian Science Monitor*, December 24. Accessed February 5, 2015. www.csmonitor.com/World/Americas/2013/1224/What-s-a-walk-in-the-park-worth-in-Peru.

Neuwirth, Robert. 2005. *Shadow Cities: A Billion Squatters in a New Urban World*. New York: Routledge.

Schumacher, E.F. 1973. *Small is Beautiful: Economics as if People Mattered*. New York: Harper & Row Publishers.

Spencer, Benjamin, Susan Bolton, and Jorge Alarcon. 2014. 'The Informal Urban Communities Initiative: Community-driven Design in the Slums of Lima, Peru.' *International Journal of Service Learning in Engineering*, 9(1): 92–107.

Spencer, Benjamin, Susan Bolton, and Jorge Alarcon. 2015. 'The Informal Urban Communities Initiative: Lomas de Zapallal, Lima, Peru.' In *Now Urbanism: The Future City is Here,* edited by Jeff Hou, Benjamin Spencer, Thaisa Way, and Ken Yocom. London: Routledge.

Spencer, Benjamin, Susan Bolton, and Joachim Voss. 2013. 'Demographic Survey Conducted in the Eliseo Collazos Neighborhood of Lomas de Zapallal, Lima, Peru.' Unpublished study.

Szreter, Simon and Graham Mooney. 1998. 'Urbanization, Mortality, and the Standard of Living Debate: New Estimates of the Expectation of Life at Birth in Nineteenth-Century British Cities.' *The Economic History Review, New Series,* 51(1): 84–112.

United Nations. 2013. *The Millennium Development Goals Report.* New York: United Nations.

14

Varying degrees of impermanence

Art and landscapes as critical provocation

Roberto Rovira

Art and landscape share common ground in the temporal and in their profound connection with making as a way of deriving meaning. Installations, unencumbered by the needs of permanent architecture as passing media, provide a means with which to experiment in three dimensions using time as an essential agent. As an impermanent medium rooted in the sublime allure of the natural world, the landscape installation provides an opportunity to imagine the possible through a critical if temporary provocation. The artistic process informs the design process given its power to evoke and ignite a sense of a site's imagined possibilities.

> *Our recollection still remains virtual; we simply prepare ourselves to receive it by adopting the appropriate attitude. Little by little it comes into view like a condensing cloud; from the virtual state it passes into the actual; and as its outlines become more distinct and its surface takes on color, it tends to imitate perception. But it remains attached to the past by its deepest roots, and if, when once realized, it did not retain something of its original virtuality, if, being a present state, it were not also something which stands out distinct from the present, we should never know it for a memory.*
>
> Henri Bergson (Bergson et al. 1911, 134)

The complex relationship between memory and perception plays a profound role in the way that we understand, intervene, and participate in the processes that shape and create landscapes. As a medium where the effects of natural phenomena coexist with the impacts of human intervention, landscape embodies both the platform that registers the effects and the causes that give it shape. As such, it is an actor, audience, and stage in its ongoing transformation.

Art and landscape share common ground in the temporal. The agencies of perception, recollection, and imagination become the elements of insight and hypothesis through which we can come to terms with and meaningfully alter landscape's course. Installations, as passing media unencumbered by the needs of permanent architecture, provide a means with which to experiment in three dimensions using time as an essential agent. As an impermanent medium, the installation provides an opportunity to imagine the possible through a critical if temporary provocation of a site's possibilities. Installations have the capacity to impart the memory of a spectacle, to insert a shift into the grain of a site, and attempt to communicate an otherwise unseen, extraordinary richness capable of revealing profound insights, poignantly and opportunistically. As art, the installation has the capacity to engage the subtleties of the in-between, the ephemeral, and the passing. An installation can assert itself as a powerful instrument through which ecologies and relationships can be revealed, and through which the indeterminate processes, dynamic relationships, and transformation of land, city, and environment can be exposed.

In the Western imagination, the landscape has historically aligned itself with an idyllic vision of the natural world (Schama 1996). An otherworldly purity romanticized by lyrical and artistic renditions of pastoral life and depictions of natural scenery inform a cultural identity that is largely forged by landscape's mythopoetic power. In the United States, the celebration of the natural world through art can be said to have inspired westward expansion. The visual and

Varying degrees of impermanence

written accounts of the landscape ranged from Albert Bierstadt's lavish depictions of the American West through painting, to John Muir's and Frederick Law Olmsted's exultations of Yosemite. Olmsted asserted in 1864:

> *The union of deepest sublimity with the deepest beauty of nature, not in one feature or another, not in one part or one scene or another, not in any landscape that can be framed by itself, but all around and wherever the visitor goes, constitutes the Yosemite the greatest glory of nature.*
>
> (Roper 1973, 268)

John Muir's poetic accounts of the West equally spoke of an almost spiritual connection and ecological communion between the natural world and the universe that is attributed by many as the catalyst that influenced policy and led to the creation of the national park system in the United States. Muir reveled in the interconnectedness of the natural world and the universe and attributed the sublime wonder of the natural world directly to the hand of God. His 1911 lyrical journal *My First Summer in the Sierras* notes, 'When we try to pick out anything by itself, we find it hitched to everything else in the Universe' (Muir 1911) and his chapter titled 'The American Forest' in *Our National Parks* (Muir 1901), by some considered at the root of the American conservation movement, goes as far as personifying God in their making:

> *The forests of America, however slighted by man, must have been a great delight to God; for they were the best he ever planted. The whole continent was a garden ... pressed and crumpled into folds and ridges, mountains, and hills, subsoiled with heaving volcanic fires, ploughed and ground and sculptured into scenery and soil with glaciers and rivers – every feature growing and changing from beauty to beauty, higher and higher.*

Through word and image, the depiction of landscape became synonymous with limitless promise and potential. In these and many other accounts, landscape almost always embodies something infinite, intractable, and ineffable. The art and poetry used to frame the natural world and its phenomena transcend explanation and description, and often celebrate, incite, and inspire emotions that go beyond the physical limits of time and space and, like art, fan the flames of imagination.

For someone as prolific and engaged in the transformation of landscapes and cities as Frederick Law Olmsted, the link between imagination and the natural world must have been especially poignant. Not only was nature's innate beauty to be revered and admired, but it was, in fact, the very medium whose promethean power he harnessed to bring about far-reaching urban and regional transformations whose impacts are significant even today. Olmsted reframed the human relationship to the land, often using unprecedented, infrastructural scales like Central Park and Boston's Emerald Necklace to do so in his capacity as a landscape architect, an occupational title he christened. Through his work and that of predecessors like Lancelot 'Capability' Brown, who used the designed landscape to re-present the natural world by quite literally composing it as a painting, we find the 'reciprocal bond between imagination and resemblance' that Michel Foucault uses to explain the 'kinship' between nature and human nature.

> *It is true that imagination is apparently only one of the properties of human nature, and resemblance one of the effects of nature ... human nature resides in that narrow overlap of representation which permits it to represent itself to itself.*
>
> (Foucault 1973, 71)

The landscape has an inherent power to be nature while re-presenting nature. Imagination is that inherently human quality that allows us to see both nature and its representation as one continuous and sometimes deceivingly seamless fabric. By harnessing nature and imagining its possibilities, we may, in fact, be better able to understand ourselves, or at the very least critically question our identity through the landscape.

Heidegger's ruminations on knowledge provide further commentary on the connection between art and being and are relevant vis-à-vis landscape. He describes the Greek concept of *techne* as a quasi-existential act that bears knowledge and imparts a sense of being through art-making: 'Knowledge is the ability to put into work the being of any particular [being] ... The work of art is a work not primarily because it is wrought, made, but because it brings about Being in a being' (Heidegger and Manheim 1959, 159). Art, like landscape-making, is portrayed as an existential exercise whereby knowledge of self and identity is manifest. Landscape as a medium that can camouflage itself as both nature and its representation, therefore, makes this existential exercise all the more elusive since the landscape is implicitly both 'the forest and the trees,' and is, therefore, difficult if not impossible to separate from its representation. Our conception of nature and landscape and the boundary between the two is often intractable and difficult to discern because it typically embodies copies upon copies of itself, layers upon layers, media on top of media in an imbricate arrangement lacking a clear boundary, reference, or starting point. Unlike an archeological excavation

Varying degrees of impermanence

that can be indexed through artifacts and concrete time frames, the landscape is both the artifact and the medium that uses itself to build itself and reveal its story. Geological time, ecological time, anthropocentric time is all collapsed in the same space. Their continuities are inextricably intertwined.

It should come as no surprise then that art has an important role to play in the somewhat unstable and fluid medium of the landscape. In the absence of clarity as to when and where a landscape as a discrete entity begins or ends, art can fill the void by imparting knowledge and critically asserting an identity through the act of making in the way that Heidegger describes it. Perception and imagination go hand in hand in the artistic process. Art can impart 'being into being' and can provoke imagination by creating situations and relationships that engage perception on multiple levels via both overt and subtle ways. The landscape has the power to connect to the mythopoetic power of a natural world charged with otherworldly immanence in the way that Olmsted, Muir, and many others throughout history have seen it. Landscape-making resembles art in its ability to invent and provoke relationships through juxtapositions between natural and proposed conditions that are in a constant state of transformation and exchange. Co-opting the natural processes involved in making landscapes (earthwork, microclimate, watersheds, horticulture, etc.) becomes a profound vehicle with which to establish identity and relevance, and shape the perception of our place and relationship to the natural. Landscape interventions that influence, participate and are impacted by ongoing natural transformation not only assert human existence, but they confirm and transcend it.

Any intervention in the landscape, therefore, necessitates ongoing engagement and making. Entropy never stops and neither can the processes that attempt to make sense of it. The need to understand and come to terms with our immediate existence through making must, therefore, find ways to engage ongoing temporal processes. Landscape installations are one such means with which to do so since they are implicitly impermanent and passing. Installations, as ephemeral media unencumbered by the needs of permanent architecture, provide a means with which to experiment in three dimensions using time as an essential agent. Installations are assembled and disassembled and provoke new and old relationships in the process. As an impermanent medium, the landscape installation provides an opportunity to imagine the possible through a critical if temporary provocation. An installation has the power to disrupt the grain of a site, persist in our memory, and materialize unexpectedly in our peripheral vision, all the while questioning the nature of its context while ushering in possibility and piquing imagination.

Roberto Rovira

Ice Mappings, an installation in Miami, Florida, that documented the progressive melting of 30 blocks of ice frozen with the petals of over 400 roses, provides a relevant example. The project documented the process of the ice's disappearance and the consequent deposition of the petals on the ground in the space of 24 hours (Figures 14.1 and 14.2). The strong geometry of the arrangement meant that the shape, known as an 'Andean cross' in South America, would slowly find its way to the ground and enter another stage in the entropic decay/evolution of the ice and the flowers. The aqueous and the vegetal seemingly disappear in the space of one day, while the reminders of their presence remain, however subtly, on the ground. In passing, not only does the installation create a very noticeable spectacle that is provocative for its unexpectedness and its striking disturbance of its context (i.e. no one would expect to see dozens of 400 pound blocks of ice laid out with such intention in a subtropical setting), but it creates a temporary environment that informs the way the public approaches, navigates, and interacts with its spatial arrangement, senses its microclimate, and feels its texture and light. As a hyper-accelerated process of decay that in its way emulates the massive effects of glaciation whose effect is in evidence thousands of years after their disappearance, *Ice Mappings* leaves its trace and footprint, and in the process critically questions how long a landscape needs to exist to make an impact.

Figure 14.1 The *Ice Mappings* installation by Roberto Rovira used 400 pound blocks of ice frozen with the petals of over 400 roses.

Varying degrees of impermanence

Figure 14.2   Ice Mappings installation close up. The blocks' gradual melting lasted nearly 24 hours, during which the ice formation slowly deposited the petals on the ground.

The relationship between landscape and art resonated with the idea of 'site constructions' described in Rosalind Krauss's seminal 1978 essay 'Sculpture in an Expanded Field,' where she talks about the 'possible combination of *landscape* and *non-landscape*' and *marked sites* that began to appear in the 1960s in works by artists like Richard Serra, Dennis Oppenheim, Nancy Holt, and others (Krauss 1985, 238). These works made an attempt to intervene into the 'real space of architecture, sometimes through partial reconstruction, sometimes through drawing,' and often with the application of impermanent marks in the landscape like De Maria's *Mile Long Drawing* which was 'drawn' on a lake bed, and Oppenheim's *Timelines* which drew patterns in the snow and in river beds. We might call these installations today. Their presence in the landscape, often at site scales common to landscape practice, provided opportunities to reframe the relationship between landscape and viewer. In Serra's *Shift*, which used a series of constructed walls in an undulating rural landscape in Canada, he contrasts his approach with that of Renaissance space:

> *What I wanted was a dialectic between one's perception of the place in totality and one's relation to the field as walked. The result is a way of measuring oneself against the indeterminacy of the land… The machinery of Renaissance space*

> *depends on measurements remaining fixed and immutable. These steps relate to a continually shifting horizon, and as measurements, they are totally transitive: elevating, lowering, extending, foreshortening, contracting, compressing, and turning. The line as a visual element, per step, becomes a transitive verb.*
>
> (Krauss 1985, 264–267)

While falling short of explicitly describing these as landscapes with ecological and constructive properties of the kind that are common to landscape architectural discourse and landscape making, they nevertheless become landscape works with landscape effects and preoccupations. Of note is Serra's admission of how his work relates to an 'indeterminacy of the land,' a term that often comes up when considering landscape not as a gallery would, but rather as an open-ended stage upon and through which processes pass.

Site constructions by artists like those included in Krauss's roster provide a framework that engages the indeterminacy of the land and the processes and systems that affect it. The language of such art is the familiar language of landscape. The setting and the means of making are equally familiar: watersheds, grading, climate, and erosion, to name a few. Their interventions in the landscape cannot be viewed or conceived without the context and the specificity of the landscape. As such, they are vehicles of documentation, imagination, and provocation all at once, helping to comprehend the circumstances of a site and one's relationship to it, while also pushing for new meanings, new relationships, and new knowledge about site as much as self, bringing being into being through the act of making.

Understanding site conditions and relationships by becoming keen observers and instigators like an artist might be, can often lead to powerful site revelations with equally powerful landscape potential. A subtle difference in grade that catches windblown bottlebrush (*Callistemon citrinus*) on the edge of a pavement can, for example, significantly enhance the visibility and experience of a walking path (Figure 14.3). Though highly unintentional to the design, the effect is not that far removed from the striking and disruptive potential of a passing installation. On their own, bottlebrush, cherry blossoms, blazing red sugar maples may indeed be worthy of exultation. When viewed as temporal phenomena with the power to contribute beyond the exulted moment when blooms peak in the spring or vibrant leaves are about to drop in the fall, for example, they hold even greater potential. If they are conceived for their potential to have an impact even when they are beyond their obvious peak, they become instrumental in imparting lasting meaning to any landscape at any time.

Varying degrees of impermanence

Figure 14.3   Red bottlebrush (*Callistemon citrinus*) debris catches at the boundary of lawn and sidewalk given the subtle difference in grade.

Such is the role of *Tillandsia* in the *Sky Lounge* project at Florida International University in Miami. Otherwise known as 'air plants' for their ability to thrive while attached to branches and tree canopies and only getting nutrients from the humid air, this type of bromeliad is a common subtropical sight that often makes its presence known after a storm when winds knock the more loosely attached specimens to the ground. Suspended from the structure of a precast concrete brise-soleil at the top of a four-story building courtyard, the *Sky Lounge* uses braided stainless steel nets as the attachment infrastructure for the air plants. Three thousand were attached to the nets as 'ecological starters' in the otherwise empty courtyard of this brutalist 1970s building. *Tillandsia* propagates from the base of the mother plant at the rate of one to three new specimens per year. The mother dies in the process, and the pups send out new roots that attach to the netting and themselves, thereby adding to the density of the planting with a net gain of one to two plants per year. As in the natural environment, a few specimens fall to the ground on an ongoing basis, but in this case, rather than remaining on the forest floor, the plants get picked up by the more than 13,000 passers-by who traverse the space every semester. Some take the time to nest the plants into the adjoining wall trellis while others take them home as souvenirs and expand the footprint of the installation, making them unwitting participants in extending the initial project in both tangible and intangible ways (Figure 14.4).

Landscape and art can intelligently inform the ongoing process of urban transformation. Rather than consider the city as a finished set of objects and more of a loose collection of sites and processes in various states of completion and decay, a city can provide rich opportunities to intervene via landscape installations that capitalize on this temporality. The *Migrating Forest* in Providence, Rhode Island (Figure 14.5) and the *Drydock Loom* in Mare Island, California (Figure

Figure 14.4 Florida International University's *Sky Lounge* by Roberto Rovira creates a shaded, flexible space with over 3,000 'air plants' (*Tillandsia* spp.) that hang from braided steel nets overhead. In their natural forest habitat, as in this space, the epiphytes naturally propagate at the rate of one to three per year, during which time some drop to the ground and might be relocated by visitors who inadvertently expand the footprint of the project in the process.

14.6) take advantage of timely contextual conditions to make their ephemeral mark. In the *Migrating Forest*, over one hundred trees were used to create an overnight evergreen forest from discarded Christmas trees in early January. The trees made their way through the city over the course of two weeks as the installation team relocated them over several blocks at night. A familiar evergreen smell transformed the experience of the urban spaces and created compact passageways through which the public moved on a daily basis. In the *Drydock Loom*, an abandoned naval shipyard, remarkable for its colossal infrastructures for shipbuilding and tending, became the setting of an installation that used several miles of blue yarn. Upon entering the space of the empty dry dock (a floodable void at the edge of the water used to access the hulls of ships for maintenance), the viewer would progressively see the vibrant horizon of blue lines separated by only a few feet from each other. On its own, a line of blue yarn would nearly be imperceptible. When viewed together, they create a striking cloud of blue that hovers above the gigantic space and undulates with the wind, much like water might if the space were flooded as it habitually was for decades. Spaces like these

Figure 14.5 The *Migrating Forest* installation used over one hundred discarded Christmas trees and 'transplanted' them into a tight urban alley. The forest was subsequently moved to two distinct locations several blocks away over a two-week period. Founded by Roberto Rovira in Providence, Rhode Island, in 1996, *Guerrilla Gardens* focused on developing the medium of the 'semi-anonymous' temporary installation such as the *Migrating Forest* as a way of expressing the potential of landscape and architecture in various urban spaces.

Figure 14.6 In the *Drydock Loom* installation, Roberto Rovira used 13,000 feet of yarn spaced 2ft apart and approximately 16ft off the ground in the Mare Island Naval Shipyard located in Vallejo, California. The hovering blue lines alluded to the adjacent river whose water used to flood the space when the shipyard was in operation.

are ripe settings for landscape interventions bent on capitalizing on the unplanned, the transient, and the in-between conditions of an urban fabric. If a city's extensive ground plane is considered as more than a collection of objects all aiming for Vitruvian permanence, and more like fabric that allows events to unfold in time (Corner and Balfour 1999), the installation can strategically insert itself within its folds to catalyze possibilities and provoke the imagination.

Natural systems can be understood as a series of events bound by an ecological order where relationships unfold and organisms interact in both stark and subtle ways. No process is finite, and no state is permanent in the ever-unfolding emergence of the landscape. The ongoing process of transformation is, in fact, its defining quality. Whether a process takes twenty-four hours or twenty-four millennia to unfold, it is this indeterminacy and impermanence that gives us pause and forces a reckoning with time and temporality that transcends the human condition. Nature, whose forces and scales we often have trouble grasping, can both be sublime and oppressive, inspiring and off-putting. Art and landscape-making seem to give us license to enter into the process, leave our mark, and enhance our human experience, whether it is in the context of designing regional watersheds and coastlines, localized urban infrastructures, or the minute footprint of our backyard. The landscape installation, as a subset of landscape-making which can simultaneously be considered art, provides a vehicle for not only intervening in the natural world but for trying our hand at the language of impermanence that fundamentally defines the processes of the natural world. To have an impact in any context, one must be able to communicate in its language. With the capacity to appear and disappear as its de facto quality, the landscape installation is a flexible means with which to test ideas and relationships in timely and disruptive ways. It can be an effective tool in provoking possibilities, fanning the flames of imagination, challenging perceptions, and giving us another tool in our attempt to impart meaning into being.

REFERENCES

Bergson, H., Paul, N. M., and Palmer, W.S. 1911. *Matter and Memory*. London: S. Sonnenschein & Co., Lim., p. 134

Corner, J. and Balfour, A. 1999. *Recovering Landscape: Essays in Contemporary Landscape Architecture*. Sparks, NV: Princeton Architectural Press.

Foucault, M. 1973. *The Order of Things: An Archaeology of the Human Sciences*. New York: Vintage Books, p. 71.

Heidegger, M. and Manheim, R. 1959. *An Introduction to Metaphysics*. New Haven: Yale University Press, p. 159.

Krauss, R.E. 1985. *The Originality of the Avant-garde and Other Modernist Myths*. Cambridge, Mass: MIT Press, pp. 238, 264–267.

Muir, John. 1901. *Our National Parks*. http://vault.sierraclub.org/john_muir_exhibit/writings/our_national_parks/, accessed July 2015.

Muir, John. 1911. *My First Summer in the Sierras*. http://vault.sierraclub.org/john_muir_exhibit/writings/favorite_quotations.aspx, accessed July 2015.

Roper, L.W. 1973. *FLO: A Biography of Frederick Law Olmsted*. Baltimore: Johns Hopkins University Press, p. 268.

Schama, S. 1996. *Landscape and Memory*. New York: Vintage.

Part III

Innovative profiles

Interview I
Mikyoung Kim Design

Mikyoung Kim, Founding Principal

LANDSCAPE ARCHITECTURE – URBAN PLANNING – SITE ART

BOSTON, MA, USA

For the last twenty years, Mikyoung Kim Design has crafted an exceptional body of work, spanning a wide range of landscapes in the United States, East Asia and the Middle East. The firm is known for their culturally significant work that serve as a powerful tool to heal and enliven the public realm. While addressing pressing environmental issues, Mikyoung strives to celebrate the beauty of the collective human experience through the use of contemporary materials and technologies.

Online resources

- http://myk-d.com/about/
- facebook.com/mikyoungkimdesign
- twitter.com/MikyoungKimDsgn

The following text is an abbreviated interview conducted by Jonathon R. Anderson and Daniel H. Ortega (EDS).

EDS: How do you understand innovation?

MYK: Innovation happens when you ask questions that you don't know the answer to. Here at the office we try to create an environment where we are open to many different kinds of creative

Mikyoung Kim

Figure i1.1 Farrar Pong Residence, Lincoln, MA.
Photograph: Chris Baker.

minds and thoughts. We try to create new kinds of connections in order to innovate. I would say that we think about the office as a kind of brain center where there isn't just one brain. The top-down model of one person coming up with all ideas, and that those ideas trickle down is not innovative. Discovery comes at moments similar to environmental ecotones, those areas where ecological systems overlap and new relationships are made. Those are the richest parts of an environment because they host unpredictable interactions between flora and fauna. In our office, we believe that we can leap to a new place when different people and fresh thinkers come together and share their ideas collectively. The things that result within those collective territories of thought is the platform where innovation can occur.

EDS: How has innovation evolved your practice?

MYK: Innovation is in the process of developing design ideas. As a group, we work in a very collaborative environment that is made up of many different kinds of creative minds. We have a group of architects, industrial designers, graphic designers, product designers, artists, as well as planners and landscape architects. We often collaborate with allied design craftspeople and fabricators. For example, we recently had a metal fabricator come to our office and we were able to brainstorm with him about some ideas that we have and develop new ways of integrating material integrity into our process. I feel like the words innovation and creativity are used very freely in the creative marketplace that we live in now. I do believe that creativity should be a difficult process and one that reveals the soul of the idea. In the last few years when I have shared our work throughout the country, people come up to me afterwards and say, 'I know these four projects and I didn't realize that your office did all of them, you're really good artists.' I find that to be a compliment because I'm not sure that we are artists per se, but the artist's model is the way in which we work. When you go to an artist's retrospective, you see different periods in their work. You realize that their work has evolved and is influenced by so many things. Invention doesn't happen in each project, but you can clearly see that it happens through eight to ten-year phases. What we see in our process is that there is maybe a five- or six-year period where we are obsessed with some idea or a process that is usually tied to a specific materiality. I feel very proud that over the last eighteen years that we've been practicing, that there isn't a singular style or brand that defines the work that we do. Our work is constantly trying to invent something new and it's not to do that out of vanity, but it's really just to keep us fresh and stay interested in the work.

EDS: To what level does interdisciplinary define innovation?

MYK: When you look at innovation, the major breakthroughs in any medium, from the sciences to the humanities, new ideas often come from unexpected connections. I think that's a good model for the creative disciplines to mimic as we move forward. Within the profession, in the past, people have been guarded about the boundaries of what landscape architecture is, and there are still some remnants of that within the profession. When you think

Figure i1.2 Crown Sky Garden at Ann & Robert H. Lurie Children's Hospital, Chicago, IL.
Photograph: Hedrich Blessing.

about the word collaboration, people tend to consider images of groups standing in a circle holding hands, but the word collaborator has an edge. It can also mean a traitor, somebody who assists a foreign enemy. So in that context, collaboration comes embedded with dissonance, and that dissonance is also important in the process. In order to come up with innovative solutions, that kind of sharp elbows approach to testing ideas definitely helps the creative process. If everyone is getting along, it means that true discourse is not happening. Collaboration is a question of flexibility.

Interview I

Figure i1.3 Crown Sky Garden at Ann & Robert H. Lurie Children's Hospital, Chicago, IL. Photograph: George Heinrich.

In practice, if you are not flexible your work becomes stagnant and not interesting. If you develop a brand or a specific visual identity, or limit yourself to a certain type of project that you're willing to work on, and you stay that course for thirty or forty years of practice, that doesn't promote innovation. Before I decided to pursue landscape architecture, I was a musician. As a pianist, the voice of creativity came to me through sound and through performance. In music, much like in landscape architecture, your ability to do well is rooted in practice. Just like you practice landscape architecture, you practice your skills, and then you perform in different venues. Our office performs in many different kinds of venues with a wide range of audiences and sites. We have designed tableware for public plazas, Swarovski crystal, we do public artwork, and we also work within clinical institutions and children's hospital institutions. This brings me back to the point that I made about the many different types of designers who make up our office; we're internally positioned to practice in an interdisciplinary way.

EDS: In part, your work is predicated on the idea of celebrating the collective human experience. On what level do you consider the end-user as a collaborator in the design process?

MYK: We have a strong community-focused process embedded in what we do. We try to understand and listen to the communities that we work with, while also bringing something new and delightful to the table. We want to bring whimsy and color to the experience. So far what we have found through our process is that by talking to people and gaining their trust and in letting them know that we have their best interests in mind, that they are pretty willing to work with us in turning their stories into a visual language. While we are completely invested in listening to the community members, we also work hard to let them know that we bring an expertise to the table, and that expertise is what will manifest their stories into that visual and experiential part of their community. For us, that's innovation. It's extremely time consuming, and it may not be a type of site-related data that a scientist would collect, but it is data that is critical to the human experience of landscape. It's a real back-and-forth process that we've developed, and it's very important to us. Landscape architecture is about the interface with humanity.

EDS: How do you create a platform or infrastructure to facilitate innovation and how do you critically examine or assess this?

MYK: We are at a critical moment deciding how we go from an office where it is small enough that everyone can work together, to a larger structure that will still be collective and innovative. That's a challenge for us because our

Figure i1.4 140 West Plaza: Exhale. Chapel Hill, NC.
Photograph: Mark Larossa.

office model is not a fixed platform. We work hard to constantly evolve the foundation of thinkers and ideas so that we're able to thrive as a creative entity. Our approach to how we plan to grow is not that different from how we try to stay innovative; we try to stay young. It's really important to stay optimistic about the future and learn from young people. Thinking young, and staying optimistic and enthusiastic, fosters the flexibility that I was talking about earlier.

EDS: What role does innovation play in our future practice?

MYK: I think that what's going to happen in the future is that the titles of artist, architect, landscape architect, etc., are going to lose meaning. I think that designers are going to want to flex greater creative muscle and be more nimble in their design practices. Maybe in the future, practitioners will just be creative entities. Design is becoming a much more fluid endeavor. To remain, and promote, future innovations in landscape architecture, we're no longer going to be able to say 'I'm a landscape architect so I only design this.' If you want to be part of the future, you're going to have to say, 'You know we've never done that kind of thing before, but we're going to take on this challenge, and we're going to figure out how that's done.' We've found that clients are already receptive to that way of approaching design problems that are unique to our times.

Interview II
PEG Office of Landscape + Architecture

Karen M'Closkey and Keith VanDerSys
Founding Partners

PHILADELPHIA, PA, USA

PEG's work explores the relationship among digital media, fabrication technology, and construction. Through new media and fabrication technologies, PEG's work explores methods of systemic patterning to expand landscape's expressive agency in the shaping of the public realm.

Online resource

- http://www.peg-ola.com/about.php

The following text is an abbreviated interview conducted by Jonathon R. Anderson and Daniel H. Ortega (EDS).

EDS: How do you understand innovation?

KV: We recently formed an innovation committee at PennDesign. There's a huge emphasis on the part of the University to initiate discussions on what it means to be innovative. We are finding that it is a challenge to define innovation. In some ways, innovation is synonymous with creativity, and it becomes almost impossible to separate the two ideas. To attempt to systematize or codify innovation is difficult because you cannot refer to bullet points, or

Interview II

develop a step-by-step approach to how one is, or becomes, innovative. That difficulty also becomes compounded when you begin to consider what methods of inquiry may be required to produce innovation. For us, we find it easier to think of innovation as a process. It is not necessarily a product or a thing. The different aspects and strengths that we bring as landscape architects is the ability to think about a problem comprehensively or systematically, and one of the characteristics of systematic thinking is the ability to analyze a problem from a wider perspective. Through a comprehensive approach to analysis, you begin to uncover the unmet, or overlooked, conditions of an environment. One of the things that we do, and that we ask of our students, is to initiate a process of uncovering new ways of visualizing the landscape. We also try to be critically aware that there is great potential to initiate a course of uncovering through the process of site research and analysis. Through that uncovering, you're able to identify the different types of excesses or deficiencies related to a project site. For example, identifying where a specific system is not operating well and whether or not there are externalities affecting that system's ability to operate properly. Once those circumstances and externalities have been identified, we can then start to respond to them. The responses to those externalities, whether they be through experimental approaches to visualization, or experimenting with different tools and methods, probably best describes our current interest in understanding and pursuing innovations in landscape architecture.

EDS: How has innovation evolved your practice/program?

KM: We have changed the types of visualization techniques and technologies that we experiment with and use. For instance, some of the recent tools that Keith has begun using for our work with the Delaware River project involve fluid dynamic simulations. This has resulted in a completely

Figure i2.1 Not Garden. Test plot 2 with laser-cut weed control fabric and full growth one year later.

different type of investigation from what was possible five years ago. At that time, we didn't have the computer power or simulation interfaces readily available in a way that was conducive to design fields. We are trying to be innovative in that we now incorporate software platforms that were previously the domain of engineering, like those used by the Army Corps of Engineers. We are starting to explore the relevance that these tools and software platforms have for landscape architecture. And we want to do so in a way that fosters collaboration between landscape architects and other disciplines. That has been a big shift for us in the last couple of years.

KV: Building on what Karen previously mentioned, computational fluid dynamics allows us to engage, and model, the changes and interactions inherent to any site or system. Our work has also become deeply involved in connecting those forms of analyzing and visualizing physical phenomena to parametric models so that the analysis becomes generative and has

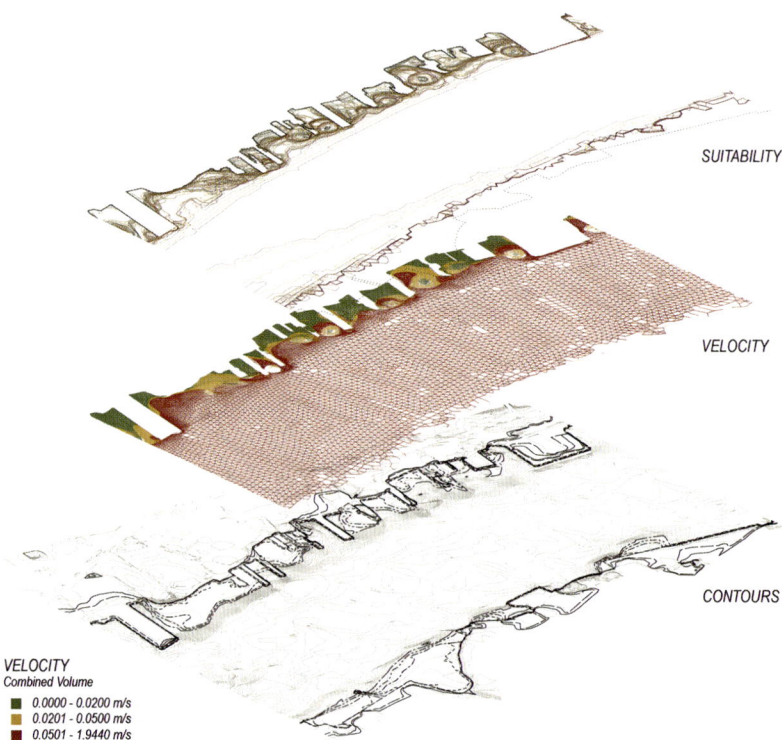

Figure i2.2 Dynamic Delaware. Hydrodynamic simulation using GIS, Aquaveo SMS/SRH-2D, and Grasshopper to determine wetland suitability zones along the Delaware River.

Interview II

some relationship to the changes and modifications that are inherent to a site. We try to engage the dynamism of landscape without relinquishing design solely to analysis. Instead, we look for how those dynamic conditions can become tools for visualizing circumstances where you might need to intervene. This type of evolutionary approach to analysis and visualization is important to us because we feel that, as a discipline, the techniques we have relied on in the past have placed too much emphasis on representing processes rather than working with processes. There is a big difference. When

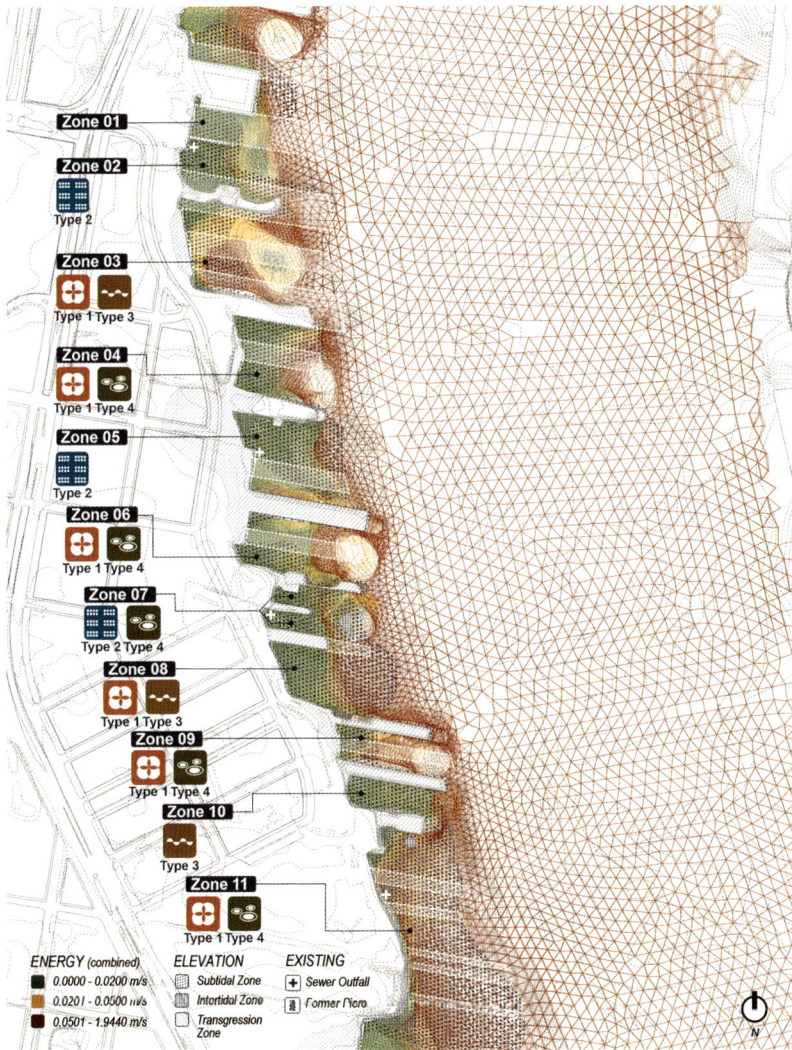

Figure i2.3 Dynamic Delaware. Resulting wetland suitability zones with biotechnical prototype options.

you start to work with processes, you begin to understand that they have numerical and metrical consequences and that those consequences can be generative. We try to teach our students that landscape architects need to link process and form as well as form and process. We also remind them that when thinking about form that it is both informed, and it also performs.

EDS: To what level does interdisciplinary define innovation?

KM: Cross-disciplinary collaborations begin to situate innovations in landscape architecture more openly. Pressures from externalities like global warming have motivated landscape architects to respond in a way that 'forces' us to recognize that we can't work on these issues by ourselves. The kinds of collaborations needed to deal with systemic externalities will allow for multiple disciplines to collaborate in ways that will inform practice. These collaborations will lead to new techniques and explorations in new modes of representations.

KV: I think that a good example of a cross-disciplinary approach can be seen in a project that we have with the Delaware River Waterfront Corporation (DRWC). The project is a part of the larger Delaware River waterfront master plan. The DRWC is trying to distinguish an area that would be beneficial to wetland reclamation, but they don't have the means to build an assessment process. In trying to help evaluate the project area, we started to do some research, and one of the things that became evident was that the two most important things you need to analyze in intertidal wetlands are elevation and energy. The evaluation component of this project is perfectly appropriate for us because we can utilize computational fluid dynamics to start to visualize the conditions where we have low force or low energy compared to the areas of high energy, which would be detrimental to any wetland. In starting this research, we realized that we needed to make connections to several individuals and groups; Franco Montalto, an environmental engineer in Drexel University's civil engineering department; the Partnership for the Delaware Estuary, which has done a series of wetland restoration projects along the Delaware; the Philadelphia Water Department; and the Army Corps of Engineers. Suddenly when you start to open up your project and your research to so many different fields of expertise, the work has to be cross-disciplinary otherwise it would be very superficial.

KM: It's these types of cross-disciplinary collaborations that are representative of how we design with nature today. We're interested in learning from the methods that the scientists and engineers are using to understand natural processes and natural systems, and to think about how those affect our work, and our discipline. But this also includes formal explorations and finding new methods of design that result from questioning what the engineers are doing, and what the scientists are doing.

EDS: How do you create a platform or infrastructure to facilitate innovation, and how do you critically examine or assess this?

KV: We just launched a research category on the PEG website, where we have added projects that include experiments and tangents related to our work. A lot of the projects in the research category are not client-based activities, nor are they fully realized research and design projects, but they are important in building up larger methods of meaning for us. For instance, with the Delaware River project we learned that data related to the edges of urban river systems is severely outdated or is simply not available; so we developed a hydro-drone where we combined a GPS fish finder/chartplotter with a remote control boat to gather bathymetry data for our research. Because of the lack of reliable information, we had to design a way to go out and collect the missing data. Developing a way to collect our own data became a critical element in being able to model, test, and articulate the different issues related to wetland evaluation. Some of the work that we're doing now at Penn is probably the most innovative work that we've done over the last couple of years. A lot of it deals with this same sort of need for getting geo-data connected to the geospatial analysis, design modeling, and simulation. I teach a seminar, for instance, where we create a structure for the students to go through the process of gathering geo-data, and bathymetry, and then use the data to delve into computational fluid dynamics. After which, the data is translated into a parametric modeling environment where they can begin to model changes to the extant condition. The big hurdle in the seminar is how data-driven processes translate into something generative. What we are really interested in, and what we are trying to convey to our students, is that once you've done the data collection and the analysis, you must identify the conditions of excess or deficiency. For instance, it becomes pretty meaningful when you see an increase or decrease in fluid velocity. That indicates some interaction of consequence at that movement in time. What then can we infer from that? These changes drive the modeling process in a way that informs where and how you might start to intervene. The values, shapes, and sizes become interesting because you can start to look at these as parts of a feedback loop. The feedback loop recognizes shifts in the overall pattern of a project, helping us to determine how to respond to those moments while providing for a built-in assessment mechanism to the project.

EDS: What role does innovation play in our future practice/education?

KV: That's a difficult question because you're not always thinking in those types of long-range terms. A lot of the time you do something because you're intrigued by it. It takes a while before the wider perspective becomes apparent. I am obsessed with doing parametric modeling because you can structure the behaviors and connections. Why these parameters are important is because you're working with systems in a way that they become measurable. This type of parametric-thinking is going to create a big shift in how we think about innovation and technology in landscape. It's easy to champion the new and innovative, however, as if it's going to solve something. Karen has a great phrase, 'A lot of the problems that we're dealing with today are the solutions of yesterday.' We tend to think that something has been solved, but instead we often just introduce a new problem. We tend to externalize, and we simplify in ways that suggest that we can solve a problem, but we're not, we're just shifting the condition

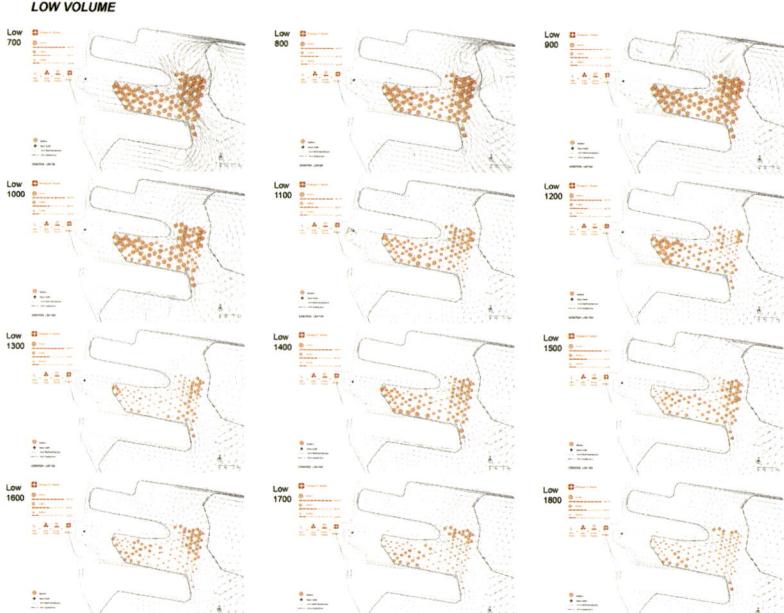

Figure i2.4 Dynamic Delaware. Hydro-electric turbine driven aeration bubblers respond to the changing velocity of the river. The increased aeration helps feed oxygen to the newly established subtidal wetland planting.

Interview II

somewhere else until it rises again. For that reason, I'm hesitant to say that innovation or technology is going to make a profound change. What I would probably say is that technology does allow us a more comprehensive way to deal with complexity, and that is a huge change. Through innovations in parametric modeling, we are going to work less with reductive, isolated, fixed representations of the world. I think that that is going to be a huge shift, both pedagogically and disciplinarily. It requires us to understand a much different way of working with time and change that we are not presently educating towards. Because the simulation is inherently time contingent and time dependent, you cannot disassociate time from the tool itself. As time-dependent technologies, you're setting up relationships and connections that are spatially and temporally dependent upon one another. You're not modeling things. You're modeling interactions and relationships, and that is the basis of how the parametric medium is structured. If you have a McLuhan-esque view, the medium is transformative in and of itself. It becomes not so much what you produce from it, but it's the entire act of working with that medium that is going to fundamentally change how you understand the world.

Figure i2.5 Dynamic Delaware. Montage of the responsive aeration bubble rings.

Interview III
Illinois Institute of Technology (IIT)

Martin Felsen, Assistant Professor, and Conor O'Shea, Visiting Assistant Professor

COLLEGE OF ARCHITECTURE

MASTER OF LANDSCAPE ARCHITECTURE PROGRAM

CHICAGO, IL, USA

The IIT landscape architecture program aims to teach landscape architects to engage small- and large-scale landscapes of urbanization through a rigorous training in geographic, ecological, and landscape infrastructural systems. Attention is given both to regenerative landscape design at a planetary level and to shaping urban landscapes that support ecological, infrastructural, and human health functions.

Online resource

- http://arch.iit.edu/study/mla-introduction

The following text is an abbreviated interview conducted by Jonathon R. Anderson and Daniel H. Ortega (EDS).

EDS: How do you understand innovation?
CO: When I heard that this book was going to be about innovation, my initial reaction was that the word innovation connotes something more technological, which, to me, is not directly

related to landscape architecture's underpinnings. However, if we reframe the question and consider innovation to be defined as moments of forward trajectory, it's helpful to look at the history of the profession over the last 150 years and identify some of those moments. For a large part of the twentieth century landscape architecture was not moving forward at any great speed, some might say it was treading water, others might say it was moving backward, but I feel that we're currently in the midst of a forward trajectory. However, I question whether landscape architecture is generating that momentum internally or if it is in response to broader political, economic, environmental, or social forces.

MF: From an academic point of view; if the twentieth century was this Big Bang of cities, and city planning and urban planning were very viable degrees, and very viable scholarly areas that produced many thoughts about innovation, we can look back now and recognize that those practices essentially formalized itself as sprawl. Yes, there were cities based around agricultural interests, there were cities based around ecological services, and other really important ideas that only landscape architects have ever pushed forward in an innovative way, but they were being utilized and reified by city planners that were dealing only with the formal components of cities. We finally figured out that city planners and architects typically believe that the fundamental unit of the urban environment is the private building and some publicly organized infrastructure. Landscape architects have always thought that the primary fundamental unit of the city is public open space that is ecologically organized. The damage that has been brought on by the designed fabric of cities is taking over. Pollution is taking over, alienation from one's environment is taking over, and all of a sudden we find ourselves with these harmful voids. The works of landscape architects are now filling those voids. The great innovations that are happening in landscape architecture right now involve the remediation of the entire environment that has been subjected to a type of holistic urban annihilation. The modern regime of landscape architects have great new ideas, and now landscape architects are getting hired by cities and developers to lead in the design of new urban environments. To bring that back here to Chicago, and to IIT, we feel that we have a significant role in the forward trajectory of ecological urbanism because we have a rich history of trying to figure out ways to create an ecologically based environment out of sprawl.

Figure i3.1 *Dialogues on Urbanization: Emerging Landscapes* promotional postcard. Front. 4″ × 6″.

Source: copyright 2015, IIT College of Architecture.

Interview III

EDS: How has innovation evolved within your program?

MF: Conor and I are both new to the MLA program. When we started, we looked at what had gone on before in terms of curricular development, and what we found was, for good reasons, the curriculum was largely focused on the concepts and technical requirements needed to graduate students with a body of knowledge that landscape architects should know. However, we also wanted to take the opportunity to align the program with the rich history of IIT and the city of Chicago. IIT's history is really interesting, and coincidently, it has a lot to say about what an MLA program should be. The history deals with Mies Van Der Rohe and his colleagues Ludwig Hilberseimer, and Alfred Caldwell. Hilberseimer renounced architectural and city planning driven modernism early in his professional life. He was essentially a Corbusian for the first decade of his career, and he realized that this kind of radical zoning, separating everything out, and designing sprawling gray-infrastructure driven cities on the edge of nowhere are not going to work. He started a class here at IIT called the Ecological Basis of Urban Planning, which was about how the natural environment, agriculture, fresh air, public health, could merge with the built environment, and how cities of the future would look based on an ecological functioning for people, not for cars. In turn, Alfred Caldwell grew the architecture curriculum toward repairing the relationship between architecture and the natural environment. Mies's idea was always that the building sits up in the landscape, stairs connect out into it, there's a thin glass membrane that disconnects the two, and that is it. Hilberseimer and Caldwell worked to counter that approach. We felt that it was important to reintroduce that ecologically focused legacy into the MLA program, so we worked with our Dean to look at the landscape architecture program and figure out how we could merge the existing curriculum with our more ecologically sensitive history as well as with the history of the city of Chicago. There are qualities of Chicago's historic landscape that are unique and could be a model for education in terms of health and happiness, quality of life. Slowly, we are trying to question this relationship of IIT's MLA program to its legacies and its context. A specific way that we are trying to do that is by hosting an exhibition about creating a dialogue amongst ourselves, and the rest of the world, around who we are and how we can redefine the MLA program in the future.

CO: Our motives behind the Spring 2016 exhibition *Dialogues on Urbanization: Emerging Landscapes* (DUEL) are a product of a dialogue between us, our

Martin Felsen and Conor O'Shea

Dean Wiel Arets, and our Associate Dean, Vedran Mimica. There are certain theoretical goals in the IIT architecture publication *Nowness*, which documents the school's current agenda, which we wanted to explore more specifically through the lens of landscape architecture. One of the primary goals behind the exhibition was to show how landscape architects are currently thinking about landscape as a lens through which to formulate ideas about planetary urbanization. We structured the showing of work so that there are eleven speculative projects and eleven built projects, with each of the eleven pairs exploring a particular sub-category of twenty-first century urbanization. The pairs also draw on ideas from recent texts in critical urban theory, and the exhibit aims to extend the advancements in research methods found in writings about planetary urbanization into the discourse of landscape architecture. Representational strategies specific to landscape architecture were a third category that we wanted to explore. We wanted to document the resurgence of GIS and the aesthetics of mapping within landscape architecture. Hopefully, the exhibition will allow IIT to make a contextual and historically sensitive claim about landscape architecture in the twenty-first century while at the same time helping the MLA program craft a stronger identity in relation to other programs and maybe even to other design disciplines.

Figure i3.2 First year IIT MLA review. March 13, 2015. Crown Hall, IIT, Chicago.
Source: copyright 2015, Conor O'Shea.

Interview III

EDS: To what level does interdisciplinary define innovation?

MF: I'm a disciplinarian. I think that interdisciplinary research and work should happen after the discipline knows what its agency is, what its theoretical basis is, what its technical constraints are, and what its expertise is all about. So, I do not believe in interdisciplinarity upfront. I believe that it should happen after there is a strong disciplinary base that's been heavily refined and set in place.

CO: I agree that interdisciplinary practice can only occur after a strong sense of self is established. It's no coincidence that the interdisciplinary studios here at IIT occur in the third year not in the first year. The idea is that any student, in any particular program, needs to develop his or her identity and understand core disciplinary knowledge before taking an interdisciplinary studio. I think landscape architecture spent the 1990s and the early 2000s revisiting its core texts and figuring revising its identity. Now landscape architects are in a position where they can lead collaborations, or oversee large projects, but it's only after having developed a strong sense of where landscape architecture is and where it came from. I think three relatively recent texts have helped form that identity: *Recovering Landscape*, *The Landscape Urbanism Reader*, and *Large Parks*. Together they have become a kind of cornerstone for the discipline. Speaking from personal experience, I know that I can always refer to those books if I am thinking about anything within landscape architecture in the early twenty-first century. If I didn't have those books to reference, I would then want to write those books. Instead, it becomes a matter of extending lines of inquiry found in those books through theory building, speculative design research, and pursuing built work. It's a great time to do so because there is very little danger of unintentionally blurring the boundaries between disciplines given that a critical core body of knowledge has been established.

MF: Interdisciplinary thinking and actions work well in the Google model where all of these different disciplines are working toward one common objective. That only works because its defined scope is based around a simulation of the real, it's not physical, there are not larger systems at work that are going to come into contact with whatever the deliverable may be. That model just doesn't work in the physical world where there are repercussions. I will also say that, even though I believe in disciplinary autonomy, I don't believe in proprietary knowledge. So, I do believe that even though the disciplines need to develop unique knowledge, they should share that knowledge in an open source way as much as possible, and it shouldn't be siloed.

EDS: How do you create a platform or infrastructure to facilitate innovation and how do you critically examine or assess this?

CO: Exhibitions and publications are one example. The recent exhibition *Dialogues on Urbanization: Emerging Landscapes* (DUEL) serves as a platform by which we can start to set, contextualize and revisit the agenda of IIT MLA.

MF: We are also reaching out to others to continue improving our local knowledge. We are also curating dialogues with the *DUEL* participants for a future publication. As far as innovation is concerned, the first goal is to innovate internally, intellectually and have people from around the world help us to develop pertinent knowledge in a way that we can then go back out with an intact, intellectual framework that has very strong roots.

EDS: If the exhibition and discussions with others begin to help you assess your intellectual content, how can that be applied to the classroom and the future structure of the MLA curriculum?

CO: Developing and disseminating gained knowledge is an important part of any program or any discipline's pedagogical endeavors.

MF: That's a good point. One of the things that we may not have mentioned is that our students helped to curate this exhibition, and it is a completely extracurricular activity that is meant to allow for us to reflect on, and assess where, the curriculum's future opportunities might exist. The exhibition as a type of dissemination will help others to help us move forward.

CO: Extracurricular actions like these should allow for more internal innovation, given that there's not oversight with respect to specific curricular or departmental objectives. Given the pace at which curricula are typically evaluated, I think that the freedom that something like an exhibition or symposium allows for may encourage or speed up innovation more quickly than specific curricular agenda items may.

MF: In that sense, the process for this extracurricular activity was needed just to stitch together a lot of the theoretical principles and ideas that are inherent to the vision of the IIT MLA program. Now that we have done this, we can, with the help of others, start to move toward accomplishing that vision. Extracurricular activities, like workshops, exhibitions, and symposia, are becoming a foundational component of the program.

EDS: What role does innovation play in our future education?

MF: Innovation in landscape architecture is nothing new to the discipline. It's working more with natural systems and convincing others to work less with artificial systems. We can see all of the unintended consequences and all

Figure i3.3 Adriaan Geuze tours *Dialogues on Urbanization: Emerging Landscapes* during a special preview with the IIT MLA program and special guests. March 23, 2015. Crown Hall, IIT, Chicago.

Source: copyright 2015, IIT College of Architecture.

Figure i3.4 Professor Conor O'Shea of the IIT MLA program introduces *Dialogues on Urbanization: Emerging Landscapes* to Adriaan Geuze and special guests. March 23, 2015. Crown Hall, IIT, Chicago.

Source: copyright 2015, IIT College of Architecture.

of the problems that the artificial approach is now wreaking on the world. Landscape architects have the greatest potential for innovating with nature to develop new safeguards against many of the environmental and social problems that we have. I see future innovations in landscape architecture as being related to developing technologies around nature. Whether the natural technologies that are pursued are completely replicated or simulated, the understanding of ecological processes and systems will allow for landscape architects to innovate professionally and intellectually. Because of that professional and intellectual growth, landscape architects will lead in the development of new kinds of solutions to the biggest environmental and quality of life challenges that we have.

CO: How innovation impacts the long-term health of the discipline is a really important question. I don't think it's a matter of constantly innovating at the same speed, or maintaining a constant level of momentum. I think it's a matter of easing up on the gas from time to time to take stock of where we are at, which is something that I think we are trying to do here at IIT. It's impossible to predict the future, but it's helpful to look back at the last 150 years of landscape architecture in North America and think about the moments when the discipline has had traction in influencing urbanization. We are definitely in a moment like that right now and probably will be for another ten or fifteen years. Exciting new books are coming out, and everyone is working hard at theorizing the present condition but the possibility that landscape urbanism becomes a distinct spin-off of landscape architecture can potentially force landscape architectural education to revert to focusing on smaller-scale issues. This is a very real concern. We have seen this before with city planning spinning off from landscape architecture at Harvard in 1929. To continue innovating, we as landscape architects must continually question and revise our discipline's core.

Interview IV
Rhode Island School of Design (RISD)

Suzanne Mathew, Assistant Professor

MASTER OF LANDSCAPE ARCHITECTURE PROGRAM

PROVIDENCE, RI, USA

RISD's MLA program is unique in that it gives students access to a wide range of fine art and design courses on campus. The MLA curriculum is seen as a laboratory where material investigations and conceptual explorations intertwine with individual studio research and practice. In addition, the program revolves around environmental and global issues, with recent involvement in projects in Bangladesh, Costa Rica, Ghana, and beyond.

Online resource

- http://www.risd.edu/academics/landscape-architecture

The following text is an abbreviated interview conducted by Jonathon R. Anderson and Daniel H. Ortega (EDS).

EDS: How do you understand innovation?

SM: I would say that innovation is anything that defines a new approach, a new way of looking at something, or a new technique that goes beyond established methodologies. I would also say that innovation often blends the old and the new: that established methods and practices are improved upon or transformed by emerging theories and practices. This happens through experimentation and invention, and also through the introduction of new technologies, materials, and alternative points of view. In design, I think that we are constantly developing new practices because we are addressing emerging issues that come from changes in our environment, in our technologies, and in our culture. Our field is constantly evolving, and so our practices are constantly adapting as well. We have a base of expertise that must constantly grow as digital technologies change building practices. We are (or should be) constantly assessing the mutual affect of our building practices on the environment, and the environment on built form. I think this is what makes design a dynamic field; I'm not sure we necessarily discuss *'innovation'* because I don't think we operate on the assumption that our practices, or that the things we make, will not change. I think that 'best practices' in design are a hybridization of the old and the new. We require knowledge of historical practices, so that we do not lose our understanding of the context we are working within, and a willingness to engage new technologies, so that we are able to adapt our practices to the changing world.

EDS: How has innovation evolved your program?

SM: Innovation is part of the mission at RISD, and it is embedded in the curriculum of the landscape architecture department in the form of material experimentation, multidisciplinary learning, and the hybridization of technologies and practices from within and beyond the discipline. At RISD, we don't have one way of approaching something. We take full advantage of the 16 art disciplines within the school and invite conversation and collaboration to occur with students and faculty across departments. The potential for multidisciplinary and interdisciplinary collaboration is communicated to the students as a pedagogical goal, and there is a focus here on doing it through a process of *critical making*. Critical making merges experimentation, production, and craft, with critical analysis, and an attitude toward developing new ways of doing things. We have a broad base of disciplines to pull from here and we are able to share expertise in a way that uncovers new questions, and leads to new approaches to answering these questions. When studio problems are framed, they're often framed in response to what we see happening here, right now, in the different disciplines on campus, as we look at them in relationship to the cultural and ecological issues we investigate within the landscape architecture department. For example, Scheri Fultineer, our department head and Associate Professor in Landscape Architecture, and Edythe Wright, an Adjunct Professor in Sculpture, recently co-taught a studio called *Creating Sculptural Habitats*. The multidisciplinary studio included sculpture students and landscape architecture students, and it focused on creating sculptural forms that could provide habitats for oysters. In bringing these two disciplines together, the studio fostered more diverse conversations about the role of aesthetics, the role of human engagement with physical objects in the landscape, and, in this case, the experiential phenomena of a coastal landscape. That sort of multidisciplinary interaction creates new methods for exploration in a way that ensures that you're not just borrowing from a discipline you don't fully understand, but rather you are sharing and cross-pollinating expertise. You could look at any number of interdisciplinary studios here at RISD, and you would find that ultimately they each operate under the same premise; how do we bring different disciplines together in a way that creates new and unexpected responses to the questions being asked.

EDS: To what level does interdisciplinary define innovation?

SM: Innovation in design gets us to a point where we can start accessing new modes of thinking, or new ways of questioning, the topics that are central to landscape architectural practice. Here at RISD, the MLA students who explore other departments or collaborate with students from other disciplines are able to learn how to work with different materials, and also become familiar with methods of making that come along with disciplines such as ceramics, sculpture, textiles, or digital media. This type of cross-disciplinary learning gives the students new ways to imagine how landscapes can be made, and how landscape architecture can be practiced. I would also say that in addition to the benefits of interdisciplinary learning, the multidisciplinary environment also frames the particular point of view of our landscape architecture department. We operate within an art school, and therefore the importance of making and craft, of working with your hands as well as with digital tools, is part of the larger culture of the school and central to how we teach landscape architecture. Something that I have noticed, moving between departments, is that landscape architecture operates at a scale that is very different from the other disciplines here, and because of that we have the opportunity to explore how they negotiate material and scale. In that way I think we bring something very specific to the table here, in that the landscape architecture department operates at a much larger scale than many of the disciplines here, and within a context that bridges culture, ecology, and the built environment with material and art-based investigations. I think our location within a multidisciplinary art environment means that there is limitless and exciting potential for what landscape architecture can become when it is allied with other disciplines that are rooted in practices of making.

Suzanne Mathew

EDS: Are there mechanisms to facilitate those collaborative projects? Are they faculty led, or are they administratively assigned?

SM: I think that collaboration is at its best when it comes from an organic overlap or sharing of research interests. There are formal mechanisms to help that happen at RISD, including research grants for collaborative research, support for faculty to develop interdisciplinary curriculum, and shared labs, such as CO-WORKS, which has been developed with the explicit purpose of bringing together a variety of 2D and 3D making practices in order for students and faculty to develop new methods of critical making. Additionally, structure to the student schedule makes space for them to explore interests outside of their department. In the landscape architecture department, our students are able take a range of electives offered by the other departments, and these are interspersed with the core landscape curriculum to encourage an exchange of ideas and practices. At RISD, students also have a winter session semester, which has been specifically designed to allow students to immerse themselves in intensive explorations in another discipline. The experiences gained in those electives typically cross-pollinate and infiltrate their landscape architecture work. There is a student in one of the landscape architecture studios right now who is also taking a ceramics class. He is working in an extremely iterative way to perfect a series of bowls. Through the experience of shaping those bowls at a one-to-one scale, he'll have a profound opportunity to consider whether he can shape the ground at a similarly fine level of detail. Experiences like this change the way students explore problems faced in landscape architecture work, and ultimately change their understanding of landscape architecture.

EDS: How do you create a platform or infrastructure to facilitate innovation, and how do you critically examine or assess this?

SM: We build assessment into the student's design process and in our curricular development. For example, from the first, studio students take in the MLA program, students are introduced to the process of critical making. There is an emphasis on an iterative process in design where you're not only physically making something, but you make things in an analytical way that furthers the design process. Through that approach, you make something, you stop and observe, and then you make something again, and once you understand the cyclical process as being iterative, each piece becomes an analysis of the last. This means that the iterations are not simply intuition-based progressions, but they critically analyze and respond

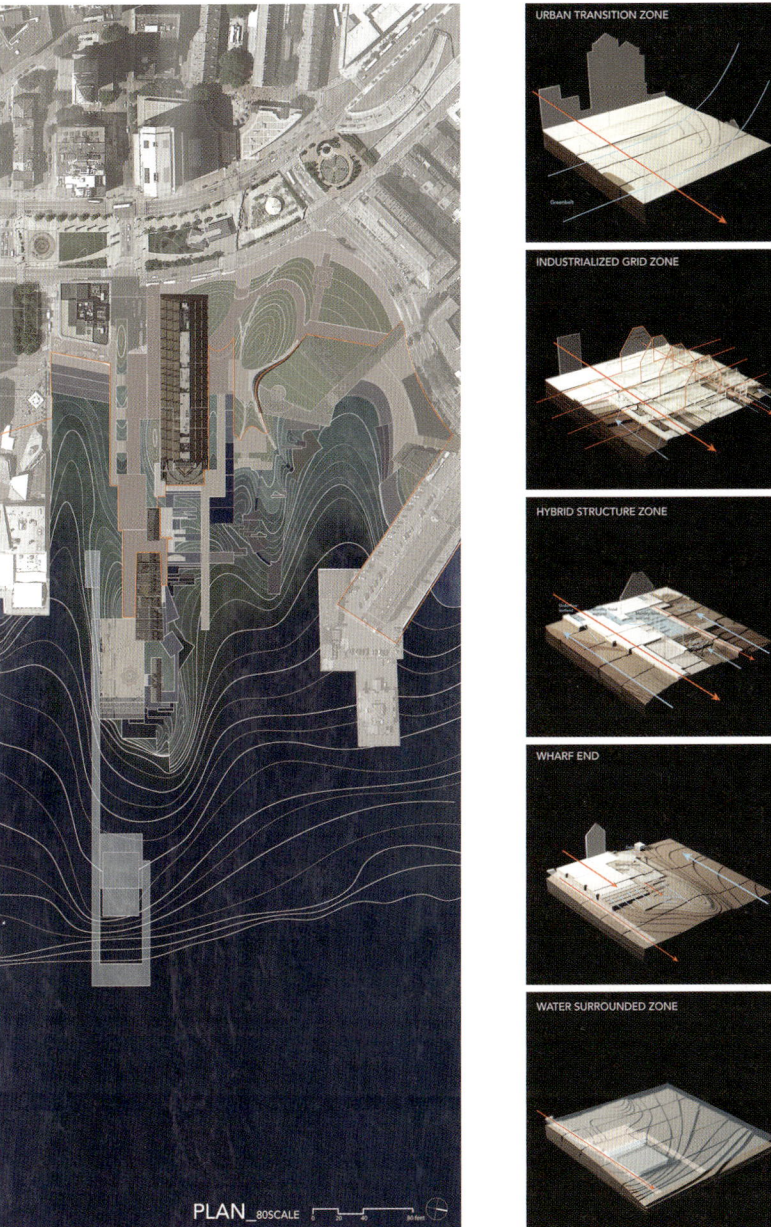

Figure i4.1 Zhi Wang, RISD MLA Graduate Thesis 2015. 'Walk Into the Sea.' Long Wharf Hybridized Landscape Pier Dynamics. This thesis project proposes a new hybridized landscape pier infrastructure to address the impacts of sea-level rise on historic waterfront structures in Boston.

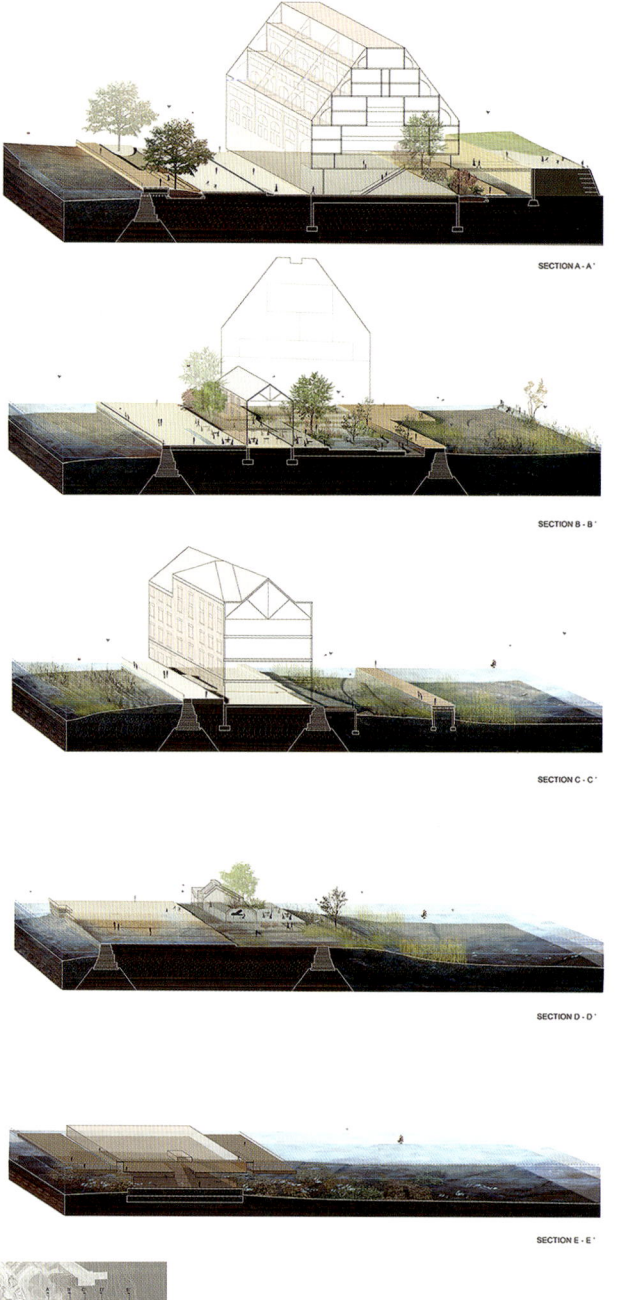

Figure i4.2 Zhi Wang, RISD MLA Graduate Thesis 2015. 'Walk Into the Sea.' Long Wharf Hybridized Pier Structure.

to what it is that you've just made. The process becomes highly informative and generative. It's important that students are clear about what they are trying to address when making something, while at the same time being able to allow intuition to guide the process. That ability to react to visual, tactile, or intuitive thought is an important part of the creative process. It's making with intention and invention, and then mining the potential in the thing that you made. The landscape architecture faculty here at RISD understands that the process of assessment and reflection is a key step in the process of critical making. If you are not analytical about your work, if you don't stop to assess that work, and critique that work, then you are not moving forward, and you won't be able to innovate.

EDS: What role does innovation play in our future education?

SM: Well, I think I've said this in another way, but innovation is intrinsic to design thinking. But in terms of how it relates to the future of education and practice in the field, I believe that our ability to identify and define critical issues within the field, but also to create new ways of practice, allows us to remain agile as designers, and allows us to stake out new territories to operate within and apply our expertise. That agility begins in school through pedagogy of research and experimentation, and prepares students not only to respond to the critical issues of today, but also to be able to anticipate and develop methods to address the critical issues that will evolve in the future. Landscape architecture would be static if we were unable to incorporate new ideas, to develop new techniques and perspectives that can adapt to our changing environment. New modes of thinking are tested through practice, and in my experience many of those new modes begin in education, in the academic environment. I think that's why a lot of people become educators in the first place, we're here because we think there's more than one way of doing something, and we are aware that the ideas shaping the profession are constantly changing. One of the best places to be is at the forefront of that dialogue, the dialogue of how we push the field and profession forward. Landscape architecture programs and departments stay agile by not only holding on to specific types of expertise, but by adding and testing new kinds of expertise, and by engaging in new technologies so that we can test them, adapt them, and put them to use in understanding the questions that landscape architects are asking.

INDEX

3D scanning, 43
3D printing, 109

adaptable, 107
aesthetics, 171
agency, 10, 41, 128, 148, 246, 259
agricultural revolution, 196
algorithmic, 140
anamorphic, 95
animation, 69, 120
anthropogenic, 138
architecture, 189
art, 224
artifacts, 54, 79, 109, 130, 213
artisanal, 207
assessment, 36
autonomous, 94

borderless, 173
boundary, 196, 226
building, 108, 190
built environment, 91, 165, 189

cartography, 10
civic infrastructures, 29
CNC, 51, 98, 109, 213
collaboration, 32, 54, 152, 209, 241
construction, 36, 189
contemporary, 169
craft, 206
creative thinking, 49
critical making, 264
cultural shift, 79
curriculum, 257
cybernetics, 171

data, 47, 65, 76, 91, 103, 138, 152, 166
datascape, 9, 33
deficiency, 251
deindustrialization, 165
design activism, 206
design paradigm, 33

digital fabrication, 109, 206
drawing, 35, 62, 136
dynamic, 17, 44, 60, 112, 224, 247

ecological urbanism, 186
ecology, 174, 208
economic, 168
emerging, 43, 80, 104, 164, 257
engineering, 189
environmental, 56, 62, 126, 168
ethics, 171
ethnographer, 144
evolving landscapes, 45
experimental, 80, 247

Fab Lab, 209
fabrication, 109, 211, 246
forward-thinking, 2

generative, 16, 248
geofences, 76
geographic, 90
Geographic Information Systems (GIS), 12, 47, 91
geometry, 121
geomorphological, 14
geospatial, 43, 103
globalization, 165
GPS, 76, 251

hybridization, 139

IIT, 254
Industrial Revolution, 176, 209
installation, 80, 224
integrate, 45, 130

landscript, 11
laser cutting, 95, 109, 213
LEED, 64
lidar, 97

manufacturing, 138

Index

mass customization, 45
material, 95, 126, 212
mechanisms, 266
media, 78
mesh, 98
Mikyoung Kim Design, 239
modeling, 12, 36, 43, 104
modernism, 200, 257
morphological, 131,
multidisciplinary, 168, 264

NASA, 173
natural systems, 61, 234, 250, 260
network, 79, 105, 166, 178

observational domain, 130
open systems, 125
operational domain, 134
optimal, 53, 113
Owens Lake, 30

paradigm shift, 11
parameters, 32, 48, 108
parametric, 45, 108, 213, 248
pattern, 12, 90, 229, 251
pedagogical, 260
PEG, 246
perception, 185
phenomena, 128, 165
physical model, 36
placemaking, 30
political, 100, 134, 144
post-industrial, 107, 165
procedural modeling, 45
prototyping, 213
public policy, 165

rapid prototyping, 43

reconciliation, 28
representation, 60, 155, 173, 196
rigorous, 150
RISD, 263
robotically, 38

scenario analysis, 114
scripting, 9
simulation, 12, 32, 47 104, 139, 247
site analysis, 61
smart phones, 76
social behaviour, 86
sociocultural, 143
software, 13, 22, 35, 93, 213
stakeholders, 54
sustainability, 143, 165, 168
system, 125, 164, 173, 213
systematic, 22, 29, 247

tangible landscape, 43
technique, 249
technology, 17, 35, 82, 98, 166, 252
temporary, 223
territories, 10, 240, 171, 269
theoretical framework, 183
theory, 144, 259
thick description, 143
topography, 35, 48, 66, 106, 166
toxicity, 92

urban, 95, 104, 144, 165

vernacular, 201
visualization, 62, 66, 95, 136, 247

waste landscapes, 164
workshops, 218
xeriscapes, 20